The Political Economy of New Slavery

Edited by

Christien van den Anker
Lecturer in Global Ethics
University of Birmingham
United Kingdom

First published 2004 by
PALGRAVE MACMILLAN
Houndmills, Basingstoke, Hampshire RG21 6XS and
175 Fifth Avenue, New York, N.Y. 10010
Companies and representatives throughout the world

PALGRAVE MACMILLAN is the global academic imprint of the Palgrave
Macmillan division of St. Martin's Press, LLC and of Palgrave Macmillan Ltd.
Macmillan® is a registered trademark in the United States, United Kingdom
and other countries. Palgrave is a registered trademark in the European
Union and other countries.

ISBN 1–4039–1522–9 hardback
ISBN 1–4039–1523–7 paperback

This book is printed on paper suitable for recycling and made from fully
managed and sustained forest sources.

A catalogue record for this book is available from the British Library.

Library of Congress Cataloging-in-Publication Data
The political economy of new slavery / edited by Christien van den Anker.
    p. cm.
    Includes bibiliographical references and index.
    ISBN 1–4039–1522–9 (hardback) — ISBN 1–4039–1523–7 (pbk.)
    1. Slavery—History—21st century. 2. Child slaves—Social conditions—
21st century. 3. Child labour—History—21st century. 4. Slavery—Law
and legislation. I. Anker, Christien van den, 1965–
    HT867.P65 2003
    306.3′62′0905—dc21   2003053632

10   9   8   7   6   5   4   3   2   1
13   12   11   10   09   08   07   06   05   04

Printed and bound in Great Britain by
Antony Rowe Ltd, Chippenham and Eastbourne

The Political Economy of New Slavery

Palgrave Texts in International Political Economy

Series Editors: **Craig Murphy**, M. Margaret Ball Professor of International Relations, Wellesley College; and **Timothy M. Shaw**, Professor of Commonwealth Governance and Development, and Director, Institute of Commonwealth Studies, School of Advanced Study, University of London

International Political Economy aims to understand the dynamic, complex relations between the diverse and interrelated political and economic phenomena at the global to local levels. In the postwar period, world economic and political systems have undergone rapid and unprecedented change. *Palgrave Texts in International Political Economy* seeks to provide authoritative and innovative texts aimed at the graduate-level student to provide key introductions to and assessment of key areas in international political economy, both established and emerging.

Titles include:

Christien van den Anker *(editor)*
THE POLITICAL ECONOMY OF NEW SLAVERY

Palgrave Texts in International Political Economy
Series Standing Order ISBN 1–4039–3807–5 hardback
Series Standing Order ISBN 1–4039–3808–3 paperback

You can receive future titles in this series as they are published by placing a standing order. Please contact your bookseller or, in case of difficulty, write to us at the address below with your name and address, the title of the series and one of the ISBNs quoted above.

Customer Services Department, Macmillan Distribution Ltd, Houndmills, Basingstoke, Hampshire RG21 6XS, England

Contents

List of Tables and Figures

Tables

Figure

Foreword

Many consider that slavery is a matter for the past, outlawed in Britain and elsewhere in the nineteenth century, and prohibited by the first international human rights instruments in the twentieth century. The image of the transatlantic slave trade and plantations still holds strong. Yet currently millions are held worldwide in contemporary forms of slavery. Among children, the International Labour Organization estimates 8.4 million are in slavery, approximately one child out of every 175 in the world.

What all these people have in common is that they are vulnerable and suffer the worst forms of exploitation. Yet what is also clear is that slavery affects all types of people, in all areas of the world, held in many different forms of slavery. These may vary, for example, from women trafficked into domestic servitude in the UK, to children working on cocoa plantations in the Ivory Coast, to bonded labourers in South Asia. As the faces of contemporary slavery are varied, so are the causes and potential solutions. Thus we need not only to look at the implementation of international law, but also economic factors, globalization and international trade, and countries' migration policies. Perhaps more so in slavery than any other area, the interface of basic human rights standards and economic policies is most apparent.

It is also clear that contemporary slavery is no respecter of traditional boundaries – the increased global crime of trafficking in people affects most countries, from the most developed such as the UK or USA through the former Eastern bloc countries to the traditionally viewed 'under developed' countries of the South. While the underlying driver of this may be poverty, other social and economic factors such as the desire to migrate are important. These diverse situations call for a more sophisticated response than the standard development agenda.

Anti-Slavery International has been working since 1839 to eliminate all forms of slavery and the slave trade. In this time we have learnt that, complex and immense though the problem is, solutions are possible that bring about real, sustainable changes in the lives of people. Increasingly both individuals and governments are becoming more aware of the problem, and are working for solutions. But much still remains to be done. Awareness of issues surrounding slavery needs to be increased; individuals can have a role in campaigning, pressurizing governments and companies to ensure human rights and labour standards. For solutions to be effective and sustainable the complex issues surrounding modern slavery need to be thoroughly understood and analyzed. The selection of chapters in this book is an invaluable tool in bringing together a variety of academics and campaigners to consider the diverse strands that contribute to modern-day slavery. It will also help those concerned with the elimination of modern-day slavery to understand the causes of and potential solutions to this continuing serious violation of human rights.

MARY CUNNEEN
Director
Anti-Slavery International

Acknowledgements

The production of an edited collection like this one involves work and support from too many people to thank personally. Here, I would like to thank the British International Studies Association for their financial support of the workshop where the chapters in this book were first presented. A big thank you to Helen Harris at the Centre for the Study of Global Ethics who ensured the workshop was able to run smoothly. Thanks are also due to Tim Shaw for his contributions to the workshop and for adopting the present volume as a part of his International Political Economy series. Many thanks, too, to Palgrave's Amanda Watkins for her support of this project. I would also like to express my gratitude to all contributors for their commitment and their flexibility in accepting my editorial suggestions. Many thanks to Louise Shorter, who kindly helped to get the final manuscript looking the part. Finally, thank you to all readers who take the time to read our work and pass on the baton in the campaign against contemporary slavery.

CHRISTIEN VAN DEN ANKER

Notes on the Contributors

Bridget Anderson has worked with Kalayaan since it was set up in 1987. She is an academic based at the Institute for Social and Cultural Anthropology at the University of Oxford. Her research interest is migration and her recent publications include a book on domestic labour and migration, entitled *Doing the Dirty Work? The Global Politics of Domestic Labour* (2000a).

Christien van den Anker is a lecturer at the Centre for the Study of Global Ethics at the University of Birmingham. Her main interests include the intersection of international normative theory, globalization and human rights. She is currently preparing a book on global social justice. She is the convenor of the British International Studies Association Working Group on Global Ethics.

Amanda Berlan is a research student at the Institute of Social and Cultural Anthropology at the University of Oxford. She is currently completing her PhD thesis on child rights in Ghana, where she previously carried out research on Fair Trade and cocoa farming.

Jeroen Doomernik is Lecturer in Political Science and Programme Manager at the Institute for Migration and Ethnic Studies, University of Amsterdam. He has published on Turkish Islam in the Netherlands and Germany, Soviet Jewish immigrants in Berlin and was commissioned by the Dutch government and several international organizations to evaluate, in a comparative perspective, immigration and integration policies. His current research is on irregular migration in general and human smuggling in particular.

Arne Dormaels is an academic assistant in Criminal Law and researcher at the Institute for International Research on Criminal Policy, University of Gent. He holds an MA in Criminology.

Nigel Dower is Senior Lecturer in Philosophy in the University of Aberdeen. His main interests are in the ethical issues raised by international relations, development and the environment. His recent publications include *World Ethics – the New Agenda* (1998) and *An Introduction* *to Global Citizenship* (2003). He is president of the International Development Ethics Association.

Emma Dowling holds a first degree in International Studies and Politics from the University of Birmingham and is currently studying for an MSc at the Centre for the Study of Global Ethics, University of Birmingham. Her main interests include the study of economic theory and ethics, dimensions of power and gender studies within a global context. She is also an active member of the social movement ATTAC (Association for the Taxation of Financial Transactions for the Aid of Citizens) within and beyond the UK.

Victoria Firmo-Fontan is a Post-Doctoral Research Fellow at Sabanci University, Turkey. She holds a PhD from the Centre for Peace and Development Studies at the University of Limerick, in the Republic of Ireland. Positions held include a research associate position in the Centre for Behavioural Research at the American University of Beirut, Lebanon, and a Marie Curie research fellowship at the University of Deusto, Spain. She specializes in issues of armed resistance and human trafficking. She has held several diplomatic postings in Bosnia-Herzegovina and Kosov@.

Ivan Manokha is a PhD student at the University of Sussex working on the discourse of human rights in the global political economy.

Bruno Moens is executive director at Payoke, Antwerp, Belgium. He holds an MA in Criminology.

Rachel Nizan holds an MA in Latin American Area Studies from the Institute of Latin American Studies in London. She spent a year working with street children in Honduras, doing both social work and research. Her main interests include children's rights, human rights, development and trade.

David Ould is deputy director of Anti-Slavery International. He has been closely involved with UK campaigning on issues of the commercial sexual exploitation of children and the use of bonded child labour in the hand-knotted carpet industries of South Asia. He helped to establish ECPAT UK and Rugmark UK to work on these issues and is on the boards of both groups. He is the representative for Anti-Slavery International on the Ethical Trading Initiative, a UK-based group that brings together companies, trade unions and non-governmental organizations (NGOs) to set common standards for companies trading in the South and to work together to trial different approaches to the monitoring and verification of these standards. He is also the treasurer of Kalayaan, a UK-based NGO working in support of migrant domestic workers.

Nele Praet is case manager at Payoke, Antwerp, Belgium. She holds an MA in Criminology.

Krishna Upadhyaya is bonded labour programme officer at Anti-Slavery International in London. He has an MA in Human Rights from Mahidol University in Bangkok and has worked for regional and national human rights organizations in Asia, focusing on bonded labour. His main areas of interests are democratization, civil society and labour rights.

Geraldine Van Bueren, a barrister, is Professor of International Human Rights Law at Queen Mary, University of London and W.P. Schreiner Professor, Faculty of Law, University of Cape Town. She is a consultant to the Commonwealth and to the United Nations.

List of Abbreviations

AABA	Association for Accounting and Business Affairs
APFL	All Pakistan Federation of Labour
ASI	Anti-Slavery International
ATOs	alternative trade organizations
BASE	Backward Society Education
BHRRC	Business and Human Rights Resource Centre
BiH	Bosnia-Herzegovina
CCOO	Confederación sindical de comisiones obreras
CEDAW	Convention on the Elimination of Discrimination against Women
CFDT	Confédération française démocratique du travail
CING	Children in Need Ghana
CKGR	Centre for Equal Opportunities and Anti-Racism
CRC	Convention on the Rights of the Child
CSR	corporate social responsibility
CWIN	Concerned Centre for Child Labour in Nepal
DEW	Development Education for Women
DR	Dominican Republic
EAP	economically active population
EIU	The Economist Intelligence Unit
ETI	Ethical Trade Initiative
EUPM	European Union Police Mission
FHIS	Honduran Social Investment Fund
FNV	Federatie Nederlandse Vakbeweging
FOSDEH	Social Forum of External Debt and the Development of Honduras
GAATW	Global Alliance Against Trafficking in Women
GEFONT	General Federation of Nepalese Trade Unions
GNCC	Ghana National Commission on Children
HIPC	heavily indebted poor country
HRW	Human Rights Watch
IAM	Information and Analysis Centre concerning Human Trafficking
ICCO	International Cocoa Organization
ICEM	International Federation of Chemical, Energy, Mine and General Worker's Union

IDB	Inter-American Development Bank
IDC	Institute of Development and Communication
IEBL	inter-entity boundary line
IHNFA	Honduran Institute of Childhood and Family
IITA	International Institute of Tropical Agriculture
ILO	International Labour Organization
IMF	International Monetary Fund
INSEC	Informal Sector Service Centre
IOM	International Organization for Migration
IPEC	International Programme for the Eradication of Child Labour
IPTF	International Police Task Force
LDCs	less developed countries
MDWs	migrant domestic workers
NATO	North Atlantic Treaty Organization
NGOs	non-governmental organizations
OHR	Office of the High Representative
OSCE	Organization for Security and Co-operation in Europe
PAN	*Plan de Acción Nacional* (Honduras)
PILER	Pakistan Institute of Labour Education and Research
PRSP	poverty reduction strategy paper
RIDE	Rural Institute for Development Education
SACCS	South Asia Coalition against Child Servitude
SAPs	structural adjustment programmes
SCF	Save the Children Fund
SFOR	NATO Stabilization Force in Bosnia–Herzegovina
SIMPOC	Statistical Information and Monitoring Programme on Child Labour
SUD	Solidarité Urgence Développement
TARA	Trade Alternative Reform Action
TCGA	Toledo Cacao Growers Association
TGWU	Transport and General Workers Union
UGT	Unión General de Trabajadores
UNDP	United Nations Development Programme
UNHCHR	United Nations High Commissioner of Human Rights
UNHCR	United Nations High Commissioner for Refugees
UNICEF	United Nations Children's Fund
UNMiBH	United Nations Mission to Bosnia-Herzegovina

UNPD	United Nations Population Division
UNTAC	United Nations Mission to Cambodia
UWA	United Workers Association
WAJU	Women and Juvenile Unit of the Police Department
WB	World Bank
WFCL	worst forms of child labour
WTO	World Trade Organization

Introduction: Combating Contemporary Slavery

Christien van den Anker

Why a collection on contemporary slavery?

Slavery was outlawed in Britain and in the rest of the world in the nineteenth century. Yet the practice has never been completely eradicated and recently several contemporary forms of slavery have caught public attention. The ship with child slaves on the coast of West Africa, the abuse of migrant domestic workers discovered in western cities, child labour in the carpet industry in India and in mines in Africa and Latin America have all attracted media attention in recent years. The work of Anti-Slavery International, still campaigning against slavery since its role in the abolition of slavery in the nineteenth century, has contributed to more and more people becoming aware of the existence of contemporary forms of slavery. Although research exists on all the forms of slavery mentioned above, researchers often do not use the term contemporary slavery to describe the subject of their work. Books focus, for example, on migrant domestic workers, on child labour or on bonded labour.

An edited collection on contemporary slavery allows us to show the variety in forms of contemporary slavery while bringing out the parallels in causes and potential remedies. Using the term contemporary slavery helps to show the urgent need for more people and governments to take steps towards ending this practice.

The definition of slavery is contested; African states have argued that the term should only be used for the transatlantic slave trade (see Chapter 1 in this volume). Although the use of the term slavery may conjure up oppressive images and has led to sensationalist reporting in the media, as well as to ill-thought-out actions by well-meaning members of the public, it still makes sense to describe certain practices

1

as slavery in order to call for more resistance and to distinguish slavery from intense exploitation. On the other hand, the authors are aware that creating justice involves more than combating slavery and even more than implementing fundamental human rights. The violations of other rights are not less deserving of campaigns and policy change. Yet, there is something especially baffling about the fact that slavery, outlawed since the nineteenth century and one of the first human rights violations to become the subject of an international convention, is still continuing to this day. Most of the measures suggested to combat slavery will protect human rights more widely.

What are the aims of the book?

The present volume results from a unique workshop at the Centre for the Study of Global Ethics at Birmingham University in May 2002, bringing together academics and campaigners on issues related to contemporary slavery. The book's foremost aim is to contribute to ending contemporary slavery. To that end, the book provides several analyses of current forms of slavery in the context of globalization, migration and a variety of local factors (Part I). In addition, it introduces the results of recent empirical research on various current forms of slavery in different parts of the world (Part II). The final aim of the book is to provide strategies and frameworks for change (Part III). All chapters show the complexity and diversity of specific forms of slavery in countries and regions, while at the same time teasing out parallels and links between types of slavery. In order to design effective policies to combat contemporary slavery, this work is crucial. The chapters introduce and clarify distinctions between slavery and other worst forms of (child) labour and exploitation. Most chapters provide an up-to-date overview of international law and policy-making on combating contemporary forms of slavery and provide an assessment of existing strategies to combat slavery. To make the book forward-looking and to strengthen its impact on reality, most chapters list practical goals to adopt in policy-making and the chapters in Part III critically assess wider directions of international policy-making, such as Fair Trade, development ethics, global taxation and reparations for past forms of slavery.

Who is the book for?

The book is written for an audience in universities as well as the general public. Our multidisciplinary approach will provide something new for students and lecturers in fields such as global political economy, political theory, international relations, anthropology, sociology, development studies, law and philosophy. It will also contribute to the understanding of the problem of increased slavery in policy-making and NGO campaigning. By including NGO perspectives on contemporary slavery, this book will complement existing academic scholarship. NGO activists have a lot to contribute to academic discourse. They provide a perspective on strategizing for change and they are well informed on recent developments on the ground and in legislation and policy-making. More academic chapters are helpful to NGOs not only for providing vital statistics to use as ammunition in political debates, but also by providing useful reflection on questions into the causes and remedies of contemporary slavery. We hope that the unique combination of academic and NGO papers will make the book attractive to both audiences.

What is in the chapters?

Chapter 1 assesses the complex ways in which globalization affects the increase in contemporary forms of slavery. On the one hand globalization contributes to exacerbated poverty, which leaves more people vulnerable to contemporary slavery, such as chattel slavery, child labour, trafficking, bonded labour and abuse of domestic workers. On the other hand, globalization contributes to more effective campaigns to raise awareness and to better international legal mechanisms to combat contemporary slavery. The way in which globalization influences particular forms of contemporary slavery influences which types of action may be most successful in combating the practice. For example, forms of slavery directly linked to export products or multinational companies, may be combated by consumer action, yet other forms such as bonded labour in local industries and religious-based slavery may need educational campaigns and local support for victims in addition to pressure on national governments to develop and implement national and international law.

In order to make some recommendations on the principles guiding policy-making, this chapter evaluates recent initiatives to combat the worst forms of slave labour by global standard-setting and proposes to develop new policies from the perspective of principles of global justice as well as from a pragmatic point of view. For example, initiatives to end slavery may sometimes take away people's livelihoods so viable alternatives need to be available in aid of effective implementation of legislation. Most importantly, victims' needs and rights as well as their agency need to be recognized in developing campaigns and policies to combat slavery. Furthermore, a cosmopolitan approach is advocated to create justice for all.

The main issues explored in Chapter 2 are: the effects globalization has on migration patterns and volumes in general; the predominantly defensive strategies most, if not all, developed states have introduced in response; and the unforeseen consequences thereof, an increase in the smuggling of human beings being one of the most significant among them.

In the first section, the chapter presents the most recent figures on migration in Europe, showing that immigration increased in recent years after the collapse of the Soviet Union. The response to increased immigration was to establish stricter legal measures on visas, asylum and so on. The section then argues that the crossing of borders by uninvited migrants was conceptualized as a security issue. At the start of the new millennium, it has become clear that both efforts to secure borders and to tighten eligibility within the processing of claims have had no long-lasting effect. Immigration in the countries of the European Union is still considerable. The next section contrasts national and global interests. It argues that liberal democracies have to balance the protection of their own citizens with the protection of human rights worldwide. Economic globalization integrates ever larger parts of the developing world rendering them dependent on the world market. Violent swings in prices combined with very rapid population growth lead to economic decline rather than development in many countries. This produces a rapidly increasing emigration pressure, which is exacerbated when people are the victim of civil strife or full-blown war. These conflicts too tend to be the result of direct or, more frequently, indirect forces of globalization.

The chapter then goes on to analyze the smuggling of migrants. Arguably the most significant effect of the one-sided approach to immigration as a security issue lies in the rise of a specific type of business operation: the smuggling and trafficking of human beings. Its conclusion states that the words *migration* and *security threat* can only be justifiably used together in the context of the threat to the well-being and basic human rights of the migrants concerned. It then sketches some policy implications, such as the consideration that alternatives to the present policies should do justice to the declining ability of states to control the movement of people and offer better protection to the basic human rights of those who are on the move.

In Chapter 3 the deputy director of Anti-Slavery International, David Ould, presents the range of human rights abuse covered by the term

'trafficking' and looks at the trafficking of people intc
Union. His chapter calls for specific measures by gove
adopted into a EU framework decision and lists wh
governments are already bound to by law.

In many cases slavery-like exploitation is worsened by trafficking. Anti-Slavery found that trafficking can be an aggravating factor in issues as diverse as: Chinese migrant factory workers working in factories set up in the export industries of Saipan; Nepalese children working as domestic servants in India; women migrant domestic workers from poor countries, such as the Philippines and Sri Lanka, working in the Middle East and Europe; children taken from West African countries to work in other countries of the region; young men from the north-east of Brazil taken to work in Amazonia; Chinese and Vietnamese illegal migrant workers in US sweatshops and other countries; children forced to go begging, either in their own or other countries; Haitian migrant workers in the Dominican Republic sugar industry; children taken from Pakistan, Bangladesh and various countries in Africa to ride as camel jockeys in the United Arab Emirates.

The International Labour Organization (ILO, 2002) has recently issued some new statistics for child labour generally and these say that in the year 2000 they estimate that worldwide some 1.2 million children were trafficked. The chapter discusses the recent developments in international legislation and policy-making to combat trafficking. Until very recently there was considerable confusion around what the term 'trafficking' actually meant. The definition used in a new United Nations Protocol, adopted in November 2000, represents the first internationally agreed definition of trafficking. Article 3 (a) of the *UN Protocol to Prevent, Suppress and Punish Trafficking in Persons, Especially Women and Children, Supplementing the United Nations Convention against Transnational Organized Crime* provides the first statement of a definition around which there now seems to be growing international consensus.

The general agreement at international level on this definition of trafficking is illustrated by a recent report by the UN Special Rapporteur on Violence against Women who looked at four different scenarios and considered whether the women were victims of trafficking (Coomaraswamy, 1997). Despite this agreement, there remains a lack of consensus about what should be done on behalf of the women, children and sometimes men who are the victims of trafficking, particularly what states and governments have an obligation to do on their behalf once these victims regain their freedom. Is the obligation restricted to upholding the law by seeking to prosecute traffickers?

ıt does a government's responsibility go much further? Anti-Slavery thinks it does.

Anti-Slavery and other NGOs were particularly vocal in calling for protection measures to be included in the European framework decision. This is because they have direct experience of assisting victims of trafficking and other extreme forms of exploitation. Anti-Slavery International found that efforts to outlaw and punish various forms of slavery will only work if governments at the same time provide protection and measures to rehabilitate or reintegrate victims.

In considering the rights of victims of trafficking and other forms of slavery under international law, Anti-Slavery and others have identified dozens of measures that states have an obligation to take to protect and assist the victims. The message of this chapter is that slave labour is not a problem that has reappeared just recently, but rather a serious pattern of abuse, which the world's richest societies have tended to ignore, assuming it cannot still exist either at home or abroad. They have ignored it because it undermines their confidence in their own ability to put an end to the gross violations of human rights from the past, such as slavery in the Americas in the nineteenth century or forced labour in the colonial and totalitarian regimes of the mid-twentieth century.

Chapter 4 presents an overview of the specific development of Belgian policy to combat trafficking in human beings. This policy is based on four pillars: the administrative level, labour law, legislation and implementation of the criminal code, and victim support. The chapter describes each of these four pillars and ends with an overview of the efforts of a Belgian NGO, Payoke, to support victims of trafficking.

Chapter 5 looks at how, months after the onset of 'Operation Infinite Justice' in Afghanistan, Afghan girls and women are subjected to an exponential increase in sexual and physical violence. In the lawless country where even the Allied troops do not dare to leave their compounds, women are more victimized than ever. Human trafficking has now reached a climax in Afghanistan whereby a girl can be sold for as little as a 100kg of wheat.

Deployment of international troops in the region will invariably increase the demand for slaves, judging by experience of what is labelled by Elwert (2000) as the post-conflictual market of violence. Bosnia-Herzegovina, as well as the Kosov@ province,[1] have been subjected to the mushrooming of brothels since the end of their respective recent violent conflicts. The objective of this chapter is to draw lessons from the post-conflictual trafficking in Bosnia-Herzegovina and to raise awareness about the risks for women of the present situation in Afghanistan.

Chapter 6 argues that paid domestic work is undertaken in most countries in Europe and it is mainly done and managed by women. Often it is not recognized properly as work. Abuse can occur more easily if the migrant domestic worker is seen as 'part of the family' or 'helping out' rather than as a worker with rights.

The chapter reflects on the use of the concept of slavery to describe the abuse that is suffered by some migrant domestic workers. Often people want to use the term slavery because it attracts media attention. Slavery is shorthand for long hours, lack of pay, and the use or threat of violence. In domestic work, violence is often casually used. The London-based support organization for victims of abuse directed at migrant domestic workers, Kalayaan, warns of the use of the term slavery to describe the plight of migrant domestic workers, as there is a pull to sensationalism. Another danger is that of racially stereo-typing both the workers and their employers. When speaking of slavery, there needs to be a villain. This may reinforce the racist myth of 'the evil Arab employer'.

Kalayaan was successful in that, after 11 years of lobbying, a change in the law meant that migrant domestic workers who had to leave their employers because of abuse were allowed to apply for leave to stay in the country – visas for migrant domestic workers, which gave them the right to change employers, were introduced.

The chapter indicates that further research needs to be done on the role of globalization and the increase in migrant domestic workers. In this respect the chapter on migration and trafficking is complementary to this chapter. Another issue for further research is the link between discrimination on the bases of gender and racism/ethnocentrism. The situation of abused male domestic workers should also be recognized as a topic for further research and NGO support.

Chapter 7 discusses the systems of debt-bondage (popularly known in South Asia as bonded labour) in India, Pakistan and Nepal. It explores the system of traditional debt-bondage prevalent in agriculture and other areas like brick kilns, quarrying, gem-cutting, the silk industries and other more recent industries like fish-processing, salt industries and among contract labourers.

In the discussion of these instances of bonded labour in South Asia some cross-cutting issues, such as the special situation of women and children, are highlighted. In addition, the chapter identifies the excluded groups of *dalits* and indigenous people as the main victims of this system. It then assesses existing legislation in all three countries and identifies lacunae in the law, especially in providing successful implementation mechanisms. This is followed by a discussion of the major components of programmatic actions taken against this system by various governmental, non-governmental and inter-governmental organizations. The chapter ends with conclusions and recommendations both in terms of reinterpreting the system and reorienting actions. The author suggests a rights-based approach to the understanding of the problem and programme-planning as a way forward. An example of rights-based analysis will be presented to contribute to the understanding of the problem.

Chapter 8 discusses the occurrence of the worst forms of child labour in Honduras as an example of a contemporary form of slavery. The author questions Western conceptions of childhood with regard to their applicability in non-Western countries and reviews the shift in perceptions of child labour in the context of Honduras. The question is asked as to what is wrong with children working and a sensitive position is developed to recommend that international law should combat the worst forms of child labour in the first instance. A recurrent theme is the distinctions between child work, child labour and child slavery. Child work is more benign and usually takes place in the home; child labour is outside the home and more harmful and detrimental to the child; child slavery is child work for no pay and under the threat of violence. Although not perfect, these distinctions do help to recognize that not all child work is harmful. Child labour increased as a result of the debt crisis in Honduras. Another major factor is the Aids epidemic; Honduras has 57 per cent of all Latin American cases. The author appraises Honduras' policy on combating the worst forms of child labour in the light of recent international legislation. The chapter ends with an assessment of the possibilities for success in combating the worst forms of child labour in Honduras. The way forward, it is argued, is to prioritize the implementation of ILO Convention 182. Longer term, all causes for exploitative child labour should be addressed. This means eradicating poverty.

In Chapter 9 the author presents her recent work on child labour in the cocoa industry in Ghana. She points out that Ghana is not representative, since the government has only recently been forced to partially liberalize the cocoa industry; they have long been the sole trading channel for cocoa exports and still set the minimum price to be paid to farmers. They have also limited the power of foreign buying companies, hence cocoa is being grown on small family farms rather than on big multinational-owned plantations. Cocoa grows better in a mixed environment. On many small family farms, child work is used regularly. Traditionally, this was seen as a good way to socialize children into work and education in schools was relatively unpopular. Today, attitudes have changed; farmers now see education as a helpful way out of cocoa farming which they do not find lucrative enough for their children. However, the Structural Adjustment Plan caused farmers to lose subsidies and made it harder for them to send their children to school. Child labour increased again and some are still using the old arguments of socialization. An interesting unintended consequence of the forced liberalization of the cocoa industry in Ghana by the Structural Adjustment Plan is that this created opportunities for direct foreign trade with farmers, which was useful for the Fair Trade movement. A myth that needs to be cleared up is that farmers receive a much higher price for their cocoa beans from Fair Trade organizations; it is mainly the additional investment in the community that creates the possibility of sending their children to school. The author argues that, because of the domestic structures of the cocoa industry in Ghana, there is a need to think broadly about child labour in this context, and to dissociate our thinking from the stereotypes of rogue farmers and rapacious multinationals often presented to us in the media. In-depth knowledge and understanding of domestic structures are prerequisite to advocating corporate social responsibility in the chocolate industry. The quest to promote education and freedom from child labour focuses on the removal of children from cocoa farms and on school enrolment. However, field-based evidence suggests that school enrolment is not a straightforward answer to child labour, as the two are closely interconnected in the vicious cycle of poverty, and that quantitative assessments should not be an exclusive measure of the need for intervention.

Chapter 10 discusses the links between the need for development ethics as a guiding framework for states, global institutions and individuals as global citizens and the struggle to combat contemporary forms of slavery. It focuses partly on the responsibility not to benefit from injustice. This would create a form of global citizenship beyond duties and obligations, incorporating present campaigns for consumers to buy Fair Trade products. The chapter responds to the question of whether a development perspective could handle problems in a globalized world at all: poverty no longer occurs neatly in so-called Third World countries; poverty in the former Soviet republics, Eastern Europe and the Balkans cannot be categorized as underdevelopment. The indicators of poverty are different there too. The author argues that the development framework could be usefully reconceptualized, especially in discourses about development ethics.

It is a common assumption that the primary ethical focus of development ethics is on the nature of well-being and the justification of the account given; for this well-being to be achieved, appropriate institutions at both the national and international levels are needed, but determining what these are is largely a matter of working out what works. This assumption will be questioned in a number of ways.

First, granted that standard models of development need ethical critique, the operational differences between the rival critiques on offer (e.g. neo-Aristotelian, Kantian, human rights) are less significant than the differences in the consequences of adopting rival normative theories of international relations or rival theories of global ethics.

Second, if effectively 'promoting' genuine development does not mean (and should not mean) maximizing it, we need to consider what ethical principles should underlie what states, transnationals and international institutions do *vis-à-vis* development.

Third, at the level of the individual, what principles ought to govern the behaviour and attitudes of individuals acting as global citizens? These issues are relevant both because individuals can play their part in global development (by acts of generosity, joining NGOs etc.) and because of how they relate to and influence their political institutions (and economic institutions), which will not change their priorities without 'citizen' pressure.

Fourth, the process of globalization makes a significant difference to how we understand the normative demands on states and individuals. This is both because globalization alters the circumstances in which priorities are decided (things become possible that were impossible or difficult before) and because it changes the nature of the ethical demands made on us.

Chapter 11 holds that arguments that new forms of slavery may have increased due to processes of globalization call for an examination of the material conditions of its victims. Systemic poverty is the driving force behind the unacceptable conditions of slavery. One of the contributing factors may be the increasing internationalization of financial markets. Therefore, it is necessary to assess how the activities of financial elites affect the lives and options open to poor people. Currency speculation is one aspect of international trade and finance that destabilizes vulnerable national currencies, consequently endangering the livelihoods of the country's citizens. It is not only the weaker developing countries that are affected by the consequences of currency speculation. Currency crises triggered by global financial speculation have occurred in Latin America, Russia, Asia and Africa, the social consequences of which have been immense. This chapter addresses currency speculation and its effects by discussing the feasibility and desirability of the Tobin tax. The argument is in favour of the tax as it poses a workable mechanism to decrease the volatility of financial markets and can yield resources to fund global solutions to global problems enhanced by poverty, such as human slavery. Furthermore, debates surrounding the Tobin tax reflect the need to question the dominant ideology of neo-liberalism, which emphasizes the priority of economics over politics by calling for less intervention in economic processes. It is evident that while financial and political elites advocate economic liberalism, their actions actually reflect the opposite. In this sense, the doctrine of neo-liberalism is proved wrong as international actors benefit from imposing a set of values upon poor countries that they themselves do not adhere to. For this reason, arguments against a Tobin tax must be unpacked to expose them for what they are: namely arguments in favour of maintaining a status quo in which human exploitation can thrive. In the final part of the chapter, the political situation and prospects for implementation of the Tobin tax are assessed.

Chapter 12 puts the development of Fair Trade in the context of global capitalism, poverty and sufferings associated with it, on the one hand, and the way global civil society and also some state governments have tried to deal with these issues on the other hand. The chapter discusses concrete examples of Fair Trade projects undertaken in a number of areas and their impact at the local level, especially evaluating how they have contributed to alleviation/prevention of slavery and slave-like labour. It subjects Fair Trade to a critical analysis, and undertakes a historical analysis into the root causes of injustice that Fair Trade deals with only rather superficially. The manner in which many former colonies were integrated into world trade some 50 years ago has largely remained the same and Fair Trade leaves in place the status quo.

In Chapter 13, the author argues for an International Charter for Reparations of Slavery. She provides two lines of argument. First, a legal precedent approach in the form of comparative historical jurisprudence. This approach shows that the slave trade was a form of piracy and piracy has been illegal for centuries. Second, the chapter outlines an argument which can succeed even against those who assert that the problem with the African slave trade was that most of it was not in breach of international law or domestic law at the time. This second approach would hold that since the international legal system is still largely based on state consent, states are free to agree amongst themselves on reparations for slavery and the slave trade.

The final part of the chapter discusses the questions of who is eligible for reparations of slavery, who has to pay and how much. The effects of the slave trade were most heavily felt in Africa, yet for some of the populations in South America and the Caribbean the effects are also still felt today. Much of the wealth of slave-trading countries such as Britain was created from slavery. However, the liability extends beyond states to commercial entities and families. There were also Africans who played a role in the slave trade. This leaves the question of what form of compensation should be provided. Since there will be very little reliance on individual claims, the author suggests dividing the awards in two: debt relief payments directly to affected states and payments aimed at civil society groups focusing on social entitlements such as education and health.

In order to have a consistent international framework dealing with reparations for past slavery, there would need to be an international body or commission to investigate claims for reparations, to assess the quantum (quantity) and to decide the form. Such a body would need to be set up under an international charter, with greater authority if under the auspices of the UN. One claim sets the figure for reparations at US$ 777 trillion. If we remember that slavery lasted for three centuries, this is not excessive.

The charter would not be the end of the process. The importance of a Slavery Reparations Commission is not only in its final result but also as an educative and conscience-raising process. The chapter concludes by holding out that reparations for slavery are an opportunity for global society to reaffirm human values.

Contemporary slavery is affecting millions of people worldwide and several workable strategies to combat this phenomenon have been developed recently. This book hopes to spread useful information on the causes and remedies of contemporary slavery and to inspire more research and political action to help end slavery. In order to contribute directly to the worldwide campaign to eradicate slavery in practice, the editor's royalties earned on the sale of this book will be donated to Anti-Slavery International.

Note

1. There is a difference between the Serbo-Croat spelling (Kosovo) and the Albanian spelling (Kosova). In order not to alienate part of her audience, Victoria Firmo-Fontan spells Kosov@ in this way.

Part I
Causes and Perspectives

1
Contemporary Slavery, Global Justice and Globalization

Christien van den Anker

Introduction

Slavery has been illegal for over a century. Freedom from slavery is an international norm, well established in international law. Yet, it is still not implemented worldwide Contemporary forms of slavery exist in all regions of the world, in the form of dangerous and exploitative types of child labour, trafficking, bonded labour and chattel slavery Usually, theories of justice, whether concerned with domestic arrangements or with the global context, propose answers to the question: what does justice require? However, in the context of thinking about contemporary slavery, the answer to this question is clear and widely shared already. This chapter is therefore concerned with the lack of implementation of the specific international norm of freedom from slavery and not with its justification in theories of justice. However, principles of justice and a cosmopolitan perspective of justice, including responsibilities towards people outside one's national borders are used to propose effective and just remedies against contemporary slavery. Two different questions will be asked: 1) what are the structural causes for the lack of implementation of this international norm? And 2) what does justice require when developing adequate policies to combat contemporary slavery? Effective implementation of human rights norms is hindered not only by lack of political will, but by several structural factors. In this chapter I assess the complex ways in which globalization affects the realization of the human right not to be enslaved. On the one hand, globalization contributes to exacerbated poverty which leaves more people vulnerable to contemporary slavery, such as chattel slavery, child labour, trafficking, bonded labour and abuse of domestic workers. On the other hand, globalization contributes to more effective campaigns to raise awareness and to create better international legal mechanisms to combat contemporary slavery. The proposed understanding of globalization as a political project whose content can be determined (instead of as a law of nature or an economic 'invisible hand' which cannot be halted) makes it possible and necessary to reflect on international measures to combat slavery, in addition to suggesting ways to improve the implementation of existing international law.

The way in which globalization affects particular forms of contemporary slavery influences which types of action may be most successful in combating the practice. For example, forms of slavery directly linked to export products or multinational companies may be combated by increased consumer action, yet other forms such as bonded labour in local agriculture and industries and religious-based slavery may need local awareness-raising and educational campaigns as well as pressure to develop and implement national and international law.

The policy recommendations in this chapter are based on an evaluation of recent initiatives to combat specific forms of slavery such as increased international standard-setting (trafficking and child labour) and fair, as well as ethical, trade (child labour and chattel slavery). The chapter ends with the recommendation of a wider perspective, taking into account recent proposals for global redistribution via taxation and more extensive development aid. In assessing ways forward, I propose to use five principles of justice:

1. respect for the rights of victims;
2. cosmopolitan impartiality (justice for all);
3. respect for the agency of victims;
4. commitment to long-term structural change of the global economy;
5. provision of support to develop viable alternative livelihoods.

Adherence to these principles implies that the presently called for rights-based approach to trafficking, for example, is better than a restrictive approach to immigration. Yet the cosmopolitan perspective argued for in this chapter advocates a wider conception of justice, creating obligations to contribute to the implementation of human rights across borders as well as a commitment to campaigning for the final two principles, which take us beyond the minimum provision of an adequate standard of living towards a more robust conception of global equality.

The concept of contemporary slavery

Theorizing about global justice is usually concerned with what justice is and with what it requires. Looking at the subject of contemporary slavery, however, there is a historic consensus that justice requires the end of slavery. Yet, despite near-universal moral and legal condemnation, slavery still exists and is on many accounts even increasing. Slavery was abolished in Britain in 1807 and throughout the British colonies in 1833. The League of Nations Slavery Convention outlawed slavery in 1926 and the United Nations Universal Declaration of Human Rights adopted in 1948 makes slavery and inhumane treatment a human rights violation in Article 4. According to Lillich (in Meron, 1984), the importance of a human right can be deduced from its status (determined by whether or not the article belongs to customary law under contemporary international law) and the restrictions on the specific article allowed for in the relevant treaty or convention. The Universal Declaration is widely considered a part of customary law and even more widespread consensus supports the position that the slavery article (along with the right to life, freedom from torture, freedom from genocide, freedom from retroactive legislation, equality before the law and arbitrary detention) forms part of customary law (Meron, 1989). Freedom from slavery is also non-derogable in times of war (along with the right to life, freedom from torture and the prohibition of retroactive legislation, being a person before the law and freedom of religion). This means that freedom from slavery is an important human right if we take the status/restriction test Lillich introduces seriously.

Other evidence for the widespread consensus on the importance of freedom from slavery is found in the support of countries for the relevant instruments outlawing slavery. The International Covenant on Civil and Political Rights of 1966 has been ratified by 149 countries (UNHCHR, 2002), which means that they are bound by its articles on the prohibition of slavery (Article 8[1]), the slave trade (Article 8[2]) and forced labour (Article 8[3]). In addition, the Supplementary Convention on the Abolition of Slavery, the Slave trade, and Institutions and Practices Similar to Slavery (1956) adds debt-bondage, serfdom, forced marriage, dowry and the inheritance of a widow to a male family member to the list of human rights violations illegal under international law. The recent Convention on the Rights of the Child specifically mentions child labour and has been ratified by a record 191 countries (UNHCHR, 2002). Most recently two optional protocols to the child rights convention were ratified by 48 state parties, outlawing the use of children in armed

conflict and the sale of children, child prostitution and child pornography. For details on international law on trafficking, see chapters 3
and 4 in this volume.

Yet, despite international law and many national constitutions outlawing slavery, the practice has never been ended. Although the traditional
form of slavery, with kidnapping, slave trading and people forced to
work in chains, no longer serves as an accurate picture of contemporary
slavery, slavery still exists in several modern guises. According to Anti-
Slavery International, the following common characteristics distinguish
slavery from other human rights violations. A slave is:

- forced to work – through mental or physical threat;
- owned or controlled by an 'employer', usually through mental or
  physical abuse or threatened abuse;
- dehumanized, treated as a commodity or bought and sold as
  'property';
- physically constrained or has restrictions placed on his/her freedom
  of movement.

Anti-Slavery International

New slavery is also defined as 'work for no pay and under the threat of
violence' (Bales, 1999). This definition excludes bad forms of servitude
and people pushed into bad labour conditions by poverty. However,
(the element of being paid or not is probably less important than the
elements of being forced to work against one's will and under threat of
violence, often with restrictions on freedom of movement through
either physical ties or by withholding of passport or identity papers.)
(In its contemporary form, slavery violates many other rights over and
above the right not to be enslaved, such as the rights to freedom,
property and fair remuneration for labour. The violence and the mental
degradation that come with most forms of slavery are violations of the
internationally protected right to be free from torture and inhumane
and degrading treatment.) Contemporary forms of slavery include bonded
labour, trafficking, the worst forms of child labour, forced marriage and
the abuse of domestic migrant workers. These now involve many times
the number of people the transatlantic slave trade ever involved.
Although reliable statistics on contemporary slavery are hard to come by
due to its illegal nature, Kevin Bales estimates that 27 million people are
contemporary slaves (Bales, 1999). Some international NGOs have put
the number as high as 200 million. Since most work on contemporary
slavery looks at one particular form of slavery at a time, there are more

estimates of, for example, child labour or bonded labour than of the total number of people trapped in contemporary forms of slavery. For recent figures, see chapters 7, 8, 9 and 12 in this volume. Here, contemporary slavery is analyzed as an overall category, since it is important to bring out the parallels in root causes as well as the differences in circumstances that are influential. These may in turn be important in finding a balance between policies that could be generalized over different forms of slavery and in different parts of the world on the one hand and policies that are specific to one type of slavery or to one region on the other hand.

The use of the term slavery is contested by some representatives of African states who argue that the term slavery ought to be reserved for the transatlantic slave trade. Although this is understandable, as is the campaigning for recognition of the harm done to people then and to communities in Africa as a continent, the parallels with contemporary slavery are stark enough to use the term in this way. Present injustice needs to be addressed and using the term slavery guarantees a wider audience. However, the term needs to be used cautiously and in clearly defined ways. Advocates of the rights of contemporary slaves need to avoid sensationalism and need to avoid focusing only on the 'most deserving cases'. Looking at different forms of abuse under the term slavery allows the possibility of identifying some common factors between them. Structural factors, or what are commonly termed root causes (in the trafficking and migration debates), are some of the elements contemporary slavery may have in common. Using the perspective of root causes, however, does not mean to say that there is one cause that determines all current forms of contemporary slavery. Still, there are a few common factors that have at least some influence, even though local factors play a role, too. According to Kevin Bales, it is poverty that makes people vulnerable to being enslaved in present times. Although there are many places where ethnicity or caste play a role, according to Bales the common denominator is poverty (Bales, 1999). I would argue that we need to take one step further and look at who is poor and therefore vulnerable to exploitation and slavery. Then it becomes clear that, although Bales is right that there is no racial justification for slavery any more as there was in the transatlantic slave trade, discrimination based on gender, race, ethnicity, religion or oppression of indigenous peoples contributes to specific groups being poor and is therefore a factor in making people more vulnerable to all forms of exploitation and thus to contemporary forms of slavery. In this chapter, I will focus on one particular root cause – increased poverty through globalization. Although I do not develop the other root causes, in two instances I will comment on gender and ethnic/racial discrimination. First, when discussing domestic violence as a contributing factor to women searching for work abroad and therefore becoming vulnerable to traffickers and, second, in the case of domestic migrant workers, where the cultural stereotypes of which women are especially good at what types of work are widespread (Anderson, 1993; and Chapter 6 in this volume).

In the remainder of this chapter, I argue that the complex process of globalization has provided a context in which new forms of slavery flourish. Even though not all forms of contemporary slavery are directly affected by globalization, indirectly they are linked through the increased poverty economic transition has brought and therefore responses should be internationally co-ordinated. The chapter argues further that policy-making should be based on certain specific principles of justice, in addition to the wrongness of slavery, in order to actually benefit the victims of contemporary slavery.

Finally, the chapter provides a focus on structural factors as well as agency, which, through actual examples, aims to show that people make the choices they can within certain parameters; it does not make sense to put easy moral blame on the people directly involved without holding responsible the people involved through longer causal chains. For example, it is easy to blame Bangladeshi employers for employing children. Yet, for the 14-year-old girl from the slum, it may be the best available option under the circumstances that she is employed in the garment industry. The political rhetoric in the West blaming local producers for exploiting child labour, masks the economic benefit that Western consumers get from cheap clothes and from keeping the economic rules of the game in place so that the majority of the world has hardly any chance of developing a mixed-base economy, without widespread poverty, with a decent living standard and adequate working conditions for all. On the other hand, the governments of, say, India and Nepal could do a lot more to implement international human rights law regarding bonded labour and forced marriages by enforcing the legislation in place in their own countries. In West Africa there is a lively trade in children from poor countries such as Benin, Togo and Mali into richer countries such as the Ivory Coast and Gabon. Parents sell their children in hope of a better future and traffickers need the children to make a living. A way forward suggested by UNICEF, which avoids the easy blame of the parents, is to make sure adults earn a wage that can support their families without having to sell their children into work.

Globalization as a political project

Kevin Bales argues that the world's slave trade has seen a rapid escalation since 1945 and a dramatic change in character. According to Bales the three factors sparking this change are:

> Firstly, the world's population has tripled since 1945 with the bulk of the growth in the Majority World. Secondly, economic change and globalization have driven rural people in poor countries to the cities and into debt. These impoverished and vulnerable people are a bumper crop of potential slaves. Finally government corruption is essential. When those responsible for law and order can be made to turn a blind eye through bribes, the slave-takers can operate unchecked.
>
> Bales, 2001

Bales' argument clearly supports the argument presented in this chapter that, at least to some extent, globalization is affecting new forms of slavery negatively. This does not mean to say that globalization is the only cause of new forms of slavery; if that were the case, any example of slavery existing before globalization or in areas less affected by globalization would be an argument against the thesis. The relationship between globalization and new forms of slavery is complex and in need of careful treatment.

Not all forms of contemporary slavery are affected in the same ways; some depend more on local practices and traditions than on the changing international economy. Both the position that globalization is the cause of all misery in the world and the view that globalization is the motor for growth and therefore brings prosperity to all are too simplistic. The role of globalization in the increase in contemporary slavery can only be analyzed by looking at different forms of slavery in different parts of the world and assessing to what extent local factors and global factors play a role.

First of all, in order to show how globalization is implicated with regard to increased slavery, the term itself needs to be discussed. Globalization consists of a complex set of processes in various spheres. Most observers would agree that globalization includes economic processes such as increases in international trade, deregulation of financial markets and the resulting flows of investments and currency speculation around the world. In addition, some have argued that globalization has several political components (Shaw, 1999). These are partly a result of economic globalization and partly an independent phenomenon. Increased international co-operation evidenced through the creation of multinational agencies and the codification of international norms in international law started as a response to human rights violations that threatened world peace. Increasingly, globalization of capitalism highlights issues to which an international political response is required. Patenting laws keeping cheap medicine unavailable in Africa have resulted in a huge death toll to AIDS/HIV and the widening gap between rich and poor with the deregulation of foreign investment worldwide has resulted in huge flows of people migrating to where they think they can find work. These issues strengthen the need for international institution-building. They also supported a tremendous growth in international NGOs. Developments in communications and travel have resulted in cultural globalization – partly top-down through multinational corporations, but partly bottom-up at alternative summits and forums, through tourism and via the internet.

The distinction between economic, political and cultural globalization is useful to make some sense of what we mean by the term globalization. Yet, there is a further point to make about the political elements of globalization. The perspective on globalization I use in this chapter in order to assess how globalization affects contemporary slavery holds that the present political and economic world order is the result of specific policy choices. Globalization in its present form and shape is the outcome of a political project aiming at universalizing global capitalism and neo-liberal principles. Economic globalization in the form of a sudden change of development strategy towards full incorporation into the world market, as part of structural adjustment programmes implemented by the IMF and the World Bank, does contribute to contemporary forms of slavery by increasing poverty and therefore vulnerability for specific groups of people. Although globalization has also provided opportunities for others, the view that globalization provides a motor for growth leaves out the difficult questions of distribution (who benefits?) and the cost of modernization to people's livelihoods. Political globalization – such as the growth of a global civil society with NGOs supporting people all over the world to get justice from their own government, from big companies and from overseas governments – can be of help to the victims of contemporary slavery. The changing conception of sovereignty and the development of international standards of human rights law and labour law are also working towards better protection of people from slavery and exploitation. On the other hand(components of globalization that contribute to contemporary slavery are: decreased border controls and cheaper international travel; increased information (or misinformation) about life in the West being affluent (through the globalization of the media);) an increased demand for the cheapest products and a lack of regulation so that flows of goods are determined by worldwide competition and labour is forced to be sold at the lowest price and under worsening conditions; increased travel and tourism, which adds to sex tourism (although the new middle classes in Asia make up the majority of clients demanding services of child prostitutes); and the use of child servants in the wider tourist industry.

Examples of effects of globalization on contemporary forms of slavery

To substantiate that globalization contributes to increasing numbers of people being enslaved, I will present examples of different types of contemporary slavery to illustrate the argument. In this section I discuss male adult slavery, child labour, bonded labour, trafficking and domestic migrant workers.

Adult male slavery

The cocoa industry in Africa has started to make use of slave labour because the world price for cocoa beans has plummeted. The lack of a worldwide fund to handle such substantial market price fluctuations leads to the local producers bearing the brunt of the economic shock. The owners of plantations can no longer afford to pay labour costs, so the use of slave labour becomes their only option other than going out of business. Eighty per cent of cocoa comes from the Ivory Coast and 95 per cent of the Ivory Coast's cocoa is tainted by slave labour (Channel 4, 2000). The economic policies required by the multilateral financial institutions such as the focus on export – usually of one primary resource – contribute to the price for these raw material exports plummeting. In this way the increasing use of slaves in the cocoa industry is an example of the effect of globalization, in particular the economic policies pursued in its name: deregulation, free trade, export-oriented growth and restructuring of local subsidies.

Child slavery

Another example of globalization affecting contemporary slavery negatively is the slave trade in children in West Africa. It is well known that in West Africa – on what was once called the slave coast – the trade in people continues.

Increasingly, children are bought and sold within and across national borders, forced into domestic work, work in markets or as cheap farm labour. UNICEF estimates there are more than 200,000 children trafficked in West and Central Africa each year. Child slavery is a significant money-maker in countries like Benin and Togo. Destitute parents are tricked into giving their children to slave-traders. A local UNICEF worker explains: 'People come and offer the families money and say that their children will work on plantations and send money home. They give the family a little money, from $15 to $30 – and then they never see their children again.

Bales, 2001

The BBC's *Correspondent* (2001) shows that the old custom of sending children to a wealthier relative to have better chances of education and of making a living has become perverted by the increased need for money, due to the globalization of the economy. Instead of sending them to relatives, children are now being sold to work for strangers in the cities or to go abroad. Parents want to believe in some El Dorado where their children will strike it lucky and be able to send money back to their families. Although the practice of sending children to relatives already existed traditionally, globalization exacerbates suffering, since being sold to strangers often leads to violence or the threat of violence. Children trafficked abroad or made to work in the city are more vulnerable to abuse and will often lose touch with their family. Latin American working children have also been affected negatively by globalization. In this case the link with globalization is that the Latin American economies have been very unstable as a result of financial crises. With the increasingly free flow of capital, speculation can harm currencies overnight. The ILO estimates that in 1995 at least 120 million of the world's children between the ages of five and 14 did full-time paid work (ILO, 1996). Many of them worked under hazardous and unhygienic conditions and for more than ten hours a day (Basu, 1999, p. 1083). However, the worldwide trend is that child labour is decreasing. In no continental region in the world is the participation rate of children as high as it was in nineteenth-century Britain, although some individual nation-states, such as Ethiopia, have a much higher rate (Basu, 1999, p. 1088). A problem with the statistical evidence is that child labour is likely to be underreported due to its illegal status and figures vary significantly depending on the definition one uses.

Some see child labour as part of a tradition or part of a culture whereas others argue that it is linked to a phase in economic development. After all, child labour was widespread in Western Europe from the age of the Industrial Revolution and in the USA from the mid-nineteenth century (Basu, 1999, p. 1083).

Existing forms of child labour vary from country to country and from situation to situation. In some cases a child may be involved in working on the family farm or in selling produce on the market. In other cases, there may be industrial labour involved. There is always an issue of children's rights at stake, since children have a universal right to free primary education according to Article 26 of the Universal Declaration of Human Rights. Their involvement in work often (although not always, as is shown in Chapter 9 in this volume) takes them away from school and therefore violates their right to an education. The lighter forms of child labour such as working on the family farm could be combined with education if there was access to proper schools (Bhatty, 1997). However the worst cases of child labour violate many other fundamental human rights. There is a widespread consensus that poverty is the main cause of child labour in developing countries (Johnson, Hill and Ivan-Smith, 1995). However, in addition to poverty, there is a complex of factors at work in the causation of child labour. Save the Children lists the interaction of micro- and macro-economic, environmental, social, cultural and political factors. On the macro-economic level they emphasize the role of adjustment and transition programmes, the decline in social sector spending and the internationalization of production (Marcus and Harper, 1996). This supports my argument.

Bonded labour

Another example to illustrate the relationship between globalization and the increase in contemporary forms of slavery is the case of bonded labour. Bonded labour has existed for centuries in countries like India, Pakistan and Nepal. Although national legislation (often even at the level of the constitution) outlaws it, many families are indebted for huge sums of money and pass on the debt from generation to generation. The system has feudal connotations in that the landowners take on a paternalistic role towards their bonded labourers. They will provide food and some form of security. In one case, a debt-bonded labourer was able to buy himself free, but returned into bondage out of choice. The reason for preferring to belong to the landowner was the safety of living according to the same rules as he had always lived. This example is not an isolated case; regularly freed bonded labourers return to their previous conditions of bondage. The deeply rooted practices need to be combatted not only through government policies to abolish them, but through measures of support and aid in finding alternative livelihoods. This implies the need for support beyond legal and economic measures, for example through projects providing emotional and educational support (Bales, 2002). The way in which globalization has affected bonded labour is again complex. Bonded labour existed before globalization and is linked to the caste system in some of the countries concerned. However, the increased poverty as a result of the economic transitions due to globalization leaves people once again vulnerable to debt-bondage and being owned by landowners. With increased price levels for necessities such as medication, families may need to borrow money to survive. As Upadhyaya argues in Chapter 7 of this volume, new forms of bonded labour are developing as a result of globalization.

Trafficking

An example of contemporary slavery that has increased exponentially recently is trafficking. Women from Central and Eastern Europe and from the former Soviet Union, including the Central Asian republics, are being trafficked into Western Europe and the Far East. Many governments still conflate trafficking with undocumented migration, particularly into prostitution. Part of the problem is the definition of trafficking. The definition of trafficking used here is based on definitions used by the UN, UNICEF and the International Organization for Migration (IOM). Forced migration or forced work after consented migration counts as trafficking, whereas consented legal travel is called migration and consented but illegal travel is smuggling. However, the notion of consent is highly contested, with some feminist lobby groups arguing that all prostitution should be considered trafficking, whereas others, like Doezema (2002), hold that coercion is a necessary element of the definition of trafficking. The former position views trafficking as merely linked to prostitution; the type of work trafficked people end up doing is often in the sex industry but not always. Research needs to look into traffickers forcing people to work in agricultural and other industries, too. In addition, by linking trafficking to the sex industry only, the movement for sex workers' rights has to deal with the problem of sex work attracting the connotation of illegality and immorality.

The immediate link between globalization and trafficking is, once again, increased poverty during economic transition towards capitalism. Whereas work was guaranteed under socialism, after the collapse of the Soviet Union, unemployment has risen enormously and the majority of the unemployed are female (Einhorn, 1996). Even people in work often do not receive their wages, thus poverty has increased dramatically in the former communist countries. Another link between trafficking and the globalization of capitalism is that the increasingly free flow of capital is not accompanied by the free flow of people. On the contrary, immigration rules are becoming more and more restrictive, so poor people hardly ever have the option of becoming legal economic migrants. Many give their life savings to mafia-like networks to travel into Western Europe. The third link with globalization is that these(networks are also growing, due to the economic chaos of transition, and they benefit from globalization in that they, too, can send capital around the world and launder money in a deregulated global economy.)

Domestic migrant workers

Finally, a more hidden form of slavery takes place right under the noses of Western citizens. Domestic migrant workers regularly suffer abuse by their employers, often without having access to remedies. The law in Britain and in many other European countries and the US, allowed diplomats to bring a servant if that was part of their culture. Servants were allowed into the country on the passport of their employer, so they did not have a visa to stay in the country legally if they left this employer. This made it especially hard for them to escape from an abusive situation. As a result of campaigning by Kalayaan (see Chapter 6 in this volume) this legal practice has now changed. However, evidence shows that many domestic migrant workers are still prevented from leaving the house; they have to work all hours and suffer violence and lack of food or a warm place to sleep. Their mental well-being is completely disregarded; they are treated as less than human. In one case in France, the woman domestic migrant worker could not read or write and did not have a sense of time or seasons once she was freed (Anderson, 1993).

Again, in this case as in the previous cases, there are several links with processes of globalization. First, poverty makes people more vulnerable and induces them to leave their home community due to lack of an alternative livelihood. Second, the increasing division between rich and poor is not only visible between countries but within countries, too. Those who have the means, can employ the poor without providing proper care through contractual obligations. Third, women's participation in the labour market has increased everywhere since the 1950s. This is partly due to independent patterns of change in social arrangements campaigned for by the women's movement and partly due to the globalization of capitalism as women are now brought in as a flexible workforce. Those women who can afford it will therefore increasingly hire help with domestic tasks. Domestic migrant workers undertake labour-related tasks in the household and also work in home-based child care. Fourth, the increase in immigration due to increased opportunities for travel and communication bring women who see an opportunity to earn money abroad to send back to their families at home. The gender and racial discrimination in the labour markets will force them into domestic work, even if they have been educated for different careers. On the other hand, as in other examples, globalization has also raised awareness of injustice in different parts of the world and brought about an increasing sense of global citizenship and responsibility for suffering across borders.

In conclusion, these examples show that globalization plays a role in all of the forms of contemporary slavery discussed. Some have existed for longer and are ingrained parts of a culture. Others, like trafficking, are relatively new and are more directly a result of an economic transition to global capitalism. It is important to characterize globalization as a political project which can be influenced by policy decisions and campaigns. In other words, the future of the people suffering from slavery depends on the design of a global system that neither exacerbates poverty nor opens the door to networks of traffickers by restrictive immigration policies. I therefore now look at existing remedies and potential ways forward.

Remedies: principles of justice, structural change and pragmatic ways forward

What does justice require? Justice requires an end to slavery in all its forms. There is global consensus on this between governments who have ratified the necessary international conventions, activists lobbying governments to implement these obligations and victims organizing in many parts of the world. Yet the struggle to end slavery runs into many obstacles. In the first part of this chapter, I argued that the globalization of capitalism, the resulting poverty, unemployment and increased migration, as well as more, generally easier opportunities for travel and communication, were contributing factors to the rise of contemporary slavery. In this second part of the chapter I identify some of the implications of this analysis for policy-making and campaigns in the struggle against slavery. At the start of this chapter, I explained that the question of what justice requires is no longer relevant when looking at the issue of slavery, as there is broad agreement on the moral wrong of slavery and the practice is outlawed in international law. However, governments are not legislating even though they are required to implement international law at home. For example in Gabon, where many children from poorer West African countries end up working in foreign and Gabonese homes, trafficking is not illegal. In Benin, a major source of trafficked children, selling children is not illegal – it is only illegal to smuggle them across borders. Many governments see trafficking as a matter of immigration, as the Gabonese minister explains in *Correspondent* (BBC, 2001). The response is to implement immigration procedures more strictly. This is harmful to trafficked persons. According to the UN Special Rapporteur on Violence Against Women,(responses to trafficking must be based on the needs of trafficked persons, and they must be tailored to protect their rights with an emphasis on gender-specific violations)(GAATW, 2001, p. 27).

Sometimes governments legislate, such as in India where bonded labour is illegal in the constitution. However, this right is not being implemented. In many cases officials are implicated in slavery practices. In West Africa mayors, chiefs of villages and others take part in falsifying documents for trafficked children; in Western European countries the adult women victims of trafficking often do not get the support from the police they need; and in Benin there are examples of slave owners who bribe police to get runaway girls back (BBC, 2001). In some cases existing international norms may not be adequately phrased to include the contemporary versions of slavery. Therefore some initiatives have focused on developing new international instruments. The ILO Convention 182 on the worst forms of child labour and the recent UN trafficking protocol are examples of this approach. In Convention 182, the ILO lists the worst forms of child labour as:

- all forms of slavery or practices similar to slavery, such as the sale and trafficking of children, debt-bondage, serfdom and forced or compulsory labour, including forced or compulsory recruitment of children for use in armed conflict;
- the use, procurement or offering of a child for prostitution, production of pornography or pornographic performances;
- the use, procurement or offering of a child for illicit activities, in particular for the production and trafficking of drugs;
- work which, by its nature, or the circumstances in which it is carried out, is likely to harm the health and safety or morals of children.

The Convention states that each country must decide which types of work are harmful and need to be targeted as a matter of urgency. This should be done after consulting employers' and workers' organizations and other interested parties. This means special attention should be paid to:

Work which exposes children to physical, psychological or sexual abuse;

Work underground, underwater, at dangerous heights or in confined spaces;

Work with dangerous machinery, equipment and tools, or which involves the manual handling or transport of heavy loads;

Work in an unhealthy environment which may, for example, expose children to hazardous substances, agents or processes, or to temperatures, noise levels, or vibrations damaging to their health;

Work under particularly difficult conditions, such as work for long hours or during the night or work where the child is unreasonably confined to the premises.

ILO, 1999, pp. 8–9

To make international law more useful in combating trafficking of human beings, the UN adopted two protocols related to trafficking: the *Protocol Against the Smuggling of Migrants by Land, Sea and Air*, and the *Protocol to Prevent, Suppress and Punish Trafficking in Persons, Especially Women and Children*, both supplementing the *United Nations Convention against Transnational Organized Crime* (UN, 2000). The latter provides the first international definition of trafficking in persons. This definition has gathered the greatest international consensus since it does not take sides in the prostitution debate. The definition used is as follows:

(a) The recruitment, transportation, transfer, harbouring or receipt of persons, by means of the threat or use of force or other forms of coercion, of abduction, of fraud, of deception, of the abuse of power or of a position of vulnerability or of the giving or receiving of payments or benefits to achieve the consent of a person having control over another person, for the purpose of exploitation.

Exploitation shall include, at a minimum, the exploitation of the prostitution of others or other forms of sexual exploitation, forced labour or services, slavery or practices similar to slavery, servitude or removal of organs.

(b) The consent of a victim of trafficking in persons to the intended exploitation set forth in subparagraph (a) of this article shall be irrelevant where any of the means set forth in subparagraph (a) have been used.

O'Connell Davidson, 2002, pp. 2–3

For a more detailed discussion of the new trafficking protocol see Chapter 3 in this volume.

These new instruments still leave governments the space to approach slavery from a law and order perspective, which may harm the victims even further. Therefore, principles of justice would still be helpful to guide practice when aiming to overcome barriers to effective implementation of international law.

Broadly speaking the implications of the argument in the first part of this chapter can be summarized into five principles that should guide policy-making in combating contemporary forms of slavery:

1. respect for the rights of victims as starting point;
2. cosmopolitan impartiality (justice for all) as the basis for policies/laws;
3. respect for the agency of victims;
4. the long-term goal of structural change to global capitalism;
5. the provision of support to develop viable alternative livelihoods.

The human rights approach defended by, among others, the United Nations High Commissioner of Human Rights (UNHCHR) (Jordan, 2002) would satisfy the first three of these principles, but not necessarily the last two. The perspective of long-term structural change in the global economic system is not part of the human rights doctrine as it stands. The provision of support to develop viable alternative livelihoods is part of NGO practice and campaigns, for example for bonded and child labourers, yet is not fully part of the agenda on trafficking.

I would like to use the remainder of this section, to outline some of the implications of holding these principles when working towards policies and action to end the practices of contemporary slavery. The first principle (respecting the rights of victims) would, for example, require governments to provide assistance for victims of trafficking who are now being deported without help to re-establish themselves at home, not taking into account the threat of violence in the home country by networks of traffickers. By withholding victim support, governments sending people home violate their rights for a second time. The second principle (cosmopolitan impartiality) would require that the strategies to combat contemporary slavery must not be based on crude self-interest of the powerful parts of the international community, such as protection of their national industries from cheap imports or their societies from immigrants suspected of using welfare benefits without contributing (Doomernik, this volume, Chapter 2). Instead, the rights and interests of all people would need to guide policy-making. This means that the contributing factors of poverty and globalization are targeted in policy-making, which includes reviewing trade regimes and supporting poor people wherever they live. The third principle, to respect agency and therefore to avoid paternalism, would require strategies to combat contemporary forms of slavery aimed at the empowerment of the potential victims. This means governments and NGOs need to recognize the agency of (potential) victims, rather than portraying them as helpless victims from the outset. The fourth principle, the longer-term goal of structural change of the global economy, is very important. The Fair Trade movement has done invaluable work in supporting poor producers. Their aim is to create alternative livelihoods, which contribute to ending slavery as well as other exploitative forms of labour (see Chapter 12 in this volume). Yet the transition of the present unjust global economy towards one based on Fair Trade will require more far-reaching measures, if it is feasible at all. However, the Fair Trade movement has made an inroad into neo-liberal economic thinking, by introducing justice and responsibility for the well-being of poor producers into trade relations. Another proposal that may prove fruitful in this respect is the Tobin tax. This is a proposed tax on financial currency speculation with the revenue being used for development goals (see Chapter 11 in this volume). This tax may be the first step towards more far-reaching proposals for global taxation such as those discussed in Pogge (1998) and Beitz (1979 and 1983). Global redistribution rather than development aid will provide structural change, although eventually the capitalist system itself needs to end in order for structural change to have the effect of ending slavery and creating meaningful work for everyone. The fifth principle, of providing alternative livelihoods, requires strategies to assist people who have been enslaved or who are potential victims of slavery, to develop livelihoods that safeguard them against being enslaved (again). This would include programmes to develop alternative means of existence for freed bonded labourers and for children who are doing the worst forms of child labour. Only programmes that provide realistic alternatives will help.

Examples of good practice are the projects implemented by the UK Department for International Development (DfID) and Save the Children, which address the underlying cause of child labour – poverty – and work towards improving working conditions and regulation (Marcus and Harper, 1996).

In the meantime, campaigners ask consumers and citizens to use their consumer power not to buy products tainted with slave labour, to demand from suppliers that they make sure labour is properly treated and to lobby their MPs to set up campaigns against wide-ranging issues, from apartheid to landmines. Governments can put pressure on international organizations and individual governments to stick with ILO core labour standards and international human rights law. International organizations need to develop standards and enforce them more effectively. These more pragmatic approaches are responses to the recent awareness of the practical barriers to eliminating slavery. For example, in the case of child labour, it has been shown that consumer boycotts or outlawing products made by children can lead to a worse existence for the child in question, with the child forced to earn money by alternative means, probably in prostitution or the drugs trade. This was the case in Bangladesh, where it was observed that attempts to bar children from working in the manufacturing industry led to some of them being pushed into prostitution (Bachman, 1995, p. 3). Yet, even if legislation is unsatisfactory, there are other measures governments and supranational organizations can take. Basu suggests that, 'Government can intervene in the market to create a variety of incentives, such as providing better and more schools, giving school meals, and improving conditions in the adult labor market, which result in a reduction of child labor' (Basu, 1999, p. 1093). Another strategy aimed at eliminating child labour is to encourage children to go to school. Making primary education compulsory has been more effective than legal bans on child labour or products made by children. It is easier to check whether a child turns up in school than whether they are absent from work (Basu, 1999, p. 1090). Some studies have suggested that child labour may sometimes make it possible for children to go to school, for example in the case of part-time labour. Generally speaking, compulsory education can play a role in limiting child labour and, even if education is not compulsory, the mere availability of good schools can do a lot to divert children away from long hours in the workplace (Drèze and Gazdar, 1996).

An additional strategy to combat new forms of slavery is to set up information campaigns and invest in education to empower those people making the choices. This is currently part of the EU strategy to combat trafficking, although, in most countries, trafficking is still considered a problem of illegal migration, and many countries use the practice of deporting victims of trafficking since they are illegal immigrants.

However, Spain, the Netherlands and Belgium now have policies in place where victims of trafficking are offered legal means to stay and work in the country if they are prepared to give evidence against traffickers. Nowhere in Europe are victims of trafficking supported to return home or to make a proper living in their country of immigration.

Other existing strategies to combat new forms of slavery are also contested and so far only partly successful. Ethical trade has made a lot of progress in getting supermarkets to sign up to codes of conduct and has been successful partly because of growing consumer pressure and awareness. However, supermarkets are still one step ahead of the game and exploit people in ways that are not against the code of conduct. For example, farmers are told exactly what the product should look like even before it is planted and the price is only agreed at the point of sale.

Conclusion

Globalization influences all contemporary forms of slavery negatively, even if they existed previously in a traditional form. However, the way in which globalization plays a role differs between forms of slavery. This implies, too, that the ways to combat contemporary forms of slavery existing in different parts of the world vary, at least to some degree. However, there are some common ways forward for all types of contemporary slavery, for example lobbying for the ratification and implementation of international law and for the introduction and implementation of national laws to punish and prevent slavery. Recently, new international law has been developed to combat new forms of slavery and the worst forms of child labour. But its enforcement is still a huge challenge and, ironically, just as with codes of conduct, new standard-setting can actually work out as a form of protectionism by the US and Europe. Campaigns to raise awareness in the affected countries, as well as in the countries that profit from the cheap labour of slaves, are also useful in all types of contemporary slavery, as are campaigns to provide alternative livelihoods for slaves and ex-slaves (and also for slaveholders in cases where their original livelihood 'forces' them to 'employ' slave labour). In all cases of contemporary slavery, provisions need to be established for ex-slaves to overcome the trauma of slavery and to be educated and reintegrated into society on a basis of equality. Finally, all current slaves and future potential slaves would benefit from lobbying for global taxation such as the Tobin tax, increased funding of development projects, growing networks of Fair Trade and exposing the poverty-increasing effects of globalization and its existence as a political project, not a law of nature.

Globalization has also contributed to the culture of opposition to injustice, by facilitating easier networking between NGOs, the growth of international organizations and international law in areas of human rights and labour conditions and, more generally, increased collaboration between states due to a changing conception of sovereignty. Some specific ways forward for different types of contemporary slavery are, for example, campaigns to show governments that the focus on immigration in order to combat trafficking results in more hassle for the victims. Governments need to be shown that the rights and interests of the victims of trafficking should come first. Other specific ways forward would be the organizing of bonded labourers into savings unions to buy themselves free one by one and awareness-raising on the issue of domestic migrant workers. Cosmopolitanism usually argues in quite abstract ways about duties and rights across boundaries. The goal of eliminating contemporary slavery raises the prospect of strengthening the cosmopolitan approach since it shows that injustice is already widely perceived as a matter of responsibility across boundaries. Consumer actions against products made by slaves show motivation to end injustice no matter where it takes place. It may be argued that the ongoing support for unjust practices is due more to lack of information than to lack of motivation to be just to people across national borders. In this chapter I proposed to use five principles as a guideline for policy-making and campaigns in the struggle to eliminate contemporary slavery:

respect for the rights of victims as starting point;
cosmopolitan impartiality (justice for all) as the basis for policies/
laws;
respect for the agency of victims;
the long-term goal of structural change to the 'rules of the game' of
global capitalism;
the provision of support to develop viable alternative livelihoods.

These principles would help us to go beyond present approaches and they would provide a perspective which would designate responsibility for contemporary forms of slavery no longer simply at the door of the immediate perpetrators, but more widely in the overall international system and its present inequality. They need to form the basis for national policies as well as for global initiatives.

2
Migration and Security: The Wrong End of the Stick?

Jeroen Doomernik

Introduction

It would almost appear as if states need security threats, either because there are institutions or individuals therein who make a living out of identifying and combating such threats to the well-being of the state, or maybe because the political community is in a permanent need of defining the 'others' (potentially dangerous) for the benefit of being able to define who we are as people who belong together. If there is some truth in this assumption, we can perhaps at least partly explain why the collapse of communism by the end of the 1980s was followed by a growing concern among policy-makers, opinion leaders and scholars for the links between immigration, foreigners and security issues. This development could be observed in most if not all Western states. In the United States, Myron Weiner (1993) was among the first scholars to discuss all the potential risks involved with (more) international migration. Theoretically those can be manifold (Weiner and Teitelbaum, 2001). In Europe, ethnic differences and their potential for conflict within immigrant receiving states was put on the agenda time and again. Well before 11th September 2001 the many Muslims who had immigrated from the countries surrounding the Mediterranean to France and north-western Europe and from former colonies in Asia to the United Kingdom had become the main targets of such discussions. Relatively minor incidents are easily blown out of all proportion[1] and the many examples of well-integrated Muslim immigrants (and their descendants) are just as ignored as any other aspect of 'normal' everyday life. It should be noted, however, that not all European states respond in similar ways to such cultural challenges. Those that are founded on the assumption of cultural homogeneity (for example, France and Germany) are more likely to see diversity as a threat than those that have more plural traditions (for instance Britain, the Netherlands or Belgium). Yet even within the latter states we have been witnessing an increased sense of alienation, projected by the native populations onto the immigrant populations in general and the Muslims among them in particular and vice versa. We can merely observe this trend and no analysis allows us to establish the causal relationships beyond reasonable doubt. But even then, the increased focus on security issues as arising out of immigration and immigrants will certainly not have helped to decrease tensions.

Above, the suggestion might have transpired that this 'securitization' of immigration and immigrants solely came about because a new threat had to be defined. This obviously would be too simple, since migration patterns and the size of migration flows started to change at around the same time that the Soviet Union started to crumble. What's more, with the Cold War being over, the West lost much interest in regions that soon thereafter were to become the scenes of massive human rights violations.

First of all, we are to have a closer look at those flows – taking the European Union as an example. Subsequently, we will discuss what types of related changes the world as a whole has gone through. The main issues to be explored are the effects globalization has on migration patterns and volumes in general, the predominantly defensive strategies most, if not all, developed states have developed in response and the unforeseen consequences thereof; an increase in the smuggling and trafficking of human beings being one of the most significant among them. This frequently appears to lead to situations of vulnerability and exploitation of migrants, in its most extreme form turning them into modern-day slaves.

Migration in a globalized world

Even though fears concerning hordes of people migrating from East to West (images of millions of prospective migrants sitting on suitcases awaiting their chances were invoked in the media) never came true, considerable migration did take place after the collapse of communist regimes in Central Eastern Europe and the former Soviet Union. In the beginning of the 1990s, Germany alone saw the arrival of more immigrants than the United States of America in the same period (Doomernik, 1997b). A large proportion of new arrivals was made up by ethnic Germans, so-called *Aussiedler*, who had an automatic right to German citizenship.[2] These migrants were among the few privileged to have a country where they knew themselves to be welcome.[3] For many other prospective or actual migrants this was very different. As a result, the number of asylum seekers increased rapidly. To them applying for asylum was the only feasible way to get a foot in the door, regardless of whether they were in need of protection or not. During the mid-1980s, the numbers of migrants asking for asylum in Europe fluctuated between 150,000 and 200,000 annually. By the end of that decade, their numbers started to rise and reached 400,000 in 1990. In 1992 they reached 676,000, two-thirds of the claims being filed in Germany alone. Many of those applications were unsuccessful in that they did not lead to a permanent residence permit, be it as a Convention refugee[4] or because of less specific humanitarian considerations. This does not mean, however, that these migrants did not settle. There were those who found alternative means of getting a residence permit (for example, through marriage, a work permit, as a student, and so on), were tolerated (currently Germany is host to half a million of such aliens) or simply remained in an undocumented state. Of the latter we, obviously, have no figures. Other immigrants too, are not always easily enumerated, especially not if figures for different countries are to be comparable. From Table 2.1, which is based on figures from the EU statistics office (EUROSTAT) (1995), we can get some idea of the volume of immigration in the EU from Central and Eastern Europe in the early part of the 1990s.[5] The table is based on stocks (in contrast to flows, documenting arrivals and departures) for 1993. If we look at the inflow of migrants in this particular year it becomes very clear that by far the largest proportion of those persons must have arrived recently (Table 2.2).

Table 2.1 Foreign nationals from East and Central Europe in selected EU countries, 1993

	Germany *	*Netherlands*	*France*	*Belgium*
Former USSR	79,049	2,123	4,661	1,160
Poland	285,553	5,362	47,127	4,812
Romania	167,327	1,851	5,114	*not available*
Hungary	61,436	1,184	2,736	720
Former CSR	63,724	802	2,433	557
Bulgaria	59,094	615	968	*not available*
Total	716,183	11,937	63,039	7,249

* excluding approximately 3.5 million *Aussiedler*, who are German nationals.
Source: EUROSTAT, 1995

Table 2.2   Immigration from East and Central Europe in selected EU countries, 1993

	Germany*	Netherlands	France	Belgium
Former USSR	99,637	1,253	920	570
Poland	75,195	1,263	1,042	735
Romania	81,769	241	931	not available
Total CEE	329,266	3,376	3,339	1,613

* excluding approximately 220,000 *Aussiedler*.
Source: EUROSTAT, 1995

Many, if not nearly all, of the migrants brought together in tables 2.1 and 2.2 arrived unsolicited and a high proportion of them will have filed an asylum request. These tables are merely an illustration, for many other immigrants arrived from Africa and Asia (for Germany: 15,258 and 29,235 respectively; it is important to note that these are aliens who have received a residence permit, thus excluding recent asylum requests: 37,570 and 50,209 respectively).

In Germany, Chancellor Kohl spoke of an emerging state crisis. The opposition parties deemed this to be a gross exaggeration but nevertheless soon thereafter agreed to a radical change in the German constitution, aiming to keep at bay as many asylum seekers as possible. Similar reactions have been in evidence in most other Western European states, especially those which have comprehensive asylum systems, although their constitutions did not require change to achieve this.

The main vehicle by which to address the asylum crises of the early and mid-1990s was thus of a legal nature: that is, definitions of who is eligible for protection, the duration thereof and the modalities attached to it. In a similar vein a number of countries of origin were defined as being safe (that is, under normal circumstances their citizens are not subjected to persecution) and others as safe third countries (countries where an asylum seeker could and should have applied for asylum before arriving at his/her final destination). Whenever either of these criteria applies, an asylum request is deemed manifestly unfounded or inadmissible. Supplementing such measures, travellers from most countries known to 'produce' asylum seekers and irregular migrants are obliged to acquire a visa before their departure. Carriers not checking the validity of this visa and the migrants' passports are liable to fines. Furthermore, agreements were made between a number of EU states to prevent asylum shopping (that is requesting for asylum in more than one member state). In addition, Europe's external borders were given more attention. Because the crossing of borders by uninvited migrants had been conceptualized as a security issue, in some states voices could be heard suggesting that the armed forces should be involved. At the start of the new millennium, it has become clear that both efforts to secure borders and to tighten eligibility within the processing of claims have had no long-lasting effect on numbers of unsolicited migrants. Immigration in the countries of the European Union is still considerable. In the northern countries requests for asylum remain high, in the South – where asylum systems are only now gradually being put in place – immigrants remain predominantly undocumented. The United States, too, has a large number of undocumented immigrants, mainly from Central America but increasingly also from China. And this in spite of a Mexican–US border turned into something akin to the Berlin Wall. In short: immigration and migrants appear to have become part of the daily experience of all developed nations. Why is this?

National versus global interests

An important reason for continuing immigration is to be found within liberal democratic states themselves. In order for states and governments to be seen as legitimate, a difficult balancing act between a number of interests is required. Economic interests, for instance, may seem to make it necessary in times of high domestic unemployment to control immigration (be it in volume or nature) whereas at the same time governments need to adhere to basic human rights. This first of all means the protection of their own citizens but it also implicitly asks for the protection of human rights in general, as specified, for instance, in an international instrument like the Universal Declaration of Human Rights or the Charter of the United Nations, even if those are not binding. For practical or political reasons the government of country A cannot always protect the fundamental rights of citizens of country B. This, however, is different when the citizen of country B is present within the borders of country A. Governments, therefore, try to prevent unsolicited immigrants from entering their jurisdiction in the first place, for once they are present, only instruments within the juridical domain remain. As we saw, these are basically definitions of entitlement. At the same time, the forces of globalization – the fruits of which are picked not least by the industrialized nations – make increasing numbers of people worldwide mobile.

Even though globalization is not as new a phenomenon as the amount of current literature on the topic would seem to suggest (Doomernik, Penninx and van Amersfoort, 1997), by the end of the twentieth century a number of factors have created a social reality previously unknown to mankind: the conjunction of economic integration and the offshoring of production to middle- or low-income countries; the free flow of information by radio, television, the Internet and (being symbolic for where they come from and stand for) consumer goods; cheap and frequent modes of global transport; and the seemingly unlimited mobility of people. Mentioning the last aspect, I inserted the word 'seemingly'. I did this because limits to mobility are almost imperceptible for citizens of the most developed nations. To the large masses of people in the developing world, however, mobility knows many limits. Yet, they are touched by all the other aspects of globalization (Adelman, 1999). As distorted and inaccurate as it may be (see, for example, Smith, 1997), they have a clear image of what the world beyond their horizons looks like, thus creating considerable incentives to move to the rich West, especially if they are confronted with economic hardship and few perspectives for positive change. In terms of root causes: the effects of economic globalization by integrating ever larger parts of the developing world (not too long ago still largely self-sufficient), rendering them dependent on the world market and its violent swings between production, demand and prices combined with very rapid population growth[6] have in many countries led to economic decline rather than development. This produces rapidly increasing emigration pressure. This is even more the case when people are the victim of civil strife or full-blown war. These conflicts, too, tend to be the result of direct or, more frequently, indirect forces of globalization.[7] In effect, the present-day world is faced with very powerful, and to a considerable extent autonomous, forces that uproot millions of people. That at least a number of those persons make their way to European and Northern American shores should thus not greatly surprise us. Currently, no more than 28 per cent of the world's refugees seek refuge in the Western world (UNHCR, 2002, p. 25). There is no reason to assume any reduction in the volume of uprooted people within the coming generations or to expect fewer of those to seek resettlement in the industrialized parts of the world. In fact, demographic imbalance in the underdeveloped world will, in all likelihood, even lead to a considerable increase in volume. War, too, will be with us for years to come. The answer receiving states try to formulate in response to this increased migration pressure is largely one-sided. Instead of addressing the fundamental causes – in as far as this would be possible in the first place – governments devise measures in the legal area and in the enforcement of border control. What we have not touched upon yet are the consequences.

The smuggling of migrants

Arguably the most significant effect of the one-sided security-based approach outlined above lies in the rise of a specific type of business operation: the smuggling and trafficking of human beings (Salt and Stein, 1997). Simply put: if migrants cannot enter a desired country of destination under their own steam because of restrictive policies and/ or border enforcement, they will rely on the help of third parties. And the more effective migration controls become, the more lucrative smuggling becomes and the higher the fees that are payable by those who are smuggled.

By smuggling we mean assisting migrants crossing borders illegally.[8] Describing and analyzing this activity, we should think of a continuum between extremes rather than an always similar act. Smuggling, for instance, may occur simply by pointing out where best to cross a border, but can also take the form of offering extensive travel package deals from country of origin to country of destination. In the latter case, we may be looking at organized crime. This is even more likely when we speak of trafficking. In this case smugglers may perceive migrants as mere goods to be exploited as lucratively as possible for financial gain, not merely helping people cross borders but also keeping them in bondage for a longer period thereafter (Williams, 1999). The term trafficking is often used in conjunction with women and children as both categories of persons are the most vulnerable to exploitation, for example in the sex trade. However, men can also fall prey to traffickers and end up in sweatshops and other industries dependent on manual labour.

Whose security?

Receiving states

States have the undisputed right to determine which aliens they let reside within their jurisdiction;[9] the only exception to this rule deriving from the Geneva Convention's non-refoulement clause (Article 33) which prohibits an alien's expulsion under certain conditions.[10] This does not mean that states always enact this right. There are numerous past instances where states did not really concern themselves with where new residents originated from, and were not bothered that they did not have the capacity to control immigration and residence, administrative or otherwise (Doomernik, 1998a). Such matters may have been dealt with locally, not centrally, as is the case in Switzerland even today. Yet, contemporary Western states all see the need to determine which aliens are allowed entry, for which purpose and duration. Increasingly, however, they are deemed to be out of control (Sassen, 1996a, 1996b; van Amersfoort, 1996; van Amersfoort and Doomernik, 1998) and unable to protect their borders against the arrival and settlement of uninvited newcomers. As we have seen, there is some basis for this view. It is, therefore, not surprising to note that the emphasis in the current debate on the links between migration and security lies on the interests of the receiving states. Furthermore, unsolicited immigration indeed poses a number of challenges, especially on welfare states.

Welfare systems are founded on the idea of insurance policies whereby the state acts as a national insurance company. There is no great problem in such a system if it carries a few free riders because the volume of their benefits is marginal to that of the total enjoyed by the population at large. However, it is imaginable that the category of free riders, that is, those drawing benefits without having contributed premiums for a prolonged period of time, becomes so substantial that the costs pose a threat to the economic well-being of the state. Such could be the case when infinite numbers of migrants settle whose arrival is not an immediate answer to labour market needs for workers. Asylum seekers and refugees are a case in point. Still, up to now, no economy has crashed because of their arrival. In fact, it is not at all difficult to find economists arguing from either perspective: mass immigration is good in macro-economical terms or plainly bad. For those looking for threats, more (potential) problems can be identified, yet, to the best of my knowledge, no serious contemporary examples can be found in industrialized nations that would merit labelling them a security threat.[11] If, however, we change our perspective from an internal to an external one, we can identify security issues, albeit of quite a different nature, that are not so prominent on the agenda of politicians, policy-makers and the media.

Perverse pre-selection

We have already noted the growing importance of the smuggling business in the arrival of asylum seekers and other unsolicited migrants to the EU and the USA. Smugglers have shown themselves to be very adept at responding to all the new measures receiving states have come up with so far. If a simple border crossing is no longer a possibility, they will bribe officials or buy 'legitimate' travel documents for their clients. This is just one example but it suffices to make clear that illegal immigration merely becomes more expensive. The subsequent effect is that only those clients who have access to sufficient financial means will be assisted. In the case of asylum seekers this implies a pre-selection; not according to whether he or she is in need of protection but by means testing. Such pre-selection – from the point of view of the protection of basic human rights, let alone the protection of the rights of refugees – is perverse.

Debt-bondage

For those without sufficient means to contract the services of a smuggler, it may mean that they are kept in debt-bondage until they have earned their fee. Sweatshop labour (usually for male victims) or prostitution (women and children) often are the only feasible options. For the former we can refer to a study done among Chinese sweatshop labourers in Manhattan (Chin, 1997, 1999), for the latter to the IOM's reports from its Migration Information Programme, which focuses on Central and Eastern European migration to Western Europe. Another forced form of repayment can consist of outright criminal activity, for example the peddling of drugs. All these are gross violations of the human rights of those concerned.

ʹ The debt-bondage may not just concern the individual migrant but also (or instead) hit those who stay behind. To families it may be a survival strategy to send one of its members abroad, either hoping for the sending back of remittances, or for the future possibility of chain migration. Either way, the family will have to invest in the departure and subsequent safe arrival of the person sent abroad. One way of doing so is by means of credit, either from an 'ordinary' loan shark or from the same organization that is to smuggle the family member into a prosperous society. The consequences can easily be serious in terms of economic survival or of being forced into activities that are criminal or incur a serious threat to the bodily integrity. Even in those instances where no debt-bondage exists, the investment made can seriously undermine the survival of a family if no or insufficient remittances materialize.

In transit

There is no way in which we can quantify the occurrence of different modes of smuggling used. This is due to a lack of research[12] and the differences likely to arise from geographical and social factors. All we know is that only a minority of migrants are smuggled by means of a complete package tour directly from country of origin to country of final destination. This means that most migrants will make one or more stops along the way. Cities like Istanbul, Warsaw, Moscow and Bucharest are temporary homes to large numbers of migrants hoping to make it into the EU. Migrants face numerous kinds of abuse. Often they have used up all their money once they land in these transit places and are thus forced to look for opportunities to replenish their budget. As described above, this makes them vulnerable to many kinds of exploitation. They may even be ripped off by unscrupulous racketeers. One example of such a scam is from Istanbul, where migrants are led to believe they are to board a ship for Greece. Payment is collected at boarding and the ship sets sail at night. In the morning the migrants disembark on a coast unknown to them and are told to walk to a village several miles down the road where they will find a police post to file an asylum request. Once near to the village, they recognize the minaret of the local mosque and realize they are still in Turkey and not in Greece (see, for example, Godfroid and Vinkx, 1999). Again, they will have to find means by which to earn money for yet another attempt.

Sleeping rough, having no access to medical care or police protection and, when whole families are on the move, no access to schooling – all pose threats to the well-being or even the survival of migrants in transit.[13] Another example of the severe risks illegal migrants face when in the hands of smugglers can be found in the numerous accounts of capsized ships and small vessels on the way from Albania to Italy (for a first-hand description see Harding, 2000), from Morocco to Spain, and from the Caribbean to the USA. When ships do not sink but instead are intercepted, smugglers are known to force their clients overboard, thus leaving law enforcement agents no choice but to fish them out of the water instead of pursuing the smugglers themselves. In other instances, people are put overboard and told to swim ashore.

Yet another example of serious risk can arise when migrants cross borders over land, be it with the assistance of others or on their own. The border between Mexico and the USA has, over the years, become very strongly guarded, at least at those spots where illegals are known to cross in great numbers. This has led them to avoid those parts of the border and look for different places to cross. The suitable, unpatrolled routes left are those that lead through uninhabited and dangerous areas. In a number of instances this has led to the death – by freezing, drowning or starving – of migrants. Less extreme, in most cases, but still often dangerous are border crossings within Europe. The recent deaths of 58 Chinese in a Dutch lorry found at Dover is a sad illustration of the dangers involved with what seemed a safe and simple journey by lorry. Also the Oder and Neisse rivers dividing Poland from Germany are known to have taken a number of victims in the past decade. All in all, since 1993, around Europe more than 2,000 migrants are reported to have perished (United Non-Profit).

Organized crime

As mentioned earlier, it is impossible to gauge the involvement of organized crime syndicates in the smuggling of migrants. We merely know that this involvement exists in general and in some migration flows in particular, for instance, in the smuggling of Chinese migrants to Northern America (Smith, 1997; Chin, 1999). Given the fact that unsolicited migration becomes more difficult due to increased immigration restrictions, there is every reason to assume that more and more professionalism is required in order to smuggle migrants into a country. Professionalism asks for division of labour and hence for organized collaboration. In other words: we should anticipate an increase in the involvement of organized crime groups in the smuggling business. This development should worry us in several ways.

First of all, it is estimated that even today the amount of money earned with the smuggling of human beings has already superseded the profits made in the drugs trade (Ghosh, 1998). This then implies that huge sums float around uncontrolled by tax inspectors and law enforcement agencies and can readily be invested in other fields of criminal entrepreneurship. Second, criminal organizations may easily be even less interested in the well-being of clients, be it in transit or upon arrival. Third, such gangs are known to actively recruit clients by misrepresenting the facts regarding what the prospective migrant will face once in the country of destination (Godfroid and Vinkx, 1999), thus increasing the problems of all concerned except themselves.

It is interesting, in this context, to note parallels between past and present rogue regimes in countries of origin. The German Democratic Republic (East Germany) in its dire need for hard currency, between 1961 and 1989, sold 34,000 dissident citizens to the Federal Republic, for between DM 40,000 and DM 95,847 each (Knauer, 1999). The advantages were obvious. It does not seem very far-fetched to assume similar operations still to take place, albeit by different methods. Until recently Iraq, for example, was a police state *par excellence* and few matters took place without the government, or its cronies, knowing about it. Yet, asylum seekers from that country recount how they fairly easily came into touch with smugglers; for example in the local bazaar. This begs the question whether the Iraqi government was involved in the smuggling out of the country of its own citizens; thus getting rid of potential or actual dissidents and making money in the process. Obviously, the long-term consequences of the emigration of large parts of the country's middle classes were disastrous but of little concern to those who prefered personal short-term financial gain.

First concluding remarks

The words migration and security threat can only be justifiably used together in the context of the threat to the well-being and basic human rights of the migrants concerned. This is not to deny that many liberal democratic states have a problem with the management of immigration flows. However, these states are all too happy to enjoy the other benefits of a globalized world; indeed, these problems are largely home-made. This is easily understood if we think of the process of globalization as increasing mobility, in terms of speed and volume, of information, goods, capital and people. Attempts to contain one, relatively small, element in this giant exchange scheme, can only end in frustration. Yet, both literally and in frustration, it is what Ghosh (1998) calls the 'huddled masses' who pay the price. Since all Western states subscribe to the human rights instruments of the United Nations, are parties to the Geneva Convention and seek to create and maintain within their borders areas of freedom, prosperity and security (as is the official aim of the European Union), they are, furthermore, under a moral obligation to address this particular 'security' threat more than any other. Globalization has made Asia and Africa into direct neighbours of Western Europe and Northern America.

Policy implications

From the above sketch of the current state of affairs in the field of irregular migration it should have become abundantly clear, first, that receiving states have, as Sassen (1996b) put it, lost control when it comes to the management of immigration processes and, second, that their stubborn denial of this fact has serious implications for the well-being of large numbers of migrants. The question then arises whether alternatives for the present immigration regimes can be found. Alternatives should take account of the declining ability of states to control the movement of people and offer better protection to the basic human rights of those who are on the move.

If it is certain that investment in more severe restrictions in the present asylum-based immigration system, and in more intensive border controls, can only exacerbate the plight of many immigrants, it seems sensible to investigate the benefits of taking the opposite route: the liberalization of immigration regimes. A number of ways can be discussed by which present regimes could be made more liberal but it seems worthwhile to first of all look at the likely consequences of completely discarding conventional immigration controls. The sole external control would then be to register the purpose of a visit when a person first entered the territory of a state whether the purpose stated was simply to visit relatives, friends, do some sight-seeing, or even to look for employment, no person should be kept from doing what they desired and no conditions should be attached, provided this person does not claim any benefits, arrives with health insurance and without the intention to commit a crime. This person could then file a claim for protection under the Geneva Convention, but that would hardly be necessary as he/she will be safe from deportation under the non-refoulement clause that is part of the Convention. From this perspective it would be taken for granted that an immigrant is willing and able to provide for his or her own upkeep. Only where this is not the case, and the Convention applies, would state responsibility come into view.

For welfare states such an approach implies a system of differentiated citizenship, that is, not every person residing within their territories can be granted equal access to society's scarce resources, let alone claim social security and/or unemployment benefits. Instead, an immigrant should accumulate rights through the duration of his/her stay and the volume of his/her contribution to society. This, obviously, can only function where a system of internal controls (at the gates of the welfare state) replaces those at the physical borders.[14] Not all states are able (those without a central population register) or willing (for example, the United States) to implement such controls.

Anyway, and as already mentioned earlier in this chapter, at present it is not very likely that governments would be willing to completely open up their borders to foreigners. Still, moving away from ever-increasing restrictionism and in the direction of more permeable borders would seem the only way out of the current 'arms race' between human smugglers and receiving states. The advantages would be numerous.

For one, the amounts of funds spent on all sides could dramatically decrease. The billions spent on border controls and the administrative procedures accompanying asylum claims and the removal of undesired aliens could be put to better use – for instance in improved protection of displaced people in their region of origin and/or economic development. Moreover, the need for migrants to rely on the services of human smugglers would be virtually eliminated, which also means less money flowing into the smugglers' pockets that subsequently would either be invested in increasing the volume of their smuggling business or in other illicit activities like drugs or arms trafficking.

Second, a more liberal regime facilitates the natural desire of people in a globalized world for mobility. In effect, migrants would arrive – probably in larger numbers than today – but are also more likely to leave once their movement has served its purpose. One observation should underline this point's relevance. In the early 1960s to mid-1970s when Western European states pursued liberal guest worker policies, the flows of migrant workers were considerable yet the stock of such immigrants present at any one time was modest in size. With the economic downturn of the mid-and late 1970s due to the oil crises, guest worker policies were terminated. New arrivals other than those necessarily allowed under international obligations (basically family reunification and asylum) were no longer welcome. In many instances this put those immigrants then present in a difficult position: should they return or stay? Staying would mean an uncertain and unplanned future in new surroundings. Returning would mean losing one's right of abode once and for all. To many this was not a promising prospect, especially not when their country of origin experienced poor economic conditions, as was often the case. As a result, many immigrants who under 'normal' conditions – that is, with the prospect of possible re-immigration – would have gone home after a number of years now saw themselves forced to stay on and to have their families join them. In effect, and contrary to what governments had expected, the stocks of immigrants rapidly increased, even though the economy could not absorb those additional newcomers. In other words, had these governments not panicked in the face of economic crisis it might very well have been that at present the size of the immigrant communities in Western European countries would have been smaller. In that way, present-day immigration policies, too, would be less problem-oriented and many of the severe problems surrounding the integration of those immigrants and their descendants would be less significant (for a full discussion of those see Doomernik, 1998b).

Third, more mobility increases the likelihood that remittances – already a very important source of foreign currency in many developing nations – are invested in countries of origin; for the upkeep of family and friends and for the migrant's own future (business) activities. In such a fashion migration contributes to the levelling out of economic disparities between developed and developing nations. Lastly, all highly developed nations are facing the prospect of ageing populations due to low fertility rates and better health care. Even though immigration is not the only answer to counter the economic effects of this, present levels of immigration are needed to maintain current population sizes (UNPD, 2000).

In short, there are good reasons for governments who feel 'threatened' by immigration and immigrants to practise what good politics should be about – developing long-term visions. As pointed out, the causes of increased mobility are very long-term in nature, and largely autonomous; the consequences can therefore not be addressed by ad hoc, short-term, responses (see Penninx and Doomernik, 1998, pp. 132–3).

Notes

1. An example from the Netherlands would be the case of an imam publicly stating that according to Islamic writings homosexuals are no better than animals and hence deserve to be killed. To a number of commentators this was yet more proof of the incompatibility between Islam and liberal democracies.
2. These are descendants of German colonists who moved east several centuries ago and had retained, to a smaller or larger extent, their German ethnic identity and language.
3. Among the others were Jews (who not only can migrate to Israel but also to the USA and Germany – a different story found in Doomernik, 1997a) and Greeks.
4. A refugee is a migrant who fulfils the criteria formulated as follows in Article 1 of the Geneva Convention: 'owing to well-founded fear of being persecuted for reasons of race, religion, nationality, membership of a particular social group or political opinion '.
5. These figures are not particularly recent because EUROSTAT tends to lag behind considerably due to the need to use uniform criteria for all member states, which, apparently, is time consuming. Publication, furthermore, appears time consuming too.
6. It would make one cynical to realize that this, too, is the result of Western interference. Especially the introduction of basic health facilities and vaccinations has greatly reduced the infant mortality rate.
7. See, for example, Westin, 1999, who makes the point that often unfinished processes of nation building, impeded by earlier colonization, cause such conflict.

8. In the latest UN draft protocol against the smuggling of migrants the following formal definition has been proposed: 'Smuggling of migrants shall mean the procurement of the illegal entry or illegal residence of a person in [a] [any] State Party of which the person is not a permanent resident in order to obtain, directly or indirectly, a financial benefit.'

9. Though from an academic viewpoint, sound arguments against this stance can be offered. See for instance the work of Carens (1999).

10. Even though it does not put states under an obligation to grant asylum it does prohibit expulsion in cases where an asylum seeker may face persecution upon his return to the country of origin. This implies that, regardless of whether persecution has taken place/may take place, the asylum seeker must be allowed to stay in the country until these questions can be answered. In the European context, similar protection is provided by the European Convention on Human Rights' Article 3.

11. Discussions abound on the dilution of a nation's culture or identity, the importation of foreign conflicts, deviant behaviour among immigrants, and the like.

12. One noteworthy exception being the survey done by Chin (1997, 1999) among Chinese who had been smuggled to New York. This survey did yield insight into the *modus operandi* of smugglers.

13. For many details on the hardships smuggled asylum seekers and refugees face, see Morrison, 1998.

14. For example, since this has become the practice in the Netherlands by means of the *Koppelingswet* (or linkage law: integrating the population and alien registers) previously hard debates about illegal/undocumented residents have nearly evaporated.

Part II
Cases and Recommendations

3
Trafficking and International Law
David Ould

Human rights must be at the core of any credible anti-trafficking strategy and...we must work from the perspective of those who most need their human rights protected and promoted...By placing human rights at the centre of our analysis, we are forced to consider the needs of the trafficked person.

Mary Robinson[1]

Introduction

Trafficking in persons has increasingly caught the world's attention over the past few years as a significant and growing human rights problem. Yet, it has proved particularly difficult to develop the necessary international legal standards and definitions to draw generally accepted distinctions between trafficking, smuggling and migration, and the accompanying coercive and voluntary elements of these. The increasing concern about levels of migration, both legal and illegal, in the rich world has made this distinction more important, but also more difficult to agree upon. Globally a market for irregular migration services has emerged, in which the mechanisms and forms of organization are still relatively unknown. As irregular migrants using these services are exposed both to unscrupulous service providers and to the immigration and policing authorities, the line between exploitation of migrant workers, and trafficking, is increasingly blurred, and the need for strong human rights protection becomes more acute.

Labour migration has been increasing strongly over the past 20 years and most forecasters expect this to increase rather than decrease, notwithstanding the restrictions and difficulties of securing travelling papers and jobs and the efforts to curb or manage such movements.

However, (it is clear that the restrictions and difficulties in place encourage people to take more risks in their desire to migrate and this puts them at risk of trafficking) According to a UN news article there are more than 185 million international or 'non-national' migrants in the world, and of these 50 per cent are women.[2] The IOM estimates that there will be more than 230 million people outside of their countries of origin by 2050. As many of these migrants are illegal such statistics have a high margin of error and the general difficulties in obtaining reliable statistics for both migration and trafficking are discussed later. Historically there were very few restrictions on migration but the international community was concerned about the continuation of the slave trade, which could be seen as the forerunner of trafficking today. Prior to the existence of the League of Nations the first efforts made by the international community to prohibit the slave trade was the Brussels Act of 1890, to which 18 European states were signatory. The Act contained effective measures to control and prevent the slave trade. It provided for a Slavery Bureau to oversee this process and to subject the sea routes preferred by slave traders to naval patrolling. Article XVIII of the Brussels Act provided that a 'strict supervision shall be organized by the local authorities at the ports and in the countries adjacent to the coast, with the view of preventing the sale and shipment of slaves...'.

Today, (it is increasingly difficult to monitor and control the traffic in persons given the dramatic increase in global migration) Following this, the Covenant of the League of Nations adopted on 28 April 1919 called on member states not only to ensure fair and human conditions of employment for all, but also to work towards the suppression of traffic in women and children for the purpose of sexual exploitation. (Later in the twentieth century, international instruments on trafficking focused on cases in which women and girls were moved across frontiers without their consent for the purposes of prostitution. These included the Convention for the Suppression of the Traffic of Women and Children of 1921 and the Convention for the Suppression of the Traffic of Women of Full Age of 1933.) Both these instruments established a duty to prohibit, prevent and punish the trafficking of women regardless of the question of consent. This wish to criminalize the recruitment of women of one country to be prostitutes in another was continued with the adoption of the 1949 Convention for the Suppression of the Traffic in Persons and of the Exploitation of the Prostitution of Others. The inextricable linkage of trafficking to prostitution in these conventions meant that the procurement of people for any other purpose than sexual exploitation was not really covered. The reality today is that people are trafficked not only for use in the sex industry, but also for many other reasons.

In Anti-Slavery International's work over the last 20 years there is evidence that slavery-like exploitation has often been exacerbated by the taking of people away from their customary place of residence to completely new locations, either in the same country or more often in different countries. Illegal migrants are particularly at risk and this is certainly the case today in many cases of slavery and trafficking. Slavery is defined by the United Nations as the partial or total ownership of one or more people.[3] Under this definition trafficking can often be seen as slavery, but it may also be seen as slave trading when people end up working as slaves when they reach their destinations. The examples given below illustrate both these areas. In some cases the link with globalization is clear but in others, such as forced begging and the examples from Brazil and Haiti, no such relationship can be established.

It is clear from information that Anti-Slavery International receives that trafficking has occurred in many widely publicized and diverse cases of exploitation of women, children and men. The following examples show that modern trafficking can be found both in the rich and poorer parts of the world. Those trafficked may have been coerced into leaving their homes, but more usually have looked for work away from home because of a lack of opportunities and have fallen into the hands of traffickers. People are trafficked across borders or within their own countries in a very similar way.

Specific examples of trafficking

In Nepal children are being deceived or abducted and taken by touts and contractors to India where they are sold to work as prostitutes in the brothels of Bombay and Calcutta or to work as domestic workers in Delhi. Some of the girls initially leave home to find work in the carpet industry of Kathmandu and are then abducted by touts working for the Indian brothels.

Children are taken from West African countries to work in other countries of the region or in Europe. In a recent case an Angolan man, Pedro Miguel da Costa Damba, was sentenced to six years in prison for document fraud. In the two previous years he had trafficked possibly hundreds of children, mainly of Angolan origin, from Portugal to the UK and then to unknown destinations.

Some five years ago information was given to Anti-Slavery International that children were being sent from Togo to other countries in

West Africa to work mainly as domestic servants, but also to provide other forms of assistance, for example to market women. Investigations showed that this was the case and indicated that children from neighbouring Benin were also being sent out of the country in quite large numbers. In order to understand the problem more thoroughly and to seek solutions Anti-Slavery International developed a small research project with a local Benin NGO, Enfants Solidaires du Monde, to investigate the trafficking of children from Benin to Gabon. A small, local team looked at children in several villages in three provinces of Benin and then went to Gabon to investigate the position of children working there. The results confirmed that a well-established trade between the two countries had been built up and that it often involved severe exploitation of the children concerned (Anti-Slavery International, 2000). Evidence was also found that some of the children were moved on from Gabon into Equatorial Guinea.

Also in West Africa many families entrust their children, mainly boys, to a *marabout* (religious leader) from the age of five or six. The *marabout* undertakes to teach them to memorize and recite passages of the Koran and, in return, the children perform various household and related duties. Traditionally, the community contributed to the upkeep of the *marabout* and the school through collections made by the children, and this was linked to the idea that boys should experience the humiliation of begging to become better men. Over the past decades the system has often become corrupted and thousands of children have been taken away from their homes in rural areas to act as a source of income for so-called *marabouts* in the towns (Anti-Slavery International, 1994).

Children are also forced to work on the streets as beggars as the result of trafficking from Albania to Italy or from South Asia to Saudi Arabia.

For more than ten years there have been well-authenticated reports of children taken from Pakistan, Bangladesh, Mauritania and Sudan to work as camel jockeys in the United Arab Emirates (UAE). Children as young as five or six are kidnapped, sold by their parents or taken on false pretences and trained to ride racing camels. They are often injured in the racing and maltreated by the trainers (Anti-Slavery International, 2002a). Despite new laws and regulations in the UAE and assurances from the government, recent evidence shows that the practice continues and children have been filmed riding in camel races in the 2002 season. NGOs in Pakistan and Bangladesh have also stopped children from being taken away from their homes by contractors believed to be taking them to the UAE.

A completely different area of trafficking involves the offering of employment to people from poor areas which involves them being taken long distances away from their homes to work. When they arrive they find that the types of work and the conditions of work are very different from those contracted. Two areas which have much concerned Anti-Slavery International in the past few years have been the employment of Haitian migrants in the sugar cane plantations (*bateyes*) of the Dominican Republic (DR) and the contracting of young men in north-east Brazil for work in the development regions of Amazonia and Rondonia.

The exploitation of Haitians in the DR sugar industry is a long-running scandal and, although the outright selling of men and children from Haiti was ended in the 1980s, the current recruitment and employment practices are often a form of trafficking. Haitian and DR contractors meet migrants on either side of the Haiti – DR border and offer them work in the DR. Often they will be told that the jobs are not in the sugar cane plantations, which are known to be awful places. Once they have accepted and signed a contract however, the Haitians are taken to the plantations and the contractors receive their fees. The contracts tie them into work on the plantations at very low wages and often the wages are reduced by such measures as under-weighing of cane cut, forcing them to shop in company stores where the prices are higher and payment by tokens which can only be exchanged in one store. Living and working conditions are also terrible and the DR army ensures that the workers abide by their contracts. In the last two years there have been signs of improvement in the *bateyes* but problems are still reported.

Similar problems are seen in Brazil. Landowners in Pará and other states in Amazonia need to find many workers to undertake forest clearance. Contractors are sent to the poor areas of Bahia and similar towns to find new employees. Young men are offered contracts at rates that would be reasonable in their home towns, but they are misled as to the arduous nature of the work and the conditions under which they will be working. They are then loaded into trucks and driven hundreds of miles to isolated estates in Pará. On arrival they are told that they must pay for the cost of travel and even the hire of tools. The work is hard, the conditions terrible and living quarters are usually minimal. In addition, the only food has to be purchased from the company store where prices are much higher than expected. The workers soon fall into debt and if they want to leave are told that they can only do so if they repay all their debt to the company store. Armed guards patrol the estates and workers who try to escape are beaten and even shot. When contracts finish, the workers are paid off and sent to the nearest small town, where they rapidly sink into debt to small lodging houses and bars and are so forced into an unending round of similar contracts. In only one of these cases, concerning Haitians, are those trafficked crossing an international border, but the workers in Brazil are just as vulnerable, and the abuse is very similar.

USA fashion companies have been purchasing finished items of clothing from operations based in Saipan, an offshore American 'commonwealth' in the Pacific Mariana Islands. Workers in the factories are mainly migrants from Bangladesh, China, Philippines and Thailand. They have often taken loans to pay the fee to an agency for finding the job. The loan was used as a way of forcing the employees to work very long hours or offset against their agreed pay in ways solely under the control of the employer. In 2001 several workers began a court case against the main US importing companies. In an agreement, reached in 2002, a group of US companies and Saipan manufacturers, including Gap, J.C. Penney, Tommy Hilfiger, Calvin Klein and Ralph Lauren, set up a $20 million fund to pay back wages to workers and create a monitoring system to prevent labour abuses. Thirty thousand current and former garment workers in Saipan are eligible to share about $6.4 million compensation for unpaid back wages (*San Francisco Chronicle*, 29 September 2002).

Recently a trade in illegal aliens from China and Vietnam moving to the USA to work in the garment industry has been exposed. Migrants have been found working long hours in bad conditions at minimal rates of pay. They are particularly vulnerable to such exploitation as they are afraid of being deported if they complain to the authorities, and are willing to work without social security or other protection.

Statistical evidence of trafficking

There is a general lack of good statistical information concerning trafficking of people. Some figures have been gathered by organizations such as the IOM, the ILO, Interpol and the United States Department of State. These figures are difficult to compare and the level of global research on the issue remains weak. In its annual report on *Trafficking in Persons*, released in February 2002 (US Department of State, 2002), the US Department of State estimated that between 700,000 and 4 million trafficked persons are victimized annually. No country is unaffected. This report is issued annually and looks at all the countries in the world for which information on trafficking in people is available. A panel then groups the countries into three tiers:

- Governments that fully comply with the minimum standards defined by the US Victims of Trafficking and Violence Protection Act, 2000.
- Governments that do not fully comply with the Act's minimum standards but are making significant efforts to bring themselves into compliance with those standards.
- Governments that do not fully comply with the Act's minimum standards and are not making significant efforts to bring themselves into compliance.

According to the Act, beginning with the 2003 report, countries in Tier 3 will be subject to certain sanctions, principally termination of non-humanitarian, non trade-related assistance and US opposition to assistance from international financial institutions, specifically the International Monetary Fund and multilateral development banks such as the World Bank. In his presentation of the 2002 report Secretary of State Colin Powell reiterated that countries in the third tier in 2003 would be subject to sanctions. In 2002, there were 18 countries in Tier 1, 53 countries in Tier 2 and 19 countries in Tier 3. While the practice of one country ranking all other countries on an issue of human rights is questionable, it has persuaded many governments to pay the issues much more attention.

The ILO has recently issued some new statistics (ILO, 2002) for child labour generally and these say that in the year 2000 they estimate that worldwide some 1.2 million children were trafficked.

Such widely disparate figures demonstrate that trafficking is a serious problem, affecting large numbers of women, children and men all around the world, but also show the need for much more research and investigation by both governments and the international agencies.

Trafficking of women

Every year millions of women (and a much smaller number of men) migrate to seek employment as domestic workers in richer countries. They come particularly from Asian countries, such as Philippines, Sri Lanka and Indonesia, but also from Latin America and Africa. The main receiving countries are in the Middle East and the richer countries of Asia (Hong Kong, Singapore and Malaysia). However, there are large communities of female migrant domestic workers in most rich countries. Anti-Slavery International has reported for more than 20 years on cases of slavery and forced labour affecting many of these domestic workers. Most of these workers make use of various contractors and employment agencies to find employment in the first place and this is often the first stage of a chain of exploitation, which clearly falls under the heading of trafficking. Interviews with Indonesian domestic workers in Hong Kong reveal a sophisticated system of debt-bondage and forced labour. Migrants take loans from the brokers, who scour Indonesian villages to persuade young women to migrate for domestic work overseas. Those sent overseas find that their wages are reduced by *ad hoc* and unagreed amounts to repay the original loan plus interest, and are afraid to leave their employment, however bad the conditions, because of threats and degrading punishments meted out to those who resist. Employers withhold passports and other personal documents as an extra method of control. To date it has proved very difficult to persuade either the Hong Kong or the Indonesian governments to protect such women. The United Nations Special Rapporteur on Violence against Women listed the following abuses suffered by women migrant domestic workers in her report to the UN Commission on Human Rights in 1997:[4]

- Debt-bondage, because women invariably have to borrow money to pay exorbitant fees to the agents, and feel bound to stay and work in order to pay off these debts.
- Illegal confinement, because employers or agents keep their passports and they are not allowed to leave the premises without accompaniment or supervision, are discouraged or even forbidden to speak to other domestic workers.
- Cruel, humiliating and degrading treatment, by slapping, hair pulling, spitting, humiliating, name calling, having no room of their own, having to sleep in corridors, on the floor even in the bathroom or kitchen; sexual harassment is usual, rape is not exceptional.
- Long hours of work without sufficient food and rest.
- Not being allowed to change jobs legally, even in the face of ill treatment.

Attention in the past five years has focused on the rise in the trafficking of women into Western Europe and other richer countries for work in the commercial sex industry. In particular, there has been much publicity concerning the trafficking of women within Central and Eastern Europe and from there to Western Europe. However, similar patterns of trafficking in women are also seen within Asia, Africa and the Middle East. Europol (Europol, 1999) has drawn up some general observations on the nationalities of women trafficked into the European

Union. These and other sources suggest there has been a move away from the developing countries in Africa and Asia towards new sources from Central and Eastern Europe, particularly post-conflict areas.

{Traffickers use various methods of recruitment today. Modelling agencies create large databases of attractive and ambitious young women seeking work abroad and these are brought into contact with traffickers who offer such work. Similarly marriage agencies dealing in 'mail-order brides' may also act as a cover for traffickers. Once the women arrive in Western Europe they may be forced into the sex industry by a mixture of threats, violence and debt-bondage.)

Changes in trafficking legislation

There were various suggestions after the Suppression of Traffic Convention was adopted in 1949 that the definition of 'traffic in persons' should be extended to cover forms of recruitment not directly linked to prostitution, when they were linked to the use of coercion or deception about the situation that awaits them. ILO Convention No. 143 recognized that trafficking occurs for purposes in addition to prostitution (ILO, 1975). In 1994 a United Nations General Assembly resolution offered a de facto definition of trafficking in women and children. Resolution 49/166 of 23 December 1994 condemned the

> illicit and clandestine movement of persons across national and international borders, largely from developing countries and some countries with economies in transition, with the end goal of forcing women and girl children into sexually or economically oppressive and exploitative situations for the profit of recruiters, traffickers and crime syndicates, as well as other illegal activities related to trafficking, such as forced domestic labour, false marriages, clandestine employment and false adoption.

Until very recently there was considerable confusion around what the term 'trafficking' actually meant. In its Resolution 53/111 of 9 December 1998 the General Assembly established an intergovernmental ad hoc committee for the purpose of elaborating an International Convention against Transnational Organized Crime and discussing the elaboration of international instruments addressing trafficking in women and children and the illegal trafficking in and transporting of migrants, in addition to illegal trafficking in firearms. This eventually led to the adoption by the UN General Assembly on 15 November 2000 of the

UN *Protocol to Prevent, Suppress and Punish Trafficking in Persons, Especially Women and Children*, supplementing the *United Nations Convention against Transnational Organized Crime*. There is a separate *Protocol Against the Smuggling of Migrants by Land, Sea and Air*. The definition used in this new UN protocol represents the first internationally agreed definition of trafficking. Article 3 (a) states:

> 'Trafficking in persons' shall mean the recruitment, transportation, transfer, harbouring or receipt of persons, *by means of the threat or use of force or other forms of coercion, of abduction, of fraud, of deception, of the abuse of power or of a position of vulnerability or of the giving or receiving of payments or benefits to achieve the consent of a person having control over another person*, for the purpose of exploitation. Exploitation shall include, at a minimum, the exploitation of the prostitution of others or other forms of sexual exploitation, forced labour or services, slavery or practices similar to slavery, servitude or the removal of organs.

> Italics added

By December 2002 the protocol had been signed by 115 states and ratified by 21. It will formally come into force 90 days after it has been ratified by a minimum of 40 states. As the initial speed of government signature has been very swift, it was hoped that this might occur during 2003.

This definition is useful because it distinguishes 'traffickers' who use 'force, deception or coercion' in order to transport people 'for the purpose of exploitation', from those involved in facilitating irregular migration or those smuggling victims of persecution from one country to another. This is a most important distinction and one that has, to date, been both incorrectly and probably deliberately muddled or ignored by many UK and other government spokespeople. They confuse the difference between people who have paid someone to facilitate their movement from one country to another, either as an asylum seeker or as an economic migrant, and those who have been trafficked by use of force or deception. Gallagher (2002) suggests that the protocols referring to trafficking in persons and smuggling of migrants allow states to divide deserving 'victims of trafficking' from undeserving 'partners in smuggling' without actually providing 'any guidance on how trafficked persons and smuggled migrants are to be identified as belonging to either of these categories'. As is so often the way in areas of slavery-like exploitation many cases of trafficking do not and will not fit the classic model of trafficking. Anderson and O'Connell Davidson (2002) point out that the risk is that the concept of trafficking will deflect attention from the exploitation of the individual and encourage the construction of moral hierarchies, as well as practical and legal barriers between victims. This would allow policy-makers to obscure the effects of their policies on the rights of the migrants.

The new definition does not regard trafficking as synonymous with recruitment into prostitution, nor is it limited to dealing with prostitution in the way that various conventions concerning the 'white slave trade' were 100 years ago. It deals with what is in effect a modern-day slave trade, by focusing on the recruitment or movement of people in circumstances involving violence, intimidation or deception, into various forms of exploitation, including prostitution, but also any other forms of forced or slave labour. This means that it covers equally the trafficking of women from Eastern Europe into Western Europe to be forced into prostitution without any right to refuse, and the trafficking of children from Togo, Ghana, Mali or Benin to work as child domestic workers in Gabon or the Ivory Coast.

Over Easter 2001, the international media highlighted the trafficking of some 30 Beninoise children on the ship *Etireno* to Gabon to work as domestic servants or street market assistants. Following pressure on the Gabonese authorities from Anti-Slavery International and partners in Benin and Gabon over the previous three years, the port authorities suddenly refused to allow the children from this ship to land. The ship returned to Benin and the children were taken into the care of local agencies, before being returned to their parents. This was rapidly followed by reports concerning the trafficking of children from Mali and Burkina Faso to the Ivory Coast to work on cocoa farms providing cocoa for some 40 per cent of the world's chocolate. As a result of the publicity, international agencies, multinationals and the governments of the countries concerned have begun to look at the issues more seriously. This has served to highlight how little is really known of the real working conditions on the hundreds of thousands of cocoa farms, the people who work on them and the inability of current laws and enforcement mechanisms to deal with such problems. It is also worth noting that stopping the trafficking is only one part of the answer, as it may only lead the children into alternative areas of exploitation if nothing is done to tackle the poverty, lack of education and jobs that put the children at risk in the first place.

Article 3(b) of the new UN protocol goes on to state: 'The consent of a victim of trafficking in persons to the intended exploitation...shall be irrelevant where any of the means set forth in subparagraph (a) are established.' In other words, (the issue of consent is irrelevant if any type of coercion, intimidation or deception occurs.)

The protocol also most importantly sets out a number of important measures that states should take to assist and protect victims of trafficking. (These include various provisions of material and psychological support, temporary or permanent residence and due consideration to safety in the case of any repatriation (preferably voluntary)) The general agreement at international level on this definition of trafficking is illustrated by a report by the UN Special Rapporteur on Violence against Women (Coomaraswamy, 1997), who looked at four different scenarios and considered whether the women were victims of trafficking:

- The first group includes women who have been completely duped and coerced. Such women have no idea where they are going or the nature of the work they will be doing.
- The second group comprises women who are told half-truths by their recruiters about their employment and are then forced to do work to which they have not previously agreed and about which they have little or no choice. Both their movement and their power to change their situation are severely restricted by debt-bondage and confiscation of their travel documents or passport.
- In the third group are women who are informed about the kind of work they will be doing. Although they do not want to do such work, they see no viable economic alternative, and therefore relinquish control to their trafficker who exploits their economic and legal vulnerability for financial gain, while keeping them, often against their will, in situations of debt-bondage.
- The fourth group comprises women who are fully informed about the work they are to perform, have no objections to performing it, are in control of their finances and have relatively unrestricted movement. This is the only situation of the above four that cannot be classified as trafficking.

Issues of concern

Despite this agreement, there remains a lack of consensus about what should be done on behalf of the women, children and men, who are the victims of trafficking, particularly what states and governments have an obligation to do on their behalf once these victims regain their freedom. The state's obligation goes further than to simply punish traffickers, to the responsibility to uphold the human rights of trafficking victims. Long experience shows that a whole set of practical measures are necessary to enable people who have been trafficked or enslaved to enjoy their human rights properly: most importantly, states have to provide some material assistance to enable former slaves to become self-sufficient economically and thus avoid perpetual dependence. The failure of states to do this on many occasions has meant that slavery has only been half-abolished,[5] that the victims are left in a limbo of dependence on their former exploiters or others, and that long-term resentment builds up, as witnessed with the claims for reparations at the recent UN World Conference Against Racism. Because of the failure of governments to compensate slaves at the end of the historical triangular slave trade, their descendants and the governments of the countries from where the slaves were taken have increasingly pressed claims for reparations. This is looked at in detail in Geraldine Van Bueren's chapter in this book. Needless to say, as in the case of any other victims of crime or major human rights abuse, the immediate health and other practical needs of victims of slavery also have to be attended to.

When confronted with the question of what protection to guarantee to victims of trafficking in the UN trafficking protocol, government representatives did what they do so often when making international law: they vacillated and fudged. Eventually they agreed a long list of assistance and protection provisions in Article 6 of the protocol, but made all of them optional rather than mandatory:

- in appropriate cases and to the extent possible under domestic law, each State Party shall protect the privacy and identity of victims of trafficking in persons, including, inter alia, by making legal proceedings relating to such trafficking confidential.
- each State Party shall ensure that its domestic legal or administrative system contains measures that provide to victims of trafficking in persons, in appropriate cases:

  (a) Information on relevant court and administrative proceedings; and
  (b) Assistance to enable their views and concerns to be presented and considered at appropriate stages of criminal proceedings against offenders, in a manner not prejudicial to the rights of the defence.

- each State Party shall consider implementing measures to provide for the physical, psychological, and social recovery of victims of trafficking in persons, including, in appropriate cases, in cooperation with non-governmental organizations, other relevant organizations, and other elements of civil society, and, in particular, the provision of:

(a) Appropriate housing;
(b) Counselling and information, in particular as regards their legal rights, in a language that the victim of trafficking can understand;
(c) Medical, psychological and material assistance; and
(d) Employment, educational and training opportunities.

- each State Party shall take into account in applying the provisions of this article, the age, gender, and special needs of victims of trafficking in persons, in particular the special needs of children, including appropriate housing, education and care.
- each State Party shall endeavour to provide for the physical safety of victims of trafficking in persons while they are within its territory.
- each State Party shall ensure that its domestic legal system contains measures that offer victims of trafficking in persons the possibility of obtaining compensation for damage suffered.

How to ensure that governments place the rights of victims at the core of their anti-trafficking policies was the objective of a two-year research study to investigate various measures to protect victims, especially those who act as witnesses in the prosecution of traffickers, completed by Anti-Slavery International in October 2002 (Pearson, 2002b). The research was carried out with local NGOs in ten countries and showed that the four countries which fared better in prosecuting traffickers, Belgium, Italy, the Netherlands and the United States of America, were those that had the most comprehensive measures for assisting victims, including temporary residence permits for those prepared to testify against their traffickers. An important part of this protection was to ensure that all persons suspected of being trafficked are given a 'reflection delay' of at least three months, as in the Netherlands. Such a delay allows trafficked persons to remain in the country legally while they recover from their situation and consider their options. To be fully effective such reflection delays should be accompanied by access to specialized services of an NGO that can ensure appropriate housing, legal, medical, psychological and material assistance. The quicker documents authorizing temporary residency are issued, the more effective they are.

Anti-Slavery International's research found a growing awareness, at all levels, of the need for a human rights framework to combat trafficking most effectively. Cases of 'best practice' in terms of protecting victims' rights exist where there is genuine understanding and goodwill on the part of the authorities involved. The United Nations High Commissioner for Human Rights summarized such a framework in her Recommended Principles and Guidelines on Human Rights and Human Trafficking submitted to the UN Economic and Social Council in July 2002 (United Nations Economic and Social Council, 2002). The report recognizes the primacy of human rights, the need to prevent trafficking, the need to protect and assist victims of trafficking and to punish the traffickers and sets out guidelines for government action. It also recommends that governments should present information on the measures they have taken to the appropriate UN human rights treaty monitoring bodies including: the Human Rights Committee; the Committee on Economic, Social and Cultural Rights; the Committee on the Elimination of Discrimination Against Women; the Committee on the Elimination of Racial Discrimination; the Committee against Torture; and the Committee on the Rights of the Child. Such reports would provide regular information on progress against trafficking around the world and also allow NGOs the opportunity to comment on the reports of their own governments.

In 2001 the EU, taking a lead from the UN, began the process of reflecting the new protocol in its law and practice, and in July 2002 the EU Council adopted a framework decision on *Combating Trafficking in Human Beings* (European Commission, 2000). The framework decision sets out to introduce a common definition of what constitutes 'trafficking in human beings' in all 15 countries and to ensure some common minimum punishment for those convicted of trafficking. Discouragingly, it says next to nothing about protecting or assisting victims of trafficking or slavery. The European Commission justified the absence of provisions to protect the rights of trafficking victims by suggesting that these would come afterwards, in a separate directive (EU Council Directive, 2002). Such a directive was published in February 2002 concerning the granting of short-term residence permits for victims of trafficking who agree to co-operate with the competent authorities. This proposes that illegal migrants who are victims of trafficking should be given a 30-day reflection period to decide whether they will co-operate with the authorities, and during this period should be given accommodation, welfare and medical support. At the end of this period those who agree to co-operate, who have severed all links with the traffickers and whose presence is considered useful by the authorities should be given short-term residence permits (initially six months). Although the provision of a period of reflection delay is a welcome development, the issue is still regarded primarily from the perspective of what would be useful to the authorities rather than the rights or best interests of the victim.

It is also worth noting that in the case of minors, the directive uses the 'best interests of the child' as a test, but this section is not binding on member states. A report prepared by one of Anti-Slavery International's partners, ECPAT UK, in 2001 (Somerset, 2001) shows that the coercive influence of the trafficker is often particularly strong in the case of minors and so prevents them from fully breaking away from their trafficker. This could make them ineligible for assistance under the directive. The EU Council framework decision on combating trafficking in human beings was finally adopted on 19 July 2002 and published in the official journal on 1 August 2002. All EU member states will have until 1 August 2004 to bring domestic legislation in line with the framework decision, which includes establishing minimum penalties for trafficking for both labour and sexual exploitation.

The European Parliament has called on the EU Council to include a considerable number of protection provisions, notably suggesting that member states must provide, free of charge: accommodation; medical and psychological assistance; financial assistance and assistance in getting vocational training or jobs; and safe and voluntary return to the trafficking victim's country of origin.[6] An additional opinion of one of its committees recommended that member states should grant 'a special permanent residence permit on humanitarian grounds' if called to do so on account of the vulnerability of someone who has been trafficked, or the dangers they are considered to be in when deported.[7] Yet others have pointed out that the current practice of several EU member states, to provide a temporary residence permit only to trafficking victims who agree to testify against their traffickers can itself be an abusive and discriminatory incentive to place themselves in danger. Anti-Slavery International and other non-governmental organizations were particularly vocal in calling for protection measures to be included in the framework decision. This is because we have direct experience of assisting victims of trafficking and other extreme forms of exploitation and are in a position to review experience over 160 years, which shows that efforts to outlaw and punish various forms of slavery, without at the same time providing protection and measures to rehabilitate or reintegrate victims, almost automatically fail. For the past five years, we have been disappointed by the failure of the measures adopted by the European Union to combat trafficking to actually help the women, children and men whom the measures are apparently designed to help. We think that adopting a framework decision to standardize the definition of an offence and to standardize penalties, without simultaneously agreeing minimum standards for protection and assistance is, at best, a lost opportunity and at worst serious negligence. Cynics suggest that the main reason for this approach is that EU government ministers concerned with immigration issues will not accept any extra obligations to allow non-EU nationals to remain in their countries or to provide them with protection. Clearly the idea that government ministers within the EU might actually want to stop anyone from exercising their basic human rights seems unlikely – and certainly unacceptable.

In considering the rights which victims of trafficking and other forms of slavery have under international law, Anti-Slavery International and others have identified dozens of measures that states have an obligation to take to protect and assist the victims. These can be summarized as follows:

- First, everyone suspected of having been trafficked must have an opportunity for temporary residence, without immediate deportation. This should include a period to recover from their ordeal in which the person concerned can decide whether they want to make a statement to the police or otherwise participate in proceedings against their trafficker. These reflection periods already exist in the Netherlands and Belgium.
- Second, victims of slavery and trafficking have a right to basic services during their temporary residence, such as appropriate housing, psychological counselling, information, medical assistance and so on. Preferably this should be offered by a specialized agency established for the purpose, probably as an NGO, and we are calling for some government support for the establishment of such an organization in the UK. Such groups have already been established elsewhere in the European Union and there is information about this in Chapter 4 in this volume with regard to Belgium.
- Third, they and their families at home must be protected from intimidation, threats or reprisals. Such protection must clearly not be linked to any decision on whether to co-operate with the authorities. If there is a real fear of re-trafficking or violence then the person should be granted exceptional or indefinite leave to remain.
- Fourth, they must have the right and opportunity to bring civil claims for compensation against the person or people who trafficked them.

In 2001, the case of a 15-year-old Nigerian girl was brought to the attention of ECPAT UK, the UK arm of an international NGO working against all forms of commercial sexual exploitation of children, including trafficking. A trafficker attempted to take the girl, who had been brought into the UK illegally from Nigeria, to Germany. By chance, the police questioned the trafficker and his victim at the port and they soon realized that the girl was not 28 years old as stated in her passport. When she could not remember the name in her passport they detained her. They let the trafficker go as he claimed that he had simply given the girl a lift and did not know her. When the girl told them the full story they did not believe her and she spent five months in a detention centre before a social worker convinced them of the truth of her story, at which stage she was given some of the support she needed. In November 2001, ECPAT UK issued a report revealing that, over the past five years, children have been increasingly trafficked into the UK and forced into prostitution. Some were prostituted in the UK and others passed through the UK to other European countries. It was impossible to define how many had been affected, but in the area of West Sussex Social Services alone, some 75 children picked up at Gatwick airport and taken into care had gone missing in the previous seven years (Somerset, 2001).

Conclusion and recommendations

One of the misleading myths surrounding slavery, since the first laws on abolition were passed at the beginning of the nineteenth century, is that the main action required to get rid of it is the enactment of a law declaring slavery to be abolished – removing its legal basis and requiring law enforcement officers to prosecute traffickers and exploiters. And yet, on its own, this has very rarely been an effective way of getting rid of slavery; it has merely been an essential precursor to a further set of much more practical steps to stop people being reduced to slavery. That is to say:

- to specify who is to ensure the release of those enslaved, and how;
- to give those freed sufficient economic autonomy to prevent them having to return to their former owners/exploiters;
- to spread the message that certain forms of employment and exploitation are no longer acceptable and will henceforth be punished.

Today, despite the increasing international attention being given to contemporary slavery and particularly to trafficking and migration, there is a real need for much better information on the issues discussed above. Such information will allow governments, local people and NGOs to seek solutions that will allow those freed from slavery to remain free. A whole set of practical measures are necessary to enable people who have been enslaved to enjoy their human rights properly. Most importantly, this creates an obligation on states to provide some material assistance to enable former slaves to become self-sufficient economically and avoid perpetual dependence. The failure of states to do this on many occasions has meant that slavery has only been half-abolished,[8] that the victims are left in a limbo of dependence on their former exploiters or others, and that long-term resentment builds up. While a legal basis prohibiting slavery is essential, it is only once slaves are free, both in their own eyes and in the eyes of their former exploiters, and no longer in a position of dependence, that the process of ending slavery has been completed. Such issues can be seen today in India and Nepal when people are freed under their respective bonded labour abolition laws, as discussed by Krishna Upadhyaya in Chapter 7 of this book. In Europe today, however, we don't have the odd case of trafficking. Anti-Slavery International does not believe the claims made by some activists that half a million or more women are trafficked into the European Union each year, but we know that there are tens of thousands of cases – a very substantial pattern – resulting in women (mainly) being forced to earn money for others in all sorts of ways, with commercial sex as the most profitable. Translating the message of experience over two centuries into the contemporary context of combating trafficking in human beings, all this means that having good law to identify trafficking as a criminal offence and prescribe realistic penalties is a necessary first and last step, but completely insufficient to actually bring about an end to trafficking by itself. Consequently, if policy-makers limit themselves to strengthening repressive laws without embarking on a corresponding set of preventative and protective measures, then they will be liable to be accused of condoning slavery and forced labour.

Slavery and the slave trade, one of the oldest forms of abuse of human beings by other humans, is alive and well. It is thriving not only on the other side of the world, in societies we might consider to be 'traditional', but also under our noses here in the European Union. The lack of avenues for legal migration is forcing potential migrants into the hands of unscrupulous agencies, including traffickers and we all have a responsibility for ensuring that such people are protected from enslavement. Slavery in the twenty-first century is sometimes portrayed by anti-globalization activists as a by-product of globalization and capitalism, increasing uncontrollably each year. The reality is that slave labour is not a problem that has reappeared just recently, but rather a serious pattern of both traditional and modern forms of abuse, which the world's richest societies have tended to ignore, assuming it cannot still exist either at home or abroad. It has been ignored because it undermines our confidence in our own ability to put an end to the gross violations of human rights from the past, such as slavery in the Americas in the nineteenth century or forced labour in the colonial and totalitarian regimes of the mid-twentieth century.

Notes

1. Mary Robinson, UN High Commissioner for Human Rights, June 2001.
2. Inter Press Service (IPS), 21 October 2002.
3. United Nations Convention on Slavery 1926.
4. Ms Radhika Coomaraswamy, E/CN.4/1997/47, paragraph 133.
5. For example, in the Islamic Republic of Mauritania.
6. European Parliament Committee on Citizens' Freedoms and Rights, Justice and Home Affairs, 30 May 2001.
7. European Parliament Committee on Women's Rights and Equal Opportunities.
8. An Organization for Security and Co-operation in Europe (OSCE) Parliamentary Assembly resolution on trafficking expressed concern that the laws in many OSCE states 'remain inadequate to deter trafficking, to bring traffickers to justice and to protect their victims' (paragraph 10). It urged states 'to harmonize their procedures' not only concerning prosecutions, but also as far as the legal, medical and psychological assistance to victims of trafficking was concerned (paragraph 15), July 2001.

4
The Belgian Counter-trafficking Policy

Arne Dormaels, Bruno Moens and Nele Praet

Introduction

In Belgium the phenomenon of trafficking in persons was thrust into the limelight in 1992, following the publication of a series of articles and a book by *Knack* journalist Chris De Stoop, who traced the international mechanisms of trafficking into Belgium and exposed the exploitation of the victims. In reaction, the House of Representatives adopted a bill for the purpose of setting up a parliamentary fact-finding committee with the task of drafting a structural policy to suppress international trafficking in women. The work of the fact-finding committee resulted, among other things, in the Act of 13 April 1995, which includes provisions for combating traffic in persons and child pornography. Another significant turning point was the introduction of the federal government's action plan for security policy of 31 May 2000 in which further attention was given to the phenomenon in view of a more structural policy.[1]

We can, therefore, distinguish two different eras. The first period runs from 1994 until mid-2000 and is characterized by an endeavour to establish a prolonged and integrated counter-trafficking policy. This period is substantially inspired by the recommendations made by the Parliamentary Investigation Committee. The second period is post-2000, following the federal government's action plan for security policy. This action plan forms one part of an ambitious and coherent project aimed at restoring the trust of the citizens in the Belgian government.

In both epochs an integrated and multidisciplinary approach – the so-called Belgian four-pillar approach – can be observed. The only difference is that with the setting up of the governmental action plan, as a result of the Coalition Agreement of 7 July 1999,[2] the phenomenon of trafficking in human beings became one of the cornerstones of a security plan which will work in accordance with the concept of complete control of every aspect of security. This control of security is implemented in the form of a chain, consisting of a preventative link, a repressive link and the after-care of both victims and perpetrators of crime.

A short history of the Belgian counter-trafficking policy

As mentioned above, the phenomenon of trafficking in human beings caught the public's attention in Belgium with the publication of the book *They are So Sweet, Sir*, in which the author discussed the commercial sexual exploitation, in Belgium, of women originating from Eastern Europe, South-east Asia and West Africa and the misperception by the Belgian government, in particular the law enforcement bodies (De Stoop, 1992). As a consequence, a Parliamentary Investigation Committee was established which was given the task of developing a structural counter-trafficking policy. The work of the committee resulted in a profound report on trafficking in human beings including a comprehensive set of policy recommendations in 1994.[3] The recommended policy is mainly characterized by the central focus given to victims of trafficking in human beings on the one hand, and on the need for a multidisciplinary approach in the fight against this form of organized crime. Contrary to Belgian tradition, the parliamentary activities and recommendations were implemented immediately by the government (De Ruyver and Fijnaut, 1994). In the first place, a circular was issued regarding the granting of residence and work permits to migrant victims of trafficking (Belgian Statute Book, 7 July 1994); this has been followed by the amendment of the Belgian Criminal Code and the Immigration Law regarding access to the country, stay, residence and removal of foreigners with a view to explicitly criminalizing trafficking in human beings and reforming legislation regarding prostitution.[4] A third initiative was the assignment of core responsibility for the humanitarian perspective and follow up to the Centre for Equal Opportunities and Combating Racism, a governmental institution, and finally, there was the obligation of the government to report annually to parliament on the implementation of the law(s) on trafficking in human beings in general.

The annual reports of the Centre for Equal Opportunities and Combating Racism kept the problem of trafficking in human beings high on the political agenda. In 2000 the Belgian Senate installed a sub-commission on Trafficking in Human Beings and Prostitution with the aim of extending the Belgian counter policy towards sexual exploitation of trafficked victims. In July 2000 this sub-commission reported on its activities and presented a number of stringent recommendations (Thijs and De T'Serclaes, 2000). This resulted in the continuation of the mandate of this sub-commission with the aim of broadening the scope to include all forms of exploitation, such as economical exploitation, which is in line with the anti-trafficking law of 13 April 1995.

Last but not least, the phenomenon of trafficking in human beings was one of the key elements in the aforementioned governmental action plan for security policy of 31 May 2000. This action plan marked a turning point since it was recognized that the most appropriate way to combat trafficking in human beings cannot be limited to the extension of a one-sided repressive legislative arsenal. A successful policy towards the combating of trafficking in human beings requires a multidisciplinary approach, the so-called 'four-pillar approach', comprising measures in the field of administrative law, labour law, as a last resort the criminal code and finally victim support.

In order to create the essential conditions for a comprehensive and integrated policy within the four-pillar perspective, the Belgian prime minister took the initiative to set up a task force on trafficking in human beings in December 2000. This was also in line with one of the recommendations made by the sub-commission of the Senate (Thijs and De T'Serclaes, 2000). This task force meets bimonthly and brings together representatives of concerned agencies active in combating trafficking in human beings. It also drew up concrete guidelines for the co-operation between the various departments and services that are (in)directly involved. In particular, the task force called for the establishment of an Information and Analysis Centre concerning Human Trafficking (IAM) within the federal police service. The task force justified its recommendation by reference to the fact that it is essential that all parties and services concerned exchange depersonalized information about human trafficking as part of an ongoing structure. The information gathered within the framework of IAM's activities may vary in form and content: embassy reports, reports from immigration officials, information deriving from NGOs active in the field, statistical data, and so on.

First pillar: administrative level

The Belgian four-pillar approach is based on both empirical research findings and on joint policy conclusions of all actors involved in combating trafficking in human beings (De Ruyver *et al.*, 1999; Van Impe,

2000). We will now discuss all four pillars (administration, labour law, criminal code and victim support) in turn. Trafficking in human beings and illegal immigration often increase with rising migration flows due to existing restrictive immigration policies. Thousands of migrants, who want to leave their country of origin for different reasons, often lack sufficient means. Moreover, migration can occur voluntarily or be forced (Hayter, 2000) and the widening gap between restrictive immigration policies and the need for migrant labour constitutes a perfect environment for trafficking (Jordan, 2002). The lack of means can be judicial (like a passport or a visa), or factual (for example, lack of money to travel via regular channels). Smugglers anticipate the victim's urge to migrate abroad, and even stimulate it, using the restrictive migration policies of the Western European countries as the reason for their existence (Siron and Van Baeveghem, 1999). Smugglers and traffickers often make use of legal channels, though not in conformity with the spirit of the laws. The Belgian parliamentary commission on trafficking in human beings and a pilot study on the Philippines (De Ruyver *et al.*, 1999) revealed a number of bottlenecks within the protection of national borders and the external borders of the Schengen territory (the so-called Fortress Europe).

In the first place there are abuses of the asylum procedures, marriage and adoption procedures, abuses of labour licences for cabaret artists, transit visas, visas for tourists, visas for purposes of family reunion, the authorization of temporary residence for au pairs; study or sport purposes, and so on. Furthermore, use is also made of false documents (forged visas) or residence titles obtained through corruption.

A second problem is the slack control on the application of the administrative visa rules, in particular within the first half of the 1990s. However, it became clear in the latest annual report on human trafficking produced by the Centre for Equal Opportunities and Combating Racism that there exists even today an enormous abuse of Schengen visas (Centrum, 2000). Individual shortcomings combined with insufficient surveillance of the embassy activities are deemed to be important factors within this area of document fraud. Since every EU member state has its own policy towards the treatment of visa applications, attention should be given to a common EU policy concerning asylum and migration.

To counter this problem a data processing system has been put in place in the Belgian visa sections of the diplomatic offices abroad. Concerned agencies such as the law enforcement bodies, the Ministry of Foreign Affairs and the Immigration Office of the Ministry of Home Affairs meet on a regular basis to enhance the exchange of information on migration issues. Furthermore a multidisciplinary team is sent out to the diplomatic offices abroad in order to collect data and train officials from the diplomatic offices to improve their knowledge on issues such as fake or forged documents. Special administrative investigation commissions have been set up within certain Belgian diplomatic offices to investigate the genuine character of foreign documents that have been submitted for legalization.

Care is needed, however, to avoid taking actions that are too severe in the administrative field, since this could actually have a counter-effect by increasing the migrant's need for assistance and recourse to traffickers and smugglers. This dualism is one of the most important challenges in the contemporary migration debate (De Ruyver and Siron, 2002). Reference could, for example, be made to the existing provisions on carrier liability as a means of preventing illegal immigration or trafficking in human beings,[5] which, in fact, prejudges the right to asylum and as a consequence increases the risk of being trapped within the trafficking ring (Vermeulen, 2002). In this regard it is important to underline that an ideal migration policy must focus on the balance between the state's interest – that is, internal cohesion and identity – and migratory pressures and therefore attune the enforcement policy and legal possibilities for migrants (Morrison, 1998).

A third problem is the gaps within existing legislation that promote various forms of abuse. For example, the Parliamentary Committee on Trafficking in Human Beings pointed out that the au pair statute too often led to abuse and should, as a consequence, be amended. Authorities discovered that a considerable number of foreign women were trafficked to Belgium as au pairs but in reality were employed as domestic workers and consequently faced economic exploitation. By Royal Decree the au pair system was brought back to its essence: further linguistic education and general cultural knowledge through a better understanding of the country's customs and living within a family.

On the issue of visas for cabaret artists, the Parliamentary Investigation Commission stressed that the employment of young foreign women as cabaret artists often masks an organized form of trafficking and commercial sexual exploitation. In the late 1980s and 1990s women from Eastern Europe and South-east Asia were recruited by impressario agencies who sold them to Belgian brothel owners with a view to their performing in cabaret shows. It became clear that the policy of issuing visas for cabaret artists led to widespread abuse. To counter the abuse, new decrees gave a more specific definition of cabaret artists and set out some specific conditions with regard to the issuance of visas.

Another trafficking mechanism is the phenomenon of fake marriages, often used as a means to legalize the stay of migrants. The Civil Code was amended pointing out that if circumstances showed that one of the two spouses had clearly no intention to build up a communal life but was seeking advantage to legalize his or her stay through marriage, the marriage should not be considered as legal. In the same regard, a directive provided local authorities with the option to refuse a marriage between a Belgian citizen and a foreigner if there is a reasonable doubt that the aim of the marriage was to legalize the stay of the foreigner. Moreover, a circular provided local authorities with specific indicators on how to detect whether a marriage is genuine or fake.

In order to combat the abuse of the political asylum procedure, often used by trafficking gangs, the Belgian government took several measures to enhance a more efficient collaboration and information exchange between the police services, the services of social inspection, the services of the inspection of labour law, the Immigration Office and the Commissariat-General for Refugees and Stateless Persons. Furthermore, the government issued specific measures to make the asylum procedure less prone to abuse.

Today the phenomenon of non-accompanied minors has become an important problem in Belgium (De Pauw *et al.*, 2002; IOM, 2001). In order to counter this phenomenon, the Minister of Justice issued a circular on the recognition of the principle of relief and assistance shelters for non-accompanied minors (Belgian Statute Book, 2002), which followed the circular of the Minister of Home Affairs concerning the identification file and the information form regarding the notifications of non-accompanied minors (Belgian Statute Book, 2002).

In particular the ministries of Home Affairs and Foreign Affairs are involved with this administrative pillar. In the first place, there is the Immigration Office of the Ministry of Home Affairs, which is responsible for the centralization, treatment and follow-up of all foreigners' dossiers in general, and of victims of trafficking in human beings in particular. The Immigration Office issues temporary residence permits, during the period of the investigation, to the victims of trafficking in human beings. Therefore, the office co-operates with the police agencies involved, justice departments and the specialized shelters for the assistance of the victims. The Immigration Office also acts as a contact point for joint initiatives within the EU and for specific initiatives with third countries. Finally, the office is also involved in the implementation of bilateral agreements on police co-operation about illegal immigration and trafficking in human beings. In this respect, the Belgian government recently adopted bilateral agreements with countries such as Albania, Hungary, Slovakia, Romania and Bulgaria where illegal immigration and human trafficking are some of the key problems faced by government (Belgian Statute Book, 2002).

On the other hand, the Ministry of Foreign Affairs is responsible for the diplomatic and consular missions which have a crucial role to play. In the past, this ministry has not fully made use of the existing possibilities to deal with the problem in the countries of origin or transit. Recently, the Minister for Foreign Affairs developed an integrated policy in order to tackle these shortcomings (De Ruyver, Van Heddeghem and Silon, 2001). Embassies located in vulnerable regions have now taken a more proactive approach as they spot new trends and stimulate prevention and reintegration initiatives in the countries of origin. An important factor can be the incorporation of these actions within broader all-embracing social-economic support to the vulnerable regions. In this regard, the Ministry of Home Affairs established a specially designed programme under which immigration liaison officers are sent out to countries whose citizens represent a growing part in the number of asylum claims. The immigration liaison officers collect data on the spot, provide assistance to the Belgian diplomatic posts abroad, collaborate with other foreign liaison officers and co-operate with the local authorities to set up information campaigns.

Second pillar: labour law

Parliamentary commissions and research projects (Siron and Van Baeveghem, 1999) identified a clear need to involve the departments of social inspection in an active and integrated way in the fight against trafficking in human beings. The Belgian experience, for example, pointed out that those women who had been officially granted work permits as cabaret artists were actually forced into prostitution by traffickers. In this respect it is important to mention that since the Royal Decree of 9 June 1999 concerning the employment of foreigners (Belgian Statute Book, 1999) the obligation exists to draw up a specific labour contract in order to provide permission to work for cabaret artists, trainees and au pair youth.

Aware that the phenomenon of trafficking in persons also forms a risk in terms of economic exploitation, the ministers for Labour, Employment and Social Affairs signed a protocol in May 2001 on the collaboration between the Department of Inspection of Social Policy and the Department of Social Inspection (Brammertz *et al.*, 2002).

This has been given concrete form through targeted controls on the use of foreign labour in general and in the identified 'high risk' sectors such as overseas restaurants, cleaners, the horticulture industry, garment workshops, prostitution, and so on, on a regular basis. In order to obtain a better overview of the situation an annual plan was drawn up in each judicial district of the sectors to be governed. This plan is based upon the collaboration and input of local actors involved in the fight against human trafficking such as the police forces, the prosecutor's office at the labour court, the liaison magistrates, the specialized centres for the assistance of victims of trafficking, and so on.

The specific competences of the departments of social inspection provide a genuine complement to the legal measures and form part of the multidisciplinary approach to combating human trafficking. It is by punishing these activities on the financial level that a contribution can be made by using various administrative fines, confiscation of goods or a request to cease activity.

Third pillar: legislation and implementation of the Criminal Code

The criminal law reaction obviously provides a last resort within the multidisciplinary and integrated approach to the phenomenon of trafficking in human beings. Following the conclusions of the Parliamentary Committee on Trafficking in Human Beings, the Belgian Parliament passed a new law on the Suppression of Trafficking in Human Beings and Child Pornography in 1995 (Belgian Statute Book, 1995). This law amended the Criminal Code as well as the Immigration Law regarding access to the country, stay, residence and removal of foreigners. It added, among others, a new Article 77*bis* to the Immigration Law in which trafficking in foreign nationals became a specific offence punishable with a sentence from one to five years' imprisonment and a fine from 2,500 to 125,000 euros. Article 77*bis* was amended in 2001 in order to penalize the rack-renter who abuses, directly or indirectly, the particular vulnerability of a foreigner, as well as those who sell, rent or enable premises to be used with the aim of making an extortionate profit.

With regard to trafficking for sexual exploitation, the law of 13 April 1995 replaced the existing Article 380 (previously Article 380*bis*) of the Criminal Code. This article provides very severe sentences of up to 20 years' imprisonment and a maximum fine of up to 500,000 euros. In line with the Council Framework Decision on trafficking in human beings,[6] the Belgian Senate introduced in May 2002 a new bill in order to punish the use of sexual services provided by a victim of trafficking in human beings.[7] The government does not intend to criminalize prostitution as a whole, but only the contemporary slavery that can be a result of prostitution. However, it is clear that the prostitution network is frequently used to exploit foreign victims of trafficking (Thijs and De T'Serclaes, 2000).

Trafficking under Belgian law is understood to involve either (a) commercial sexual exploitation, economic exploitation or (b) smuggling with the use of threats, violence or abuse of the vulnerable or precarious position of the foreigner. The latter is applied to prosecute exploitation in cases not involving prostitution. Particularly important is the fact that 'abuse of vulnerable or precarious position' is interpreted very widely and that, as a consequence thereof, the foreigner's illegal immigration status is proof enough of abuse of the vulnerable position. Obviously, Belgian law provides a very broad definition of the concept of trafficking in persons to encompass trafficking for purposes unrelated to the sex industry (OSCE, 1999). This definition does not merely apply to networks active in the trade in women, but also covers networks who smuggle asylum seekers into the country or who exploit legal or illegal foreign employees (Siron and Van Baeveghem, 1999).

The judicial onus of proof for trafficking in human beings is often tremendously hard to achieve, compared to the labour law infractions. Therefore, the Belgian anti-trafficking law defined that, in case of labour law infractions, with reasonable indications of infringements of the trafficking law, the Minister of Justice can demand, by means of a court order, the cessation of activities in expectation of a judicial decision. This provides the opportunity to react in an effective way when criminal actions are suspected.

Essential within the legal approach is the 'Directive on the investigation and prosecution policy concerning trafficking in human beings and child pornography' issued by the Ministry of Justice in 1999 (known as the COL 12/99) with the aim of establishing a uniform and coherent policy. A central role in the further enhancement and co-ordination of the relationship between the justice authorities and the other actors involved such as the police forces, social services and the departments of social inspection will be given to the so-called 'Liaison Magistrate on trafficking in human beings'. This magistrate will function as a contact point for the external actors. At least once a year the 'liaison magistrate' has to organize a meeting with concerned services in the field of trafficking in human beings with the aim of establishing and maintaining an open and respectful dialogue. Furthermore, on a case-by-case basis, the liaison magistrate may also invite any person or department whose help he or she deems useful to the investigations and prosecution regarding trafficking in persons. Additionally, he or she will also be responsible for the collaboration with the national magistrates in their role of co-ordinating of prosecutions and the facilitation of the international criminal co-operation (Brammertz *et al.*, 2002).

Fourth pillar: victim support

The Belgian system for victim support is based on a difficult compromise between, on the one hand, the desire to protect the victims and to offer them prospects for the future and, on the other hand, the necessity for an effective fight against the networks involved in trafficking. It is in this context that the victims of trafficking who agree to co-operate with the judicial authorities and agree to be assisted by a specialized shelter may be granted a specific residence status.

A general overview of three relevant legal texts will draw the conclusion that the position of institutions providing assistance for victims of trafficking in human beings, as well as the victims themselves, has improved steadily in recent years (OCSE, 1999).[8]

In the first place, there is the 'Circular concerning the delivery of residence and work permits to foreigners, victims of trafficking in human beings', issued by the Ministry of the Interior in 1994. This circular formally recognizes the statute of 'victims of trafficking in human beings'. Whenever a victim of trafficking goes to a specialized service that provides assistance to victims, and the victim can prove to the authorities that they have sought this type of assistance, they may receive a delayed expulsion order (as opposed to a direct expulsion order) to leave the country within 45 days that gives legal title to be in the country for the 45-day period. The decision whether they receive this order or not lies with the Immigration Office. If the prosecution service decides to pursue the case, the victim can receive an authorization from the Immigration Office to stay in the country for three more months. If after a period of three months the prosecutor has good reason to believe that the circumstances reported amount to a trafficking case a six-month document is delivered. A renewal of this authorization for another six months is possible until the end of the criminal proceedings against the trafficker. Yet again, assistance by a specialized organization is obligatory. Victims residing under this residence framework are offered access to employment, education, compensation, legal aid, mental and physical health care, financial support, and so on.

Trafficked persons can request permanent residency at the end of the criminal proceedings against the trafficker. The granting of a permanent residency will depend on the discretionary powers of the Minister of Interior and is based on advice by the Immigration Office and reports by the specialized centre for victim support and the local communities. The Immigration Office will therefore take into account the importance of the information reported, and also consider the degree to which the trafficked persons have integrated themselves into Belgian society. When the prosecution, based on the information of the victim, leads to a conviction, permanent residency is generally always granted. If a case is dismissed but the victim has resided for a minimum period of two years under the residence procedure, the victim can apply for a permanent stay. The deciding factor will be the level of integration into Belgian society. This is the so called 'Stop' procedure.

Second, there is the 'Joint Directive for the Immigration Office, police services, social inspection concerning assistance to victims of trafficking' issued by the ministries of Justice, the Interior, Employment, Social Affairs and Public Health in 1997. This directive was issued following new legislation on the fight against trafficking in human beings and child pornography in 1995. In this directive, three non-governmental organizations were acknowledged to be specialized institutions for providing assistance to victims of trafficking: Payoke in Antwerp; Pag-Asa in Brussels; and Surya in Liège. All three of them receive government funding and provide services to victims of trafficking, that is, sexual and economic exploitation and smuggling. Victims of trafficking who want to make use of the possibilities offered by the 1994 circular must prove that they have contacted and are assisted by one of these three organizations (or social services that have an acknowledged agreement with them) in order to receive help and assistance. The directive stresses the importance of consultation and co-operation between these three organizations and the prosecution service, the police and the social inspection.

Third, there is the already mentioned 'Directive on the investigation and prosecution policy concerning trafficking in human beings and child pornography' issued by the Ministry of Justice in 1999, which formalizes the relationship between the justice authorities and the organizations for assisting victims of trafficking. This directive provides for a set of deontological rules to be respected by the police officers active in the field of combating trafficking in human beings. Moreover, it states explicitly that the methods applied by the police forces may not neglect or interfere with the rights and the interests of the victims.

Victims who are already residing in an illegal, precarious and vulnerable position must not be forced into a worse position or a more clandestine situation due to repressive interventions by the police agencies. Therefore, the police officers are urged to recognize these persons primarily as victims and not approach them as illegal immigrants who violate Belgian administrative and social legislation. Particularly important is that this directive advises that the victims should be referred to the three institutions that specialize in the relief of trafficked victims and that the framework for victim treatment should be applied as established within the two aforementioned circulars.

In general the specialized shelters offer a victim of trafficking protection, legal, administrative, social and medical assistance. Protection should be seen as providing victims of trafficking with accommodation if he or she has no other place to stay or in case the victim might be in danger. The length of the stay at the safe house varies from one situation to another. In principle there are no limits, although the average stay at the safe house is six months.

Legal assistance is aimed at ensuring that the victim's rights and interest are defended. Obviously, most of the victims are not well informed about their legal position and rights. Moreover, victims often do not dare to tell the truth during their initial statement to the police. Therefore, the shelters will offer the victim the assistance of a lawyer. Another possibility is that the Centre for Equal Opportunities and Combating Racism, as well as the three specialist organizations, have the capacity to appear in court in lawsuits related to trafficking in human beings. The organization may form the plaintiff in its own name or on behalf of the victims who authorize it to do so.

Administrative support is directed at unravelling the cluster of administrative rules in order to facilitate obtaining a residence permit for the victims as discussed above.

Prevention projects aimed at disseminating correct information to the countries of origin and transit by informative programme or information campaigns relating to the actual opportunities in terms of residence and living and working conditions and the risk of being abused by smugglers and traffickers have gained particular attention (Koser, 2000).

Finally, the IOM conducted a pilot project for the return and reintegration of victims of human trafficking in 2001. The objective of the project was to gather and disseminate information on the services available for victims of human trafficking with the aim of setting up an instrument to assist victims to return home in a secure and dignified way. Based on the project outcomes, the Belgian government approved the subsidy of another pilot project. This involves 20 victims who had made the decision (voluntarily) to leave Belgium (Brammertz *et al.*, 2002).

Psycho-social support for victims of human trafficking: experiences in practice

The central mission of Payoke is to provide support and assistance to victims of human trafficking. Given the Belgian legal framework, that is law and regulations concerning victims of human trafficking, it should be underlined that this is not always an easy task to fulfil. Social workers in this field often feel in an ambiguous position. On the one hand they are supporting the victim with all his or her needs, yet on the other hand they have an obligation to inform the authorities as they are expected to give full information to the governmental agencies concerned in respect of the individual cases. This double role often leads to contradictory situations and it is the task of the specialist organizations to find the right balance.

Basically, Payoke provides two kinds of services: psycho-social and judicial-administrative support. The administrative assistance primarily comprises application for the residence documents under the above-mentioned residence procedure, as well as follow up. The judicial assistance focuses on informing the clients on the criminal procedure, follow-up of the criminal procedure and compensation claims. Psycho-social support entails a broad range of activities such as: lodging, housing, safety, physical health, mental health, education, employment, financial support, and so on.

Table 4.1 Number of Payoke clients: an overview

Year	Number of clients
1996	97
1997	117
1998	127
1999	119
2000	184
2001	199

Source: Payoke, 2002: 25

The intensity of the support varies from client to client and is therefore based on the individual needs of the client. Every person has different qualities, questions and needs. This makes it very difficult to give a general description of psycho-social support.

For every new client, the assistance starts with an intake procedure.[9] The intake is not always the first step in the assistance plan. Victims often find themselves in a situation of crisis so that the initial help focuses on redressing that situation. There may be a need to provide them with a safe place where they can feel comfortable and rest or in cases where the victim has been seriously injured as a result of their ordeal, they need to be referred to a doctor or a hospital. There can be various ways for victims to be referred to a specialist organization.

One of the clients' most urgent needs at their first contact with Payoke is a place to stay where they feel safe. In most cases victims are lodged in the organization's safe house (Asmodee), which is located at a secret address in Antwerp. Sometimes the victim needs to be referred to another safe house in case there is a security problem or a lack of lodging capacity.

Most clients have medical problems. Some of those problems need urgent care. In general victims have to undergo a routine medical check up. Mental health is also a very important issue. Most victims of human trafficking suffer from one or more mental health problems, such as stress or depression, and it is very important that they are provided with adequate care. Apart from individual referral to psychotherapists, focus discussion groups are organized for those who are living in the shelter.

In a safe house victims can come to rest. They have the opportunity to eat, to sleep, to take a shower or a bath, to get clothes, and to do all of this in a safe environment. In a safe house, staff offer the victims

Table 4.2   Agencies as first contact

First contact with victims through:	Percentage in 2001
Police services	42
Judicial services	2
Confiding in someone (such as out-reach workers, acquaintances, etc.)	63
Other organizations and services (such as organizations that support people without documents, hospitals, etc.)	21
Asylum centres	2.5

Source: Payoke, 2002: 27

support and a listening ear, provide them with information and so on. The social workers encourage and support the victim in his or her efforts to solve his or her problems, to feel better, to embark on education, to look for future lodging, and so on, in view of further integration. Safe-house clients experience a daily routine: getting up at certain hours, eating between certain hours, doing daily tasks, and so on. Clients sometimes complain about this routine, but in the end almost all of them feel good about it. It gives them an opportunity to get back on track with their lives and with society – a lot of the victims of human trafficking have lived very unsteady lives, especially the women who have been exploited in the sex industry. The return to a routine has a very positive, restful effect on most of the victims. Taking into account a victim's need to integrate themselves into society, special attention is given to registration for language courses and integration workshops as significant means to get access to society.

In general, clients have to stay for a minimum period of three months in the safe house. One month before the end of their stay, clients are

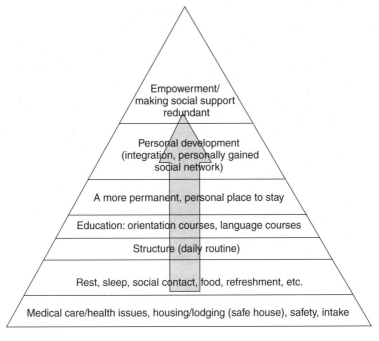

Figure 4.1 Model of support for clients of Payoke

prepared for independent living and they are followed up closely as some experience difficulties when leaving a communal life.

After leaving the residential setting the victims are referred to the ambulatory service of Payoke where a long-term assistance plan is designed with the client. As the assistance of victims varies in each case, it is difficult to give a general overview of the support. But in general, a simplified model of the evolution that most clients go through is shown in Figure 4.1.

Notes

1. Federaal veiligheids- en detentieplan (Government safety and detention plan), URL: just.fgov.be/index_ nl.htm.
2. Coalition Agreement of 7 July 1999: The way to the 21st century. URL: premier.fgov.be/e_html_index_image_swap.html.
3. Parlementaire Commissie van onderzoek naar een structureel beleid met het oog op de bestraffing en de uitroeiing van de mensenhandel, *Parl. St. Kamer*, 1993–4, no. 673/7 – 91/92, 1–369.
4. Wet van 13 April 1995 houdende bepalingen tot bestrijding van mensenhandel en van de kinderpornografie (Law of 13 April 1995 on trafficking in human beings and child pornography), *Belgian Statute Book*, 25 April 1995.
5. With the coming into force of the *Council Directive of 28 June 2001 supplementing the provisions of Article 26 of the Convention implementing the Schengen Agreement of 14 June 1985* (*OJ*, 10 July 2001, L 187) the EU member states are obliged to take the necessary steps in order to ensure that under their national laws, regulations and administrative provisions, carriers must ensure that third-country nationals who intend to enter member states possess the necessary travel documents and, where appropriate, visas.
6. Council Framework Decision of 19 July 2002 on combating trafficking in human beings: *OJ*, 1 August 2002, L 203, 1–4.
7. Wetsvoorstel tot invoeging van een artikel 380*quater* in het Strafwetboek met betrekking tot het gebruiken van diensten van seksuele aard geleverd door een slachtoffer van mensenhandel (Proposal for new legislation on the use of sexual services provided by a victim of trafficking in human beings), submitted by Marc Hordies, Paul Galand, Magdeleine Willame-Boonen, Jean-Pierre Malmendier, *Parl. St., Senaat* 2001–02, no. 2–1146/1.
8. For a comprehensive review on the Belgian victim support, see Moens, 2002.
9. An *intake* is a conversation where both parties (client and organization) exchange information and where they try to get a global view of the assessment of the client's needs and the options available to the organization to fulfil these needs.

5
Responses to Sexual Slavery: From the Balkans to Afghanistan

Victoria Firmo-Fontan

Introduction

A year after the onset of 'Operation Infinite Justice' in Afghanistan, girls and women within and around the country are subjected to an exponential increase in trafficking, resulting itself in a resurgence of sexual and physical violence.[1] In this lawless territory women are more victimized than ever, after years of drought and armed conflict, human trafficking, mainly but not exclusively of women and girls, has reached a climax whereby a girl can be sold for as little as 100 kg of wheat.[2] While the pretext for such transactions between a parent and a buyer might be that of marriage, girls may be sold several times before reaching a place where they are physically and/or emotionally coerced into performing sexual acts with clients. While the series of transactions involving the movement of the individual will be referred to in this chapter as trafficking, the coercion dynamic behind the acts of the prostitute will be identified as forced prostitution, itself very distinct from the profession of other sex workers who engage in prostitution of their own free will. Moreover, the remuneration given for the act will not be regarded as a key dynamic, as some girls may be given sporadic payment by their owner, while still being forced to work as prostitutes, either through debt-bondage, as a way to repay pimps for a freedom that will rarely be achieved, or through physical violence. As this chapter will illustrate, the former is rarely exclusive of the latter, which is why the term of sexual slavery is used.

The recent UK court ruling in favour of the former United Nations Mission to Bosnia-Herzegovina (UNMiBH) worker, Kathryn Bolkovac – wrongfully dismissed by her employer for disclosing information on the involvement of UN workers in the sex trade of Bosnia-Herzegovina – has publicly highlighted the direct link between the sex industry of 'peace' and the presence of international peacekeeping personnel in post-conflict areas. As pertaining to retributive peace, the phenomenon of post-conflict human trafficking for forced prostitution is described by Madeleine Rees, head of the UN Human Rights Commission office in Sarajevo, as drawing on the rules of supply and demand, whereby '[o]nly the international community would have been able to get to the flats and bars being made available with foreign women' (McGregory, 2002).

In the event of a successful deployment of international troops in all regions of Afghanistan, which local sources and past history suggest might not necessarily happen, the demand for female slaves will invariably rise, according to Elwert (2000), in what is labelled part of the post-conflict market of violence. In Bosnia-Herzegovina (BiH), the UNMiBH has estimated that between 750 and 1,000 trafficked women and girls are subjected to sexual slavery, while the NGO Lara, based in Bijeljina, estimates that double the aforementioned number of foreign women are presently trapped in brothels around BiH (Vandenberg, 2002). The conflicting nature of such speculations concerning the specific number of sex slaves held on BiH territory is symptomatic of the numerous problems surrounding a volatile trade. The aim of this chapter is to draw lessons from the issues surrounding the onset of trafficking to and within Bosnia-Herzegovina, in order to issue valid recommendations to prevent the worsening of the present situation in Afghanistan and Pakistan.

Trafficking: seen and unseen

The brutalization of the female body in war through rape is not a new phenomenon. However, the revelations surrounding the use of rape camps during the war in Bosnia-Herzegovina has given a new direction to the study of conflict, for its civilian dimension could not be ignored any longer (Stiglmayer, 1994). Peace studies acquired renewed academic legitimacy over their strategic studies counterpart, while the debate over the civilian nature of conflicts became centred around the subject of 'new and old wars' (Kaldor, 2000). While the field of peace studies has drastically expanded since the end of the Cold War, this chapter will contend that violence against women also seems to be repeated in peace through trafficking and forced prostitution, constituting the core of sexual slavery. Therefore, the study of new wars ought to be expanded to include a redefinition of what does and should constitute a rights-based peace. Indeed, when confronted with the everyday realities of trafficking, its persistence, prevalence and consistency, the commerce of women can be labelled as an unfortunate result of peace, as one of those phenomena that no one can avoid, and one that is much preferable to an armed conflict as such. However, the issue does not lie in a zero-sum interpretation of war and peace, but rather in the experience suffered by the individual subjected to trafficking, for victimization does not only lie in the hands of the criminals themselves, but also with the existing legal framework punishing the corrupt 'sex worker' for her 'indecent' occupation. In order to overcome some of the conceptual confusion, let us first look at exactly what trafficking entails in the Balkans and in Afghanistan.[3]

Origins

First, the person, not exclusively though primarily female, is subjected to what Galtung (1975) identifies as 'structural violence' in her own country of origin. For women who find themselves displaced to the former Yugoslavia, these are mostly Ukraine, Romania and Moldova, and most women trafficked within Afghanistan or to Pakistan, are from Afghanistan. In these countries of origin economic stress and the feminization of poverty might entice women to seek alternative employment in another state. Developed by Pearce (1978), the concept of the feminization of poverty focuses on the sex differences in poverty rates, while analyzing the processes by which women's risks of poverty might be increased. Of an estimated 1,300 million persons worldwide estimated to be poor, 70 per cent are women (Marcoux, 1997). In the developing world, although not exclusively, the processes facilitating the feminization of poverty can be attributed to traditional and religious dynamics, surrounding inheritance laws for instance, or to a lack of governmental support for single, widowed or divorced women. For example, many women interviewed claimed to have had to emigrate as a result of a lack of access to secondary education due to their sex, limiting their employment prospects, the latter also decreased by a gender segregation in employment. The patriarchal system, more severe in some countries than others, might also influence some women to leave an abusive marriage, or an alienating condition as a single mother. Some may then decide to answer an advertisement to become a waitress or a nanny in Western Europe, or a matrimonial advertisement. Others will contact an agency that allegedly specializes in finding 'work' abroad, the sexual nature of which may be known by the employment seekers, who may take their future positions as sex workers as a calculated risk. Indeed, some women who know that they risk being taken into prostitution, believe that they will be financially better off, working in a Western country, or also speculate on the possibility of marrying a 'Western man'. An argument commonly advanced in the countries of origin is that most women are aware of their future conditions as prostitutes. Interviews carried out with Romanian nationals have corroborated the aforementioned view that 'these women' who choose to emigrate know the nature of their work abroad, and therefore only have themselves to blame for their situation.[4] Not only does this type of opinion exonerate the countries of origin to carry out awareness programmes, it also trivializes the experience of women in sexual slavery. Indeed, some are aware of the risks that they are taking, however, others do not know what to expect. The aforementioned argument blames exclusively the trafficked women, who are supposedly responsible for their misfortunes. It therefore subjects them to yet another type of abuse. For many trafficked women, another harsher reality seems to be the cause of what is perceived by too many as their 'self-inflicted' displacement. George Mulheir, Country Director of Hope and Homes for Children in Romania, explains that a significant number of young women who have spent their childhood in Romanian orphanages are subsequently lost to the vortex of sexual slavery, mainly in the Balkans or the Middle East.[5] The social exclusion suffered by these young women in crowded state orphanages makes them easy prey to the sex industry upon their discharge from these institutions, where they have not been introduced to human interaction or the outside world. Moreover, while their craving for affective bonding will be utilized by unscrupulous individuals, their social inexperience will ensure the permanence of their state of captivity once displaced. Some Romanian prostitutes interviewed in Jounieh, Lebanon, did not perceive their situation as necessarily entailing captivity, although if allowed at all, they would only leave their homes, accompanied, for a maximum of one hour a week. While one might assume that their relationship with other Romanian sexual slaves aware of their own conditions could have triggered a realization of their captive status, the reality was often different, as some would not be emotionally equipped to face reality. The vulnerability of many individuals in their country of origin is therefore a strong enticement for traffickers, as it provides a certainty that they will not seek freedom once working in foreign places. This phenomenon can be compared with the state of false-consciousness experienced by women within the patriarchal order, whose questioning might entail a psychic collapse of the symbolic order they have known and abided by all their lives, resulting then in a psychosis (Grosz, 1990). The possibility of vulnerable women's empowerment might entail the questioning of their entire life, and thus create a further mental breakdown. In sum, whether or not knowledgeable of their conditions before or after displacement, 'aware' women interviewed by the author recognize that they never would have accepted to leave their countries had they known about their fate as slaves, while others who do not fully appreciate the gravity of their conditions have persistently expressed their unhappiness to the author. The 'awareness argument', utilized mainly by the few brothel clients interviewed during this research, or by countries seeking to absolve themselves from creating the need for forced migration, is therefore rendered void by the condition of slavery in which these women find themselves. The concept of slavery is developed below as referring to the fact that the women interviewed all claimed to have been sold, forced to work without or with little payment or after contracting debt-bondage. They have then been coerced and/or abused into performing sexual acts with individuals who have paid for the encounter. While this chapter is focused on the topic of forced prostitution, it should also be made clear that trafficking does not only lead to sexual slavery, it can also involve manual labour, such as in Northern Brazil, or the entertainment industry, such as the boys taken from Afghanistan to the Gulf to become camel racers (see Chapter 3 in this volume).

Destination

Most victims recruited in BiH do not make it to the advertized destination and end up being sold at auctions, mainly in Belgrade or at the infamous Arizona Market of Brcko, for prices ranging from 500 Konvertible Marks (KM) to 5,000 KM. When they arrive in their location of displacement, they might be forced into submission for several days by their owner or the keeper of the establishment, euphemistically called a nightclub, through physical violence and sexual abuse. Their passports are taken away from them and they are told that their documents will be returned when they have repaid their 'carer's' expenses to find employment for them. They are then put on the market and forced to perform sexual work every day, sometimes with only a few hours to rest. The typical day of a sex slave would entail: receiving clients in the evening until dawn; sleeping for a few hours; cleaning the nightclub; working as a waitress during the day if the establishment is also a restaurant; and then starting to receive clients again. At the time of writing, the situation for women trafficked within Afghanistan, or from the lawless region of Pakistan, is the same. However, the demand for recreation by international workers has not yet reached a climax in Afghanistan, since most internationals choose to go on 'stress leave' in Pakistan or Thailand, and may seek the company of prostitutes there.[6]

Release or escape?

In BiH, should sex slaves manage to escape from their nightclubs, they might be granted asylum in a safe place, before being deported back to their countries of origin, for the lucky few who have been able to escape with their passport. Women who attempted to escape may also be killed by their owner, or arrested by the local police and deported to the other side of the inter-entity boundary line (IEBL), where another pimp is waiting to buy them from the police.[7] As a matter of fact, after having realized that many deported women would become victims of trafficking again, the Office of the High Representative (OHR) issued a decision in 1999 prohibiting the deportations of aliens by BiH police without consulting the UNMiBH/International Police Task Force (IPTF) (Ludwig Boltzmann Institute of Human Rights, 2001). While this ensured that the women arrested would be given IOM shelter, it also resulted in the deportation of women solely across the entity line within BiH. For those taken into custody after a police raid (providing that the owner has not been tipped off in advance), another form of unfair treatment occurs whereby they will be effectively considered as criminals by the authorities, and either deported or imprisoned. How would they be tipped off, when a raid is prepared by the local police and assisted by the IPTF? The answer lies in the fact that, until recently, a blind eye has been turned to the frequent visits that some IPTF staff paid to nightclubs as clients.[8] Moreover, numerous times the local police have been involved in either maintaining the existence of the prostitution establishments, either for money or complimentary visits, or facilitating the trafficking of the women within BiH, mainly across the IEBL separating the Bosnian Croat Federation and Republika Srpska.[9] There have been many scandals surrounding the tacit acceptance of prostitution by local or international police, as well as the impunity with which some international staff were behaving in the field (Vandenberg, 2002; Human Rights Watch, 2002b). Cases of collusion and even financial co-operation between nightclub owners and IPTF staff are too frequent, involving trafficking of women, girls and also young boys.[10] Investigations and testimonies, such as that of Kathryn Bolkovac, point to the reality that IPTF monitors visit brothels and arrange for women to be delivered to their homes, in breach of their codes of conduct. As the sanctions for IPTF staff convicted of having violated the United Nations 'zero tolerance' policy are incumbent to their countries of origins, they greatly differ in consequence, from involving the mere relocation in another part of BiH for US or Jordanian staff, to being sent home at once for German officers.[11] IPTF staff are not the only internationals involved in sustaining the industry: in BiH brothels tend to cluster around SFOR bases, while in Lebanon they are located within Christian areas (euphemistically reputed within the UN 'scene' as having an active nightlife) and in Pakistan within internationally friendly areas. For the 'internationals' involved in the industry, blackmail can also be a way for the nightclub owners to be informed of a forthcoming raid.

Retributive peace

The occurrence of sexual slavery in post-conflict areas is condoned by the very individuals that should respect and apply human rights and can therefore relate to the dynamic of retribution and lawlessness present in this type of environment. Indeed, Bosnia-Herzegovina can be understood as a society experiencing negative peace, whereby its people are not fighting any more, but are not ready to share a common future. In a similar vein, no one is inclined to acknowledge responsibility for the onset of the war. While putting the blame onto one another for the war, former combatants interviewed by the author invoke self-defence when recognizing their role as fighters. In this context, peace can take various forms, not all geared towards the invalidation of polarizations. Indeed, the difference between negative and positive peace, the former exclusively focusing on the absence of armed violence, and the latter aiming at the formation of what Margalit (1999) identifies as the 'decent society' lies in the polarization of populations in a post-conflict setting. While pertaining to the ownership of responsibility or collective memory, the successful elaboration of positive peace seeks to reduce ethnic, gender and economic polarizations (Firmo-Fontan, 2003a). In a context such as that of BiH, the non-ownership of collective responsibility for the development of the conflict, rejecting a blame onto the 'other', whether it be ethnic, foreign or even gendered, has led the country to rebuild itself under the auspices of division, embodied in the partition of the country through the Dayton Peace Accords, and illustrated in the division of gender, classifying women as the dependant, to protect, provide for, control and at times brutalize, and as the 'other', a dehumanized nemesis trafficked and violated for the self-gratification of the dominant.

The increase of gender divisions in post-war BiH can be expressed by the decline of women's place in the public sphere, whether it be in the employment market or local politics, this despite international efforts to promote gender awareness (Firmo-Fontan, 2000). Within her area of investigation, located in Canton 10, the author noticed the inequalities of employment between men and women, prompted by the slow economy, and itself an expression of the feminization of poverty. Added to these inequalities are the divisions within the female gender, prompted by the separation of the women to protect, who have rights, that is, the Bosnian women, and the new 'others', trafficked women used as commodities. While the international community has been promoting gender equalities within post-war BiH, the detached attitude of international staff with regards to sexual slavery, in the same manner as that of local individuals, illustrates a general failure to understand peace beyond the cessation of armed violence, as well as to conceptualize structural violence as the prime dynamic hindering the growth of a 'decent society', whereby the institutionalization of equality stems from the cultural, the legislative, the economic and the political. The international failure to bring sustainable peace to BiH can be explained by the fact that it has encouraged short-term centralized reconstruction initiatives to the detriment of sustainable development tailored to suit specific circumstances while evolving in a multitrack setting, that is bottom-up and top-down post-conflict rehabilitation (Firmo-Fontan, 2003b). The author's experience as a democratization officer for the OSCE was symptomatic of the aforementioned trend. Indeed, as she was asked to act within the remit of the mandate that was set for her by the OSCE Head Office in Sarajevo, she was unable to suit the needs of her community specifically. This discrepancy between the field and the think-tank finds its most acute expression in the international community's approach to sexual slavery. As a matter of fact, for other internationals who do not use the services of a brothel as such, the issue becomes all too familiar and sometimes trivialized. In some instances the issue has become 'normalized'. The first official meeting that the author (in her capacity with the OSCE) had with the mayor of Grahovo, Mr Slobodan Sabljic, was held in the restaurant of the local brothel, with official representatives of the UNHCR and the Bosnian-Croat Federation government. Upon enquiry, she was told that the only two sex workers present were there of their own free will. One of them was serving during the meal. A subsequent informal interview with one of the women showed that she was from Ukraine and had to sell sex as a way to repay her pimp for buying her at the local auction. The premises of the brothel in question are rented from the Grahovo municipality to a businessman from the nearby town of Livno. When attempting to alert the international authorities, the author was informed that trafficking was not part of her mandate and that she was setting onto someone else's turf. So whose turf is it?

Legal responses

In July 2001, six years after the Dayton Peace Accords, the UN created the Special Trafficking Operations Program (STOP) to fight trafficking. Between then and 1 January 2003, IPTF and local police have conducted over 270 raids and interviewed over 800 women (Vandenberg, 2002). This part of the chapter will show that while international law has evolved towards the recognition of trafficking as a rights-based issue, international workers can still act with impunity with regards to slavery.

Better late than never, the STOP initiative has yet to be fully put into practice and harmonized between different parts of BiH. Indeed, in some parts of the country, IPTF human rights officers are given the task of monitoring borders and trafficking with no previous experience or consistent training. Moreover, the poor human rights record in some of their countries of origin does not make some of them the best candidates to uphold human rights abroad. When the author was stationed in Drvar, BiH, one Irish national, based in Banja Luka, without any training in international or human rights law, was in charge of co-ordinating the monitoring of borders against trafficking. As the issue of trafficking remains to be addressed within the Republic of Ireland itself, one might have wondered if a member of the Guarda Siochana was best suited to address the issue abroad.[12] At the time of research, one STOP team, based in Doboj, was composed of two officers, who were in charge of the care of 176 slaves working in more than 30 brothels. The team, underfunded and understaffed, had been relentlessly asking for support from HQ Sarajevo. Both officers deplored the fact that they were unlikely to receive support before the end of their 12-month assignment, jeopardizing chances of follow-up from one team to the next. They felt the problem had been addressed far too late by the international community, and their presence was a drop in the ocean: they had been able to support eight girls to leave the brothels over a period of six months.[13] They explained that when the girls are rescued, they are either deported by the local police, or if they ask, they will be allowed to talk privately with the IPTF officers, who will then provide shelter for them through the IOM, based in Sarajevo and funded by the UN Mission to Bosnia-Herzegovina (UNMiBH) and the Soros Foundation. While the integrity of the Doboj STOP team is unquestionable, other instances have shown that women are reluctant to speak to IPTF, let alone the local police, as a result of their past involvement in trafficking (Vandenberg, 2002; Human Rights Watch, 2002b). When interviewed, the women will then be encouraged to prosecute the nightclub owners. They rarely choose to proceed as they fear to be either deported as owners of illegal documents, retaliated against by the nightclub owners in BiH, or fear repercussions on their families. In one instance, a girl interviewed, who had been sold by the acquaintance of a friend, was concerned about the well-being of her daughter in her country of origin.[14] On 1 January 2003, the IPTF mission, under UN control, was replaced by the European Union Police Mission (EUPM), reducing the number of the international police assisting the development of the BiH police force from over 2,000 to 512 policemen. This has directly resulted in a decrease in international police activities with regards to trafficking, bringing the STOP initiative to a halt (Zecchini, 2003). In an effort to reassure the international public on the follow-up of past initiatives, the EUPM assisted in the raid of 24 brothels on 2 January 2003. No arrests were made. The next part of this chapter will assess the international law response to human trafficking.

Trafficking and international law in BiH

International law concerning the combat of trafficking can be applied to BiH.[15] According to Article 2, paragraph 1 of the BiH Constitution, 'Bosnia and Herzegovina and both its entities will provide the highest level of internationally recognized human rights and human freedoms.' Moreover, Article 2, paragraph 2 states that the 'rights and freedoms established in the European Convention on Human Rights and Fundamental Freedoms and its protocols shall apply directly in Bosnia and Herzegovina. Those documents will have priority over all other law.' The *United Nations (UN) Convention for the Suppression of the Trafficking in Persons and of the Exploitation of the Prostitution of Others* of 1949 does not contain a definition of traffic in persons because it does not apply as an anti-trafficking instrument as such.[16] It focuses on prostitution and calls for the penalizing of any person making profit of another person's prostitution. It only addresses the needs of women by acknowledging, under Article 16, their need for rehabilitation, while forcing them to be assisted in their return to their countries of origins under Article 18. In practice, it therefore treats them as criminals or undocumented migrants, who should be deported. This practice does not take into consideration the reasons that they chose to leave their countries, and does not motivate them to seek reparation or help if mistreated by their employers while residing in the country of destination. Article 6 of the *UN Convention on the Elimination of All Forms of Discrimination Against Women* of 1979 obliges state parties to 'take all appropriate measures, including legislation, to suppress all forms of trafficking in women and exploitation of prostitution of women'.[17] However, the provision contains no explanation or definition of the terms 'trafficking' and 'exploitation of prostitution'. The Committee (CEDAW), established under the convention in order to review state parties' compliance with their treaty obligations, recognizes the role of poverty and unemployment, wars and armed conflicts in increasing the incidence of trafficking in women. It also stresses the need for the protection of victims and prosecutions of perpetrators. Moreover, the *UN International Convention on the Protection of the Rights of All Migrant Workers and Their Families* of 1990 requires state parties to recognize all migrant workers as 'persons before the law' and to ensure their access to the legal system and non-discriminatory treatment before the courts.[18] Another relevant instrument is the *UN Convention on the Rights of the Child* of 1989.[19] Under the convention, children are recognized to have special needs and a different legal status to adults. They are therefore protected under the terminology 'best interests of the child' against any act from the state that could result in their revictimization. It also calls upon states to combat kidnapping of children and to protect them from economic, sexual or other exploitation. BiH has not signed the Slavery Convention of 1926 which abolishes slavery in all its forms, including forced or compulsory labour that develops into 'conditions analogous to slavery'. However, BiH is party to the *UN Supplementary Convention on the Abolition of Slavery, the Slave Trade, and Institutions and Practices Similar to Slavery* of 1956.[20] This convention calls for the abolition of slavery-like institutions and practices such as debt-bondage or forced marriages. As many sexual slaves are kept imprisoned as a result of a need to repay their captors for travel, auction and lodging costs, thus clearly constituting a situation of debt-bondage, the aforementioned convention could be used as an alternative to the other treaties victimizing the individual as an illegal migrant.

As described by Ould in Chapter 3 of the present volume, the term 'trafficking' was not appropriately conceptualized until the adoption in 2001 of the United Nation *Protocol to Prevent, Suppress and Punish Trafficking in Persons, Especially Women and Children, supplementing the*

Convention against Transnational Organized Crime. The protocol was ratified by the BiH government on 24 April 2002 (Human Rights Watch, 2002b). In this protocol, trafficking does not only refer to prostitution, but also includes the violence, intimidation and deception pertaining to the displacement of people into forced or slave labour (UN, 2001). Moreover, it does not recognize as legally legitimizing the original consent given by the victims of slavery. The specificity of the definition of trafficking has resulted in the elaboration of a report by the UN Special Raporteur on Violence Against Women, in which four different sets of circumstances have been established to facilitate the diagnosis of trafficking. A first group of individuals has been established and refers to the absolute coercion and dupery of which women are victim. A second group encapsulates women who were partly lied to when they accepted recruitment for employment, such as concerning their destination of work, the nature of the work they were going to produce or the extent of the debt they were going to sustain as a result of their travel. A third group comprises of women who were aware of the kind of work they were going to do, but who did not know the extent to which their movements and finances were to be restricted. Finally, the fourth group refers to women who know that they are to sell their body as a commodity for the sexual pleasure of their clients, and who are in control of their own finances and movements. This latter set of circumstances is the only one where women can be referred to as prostitutes, as opposed to sexual slaves, and do not classify as trafficked individuals. This report is the first of its kind to define so specifically the term 'trafficking' for women. However, it does not link the act directly to the issue of modern slavery, or sexual slavery, and fails to present a specific protocol to address the issues of prevention and repression of trafficking.

There is no doubt that the sharpening up of the definition of trafficking will lead to a future legal link between its practice and sexual slavery, the question that remains is when. Moreover, the rapid increase in 'humanitarian strikes' and 'democratic interference' emanating from Western powers since the end of the Cold War leaves thousands of women at risk of being victimized by their traffickers, their wealthy peacekeeping 'clients' and international law. In practice, therefore, as illustrated by the case of Doboj, most women diagnosed as trafficked individuals and freed, the 'chosen few', will have to wait to be transferred to the IOM house in Sarajevo, this pending a) a local investigation, b) a review of their case by the IPTF HQ, c) space in the safe house, all of the above possible only through the rare availability of a translator for those who do not speak the local language. This process is extremely time consuming, and only falls under the mandate of two officers, whose dedication, however, is remarkable. Since the officers assess the international community's reaction as coming too late, they stress the importance of prevention, both in BiH for women trafficked out of BiH, and in the other countries of origin. Prevention should play an essential role in the general current international efforts to curb trafficking, as well as in the effort to bring law and order to Afghanistan. So far, due to a lack of budget, the IOM activities have just been scaled back, and human trafficking has not been mentioned in the Agreement on Provisional Arrangements in Afghanistan, officially binding on 22 December 2001.[21] As well as prevention, assessed later, the impunity enjoyed by members of the international community with regards to trafficking should be addressed.

International impunity

The international response to trafficking encounters several major obstacles, due to the lack of harmonization of prosecution procedures for criminals as well as the treatment of the trafficked individuals and their 'clients'. At the time of writing, SFOR, as part of NATO, has no formal regulations sanctioning the use of prostitutes by their personnel as a result of the fact that, under Appendix B to Annex 1A of the Dayton Agreement, NATO personnel are placed under the jurisdiction of their respective nations (Human Rights Watch, 2002b). In the case of IPTF monitors, no member of the mission can be arrested or detained within BiH. They have absolute immunity from criminal prosecution. Moreover, should a Bosnian court seek to prosecute an IPTF officer, this could only be achieved if an immunity waiver was issued by the UN Secretary General. In the case of the EUPM, provisions for the prosecution of mission members are incumbent on their countries of origin. As no harmonization of procedure to punish users has been put in place, the author interviewed representatives of three European armed forces and one police service. The interviews were carried out both in a formal and an informal manner. Upon enquiry on the training of peacekeeping personnel in relation to the issue of trafficking, the Irish Defence Forces mentioned that the issue will be raised in various Human Rights lectures given at the United Nations Training School of Cunnagh. The French Inter-Army Health Services stated that they train their soldiers to be cautious of sexually transmitted diseases. The British Army was unable to inform the author on existing overall policies pertaining to the awareness of trafficking and the use of prostitutes by its troops on UN/NATO missions. Moreover, the existence of repressive policies towards the encouragement of sexual slavery seems to be left to the personnel's own countries. In the case of American IPTF monitors implicated in trafficking, whether through the 'ownership' or the use of trafficked women, the fact that they enjoy immunity under the terms of the Dayton Peace Accords means that they cannot be prosecuted upon their return to the US, as a result of a lack of jurisdiction. In the light of these statements, one can safely assume that the issue of sexual slavery is not recognized by the United Nations, or the troops it sends, as relevant to peacekeeping. At the EU level, the incorporation of a policy addressing the issue of sexual slavery might only be possible through the Common Foreign Security Policy, however, as the repression of trafficking and the issue of border control is already part of the EU Justice and Home Affairs Treaty, this former solution seems unlikely.[22] Indeed, the ethos surrounding sexual slavery appears to be one of repression of the victims themselves, as opposed to the fostering of their protection.

Prevention

Considering the complexity of the issue as well as the multifaceted nature of trafficking, effective strategies against trafficking should never be restricted to post-trafficking prosecutions and deportations. An anthropologist working in Albania emphasized the need for awareness in the countries of origin.[23] She was faced with a dilemma when introduced by locals to newspapers recruiting women for 'marriage'. While the locals did not seem to know what these entailed and either joked or considered seriously these publications as genuine offers for marriage, she was faced with a difficult choice, either to warn her interlocutors as to the purpose of the exercise, or not to. Where does the balance of ethics lie in such a case? Are the locals aware and do they not make their positions known, for concern over their own reputations as brothers or fathers of effectively enslaved women? Are they genuinely unaware of slavery? Some leaving to get married never contact their families again for fear of the shame that their conditions would bring, others return and willingly answer another advertisement, hoping that they will be more lucky and work in a better place – they would correspond to the aforementioned third category of women eligible to be qualified as trafficked.

The painful process of raising awareness involves many target groups, ranging from international workers to women victims of violence.

It could be initiated by the international community when arriving in a post-war area, or by survivors, in collaboration with their governments, local NGOs and international organizations. Members of the international community in BiH and now in Afghanistan, comprising an important number of 'users' within the peacekeeping personnel, should be made aware that often women do not work in brothels of their own free will and that in most cases, they do not make any money at all. The narrative used to raise awareness should be exclusively that of slavery, for trafficking uses the victim's body as a commodity, transported and sold through channels of organized crime. Awareness-raising campaigns are important in order to provide potential victims with sufficient information attached to migration. School children are an important target group in the issue of migration, since slaves can also be children. Awareness should also target women victims of violence in countries that are the hardest hit. A correlation has been made between violence and the rise of trafficking in Moldova and Ukraine, as women do see migration as a desperate measure to flee an abusive relationship, as much as they also leave their homes for economic reasons (Minnesota Advocates for Human Rights, 2000: quoted in Kartush, 2001).

Police training could also account for successful prevention and action against trafficking. While this account mainly focuses on trafficking into BiH, women are also being trafficked out of the country, across the entity line, and all around the former Yugoslavia. General awareness could also promote future legislative harmonization between border-states. The OSCE, given the mandate of police training under a specific pillar system of post-conflict management, is successfully training new police recruits in Kosov@ to that effect.

Conclusion

Trafficking and forced prostitution were acknowledged as stark reality faced by transitional societies following the 1990 United Nations Mission to Cambodia (UNTAC) (Fetherston, 1998). Five years later, the onset of peace in BiH reiterated international concern over the issue. However, the successful NATO campaign in Kosov@ of 1999 brought forward a sudden mushrooming of brothels across the province. While some of the lessons learned from BiH have been applied to Kosov@ with regard to trafficking, the number of brothels in the region is still unacceptable. Will Afghanistan suffer from the same flaws in international policy-making? What can be done to prevent it? International law seems to acknowledge trafficking as a fatality. Our role is to take it seriously.

Notes

1. Personal correspondence, corroborated by Human Rights Watch (2002c).
2. News International, 'Disgrace to humanity: Afghan girls on sale for 100kg of wheat', 10 February 2002.
3. It is with reluctance that the term Balkans is being used by the author, who acknowledges the existence of the literature on the westernisation of the term (Hudson, 2002).
4. Recorded interview with Laura Hampea, Bilbao, Spain, December 2002.
5. Interview with George Mulheir, Limerick, 15 May 2002.
6. Interview with Aitor Asli Victoria, Doctores sin Fronteras Mission to Afghanistan, November 2002, Bilbao, Spain.
7. The Dayton Peace Accord has partitioned BiH into the Serb Republic (Republika Srpska) and the Bosnian-Croat Federation. The partition has resulted in the formation of different police forces.
8. Unattributable interviews with OSCE and IPTF staff, corroborated by Human Rights Watch (2002b).
9. See note 7.
10. Personal communication, corroborated by Human Rights Watch (2002b).
11. Unattributable interviews with IPTF staff.
12. At the time of writing, the author has initiated an academic enquiry into the implication of legally based lap-dancing clubs within the Republic of Ireland in the trafficking of Eastern European sex workers. The present enquiry will investigate several claims made surrounding the use of lap-dancing clubs as a means of gaining entry for individuals to Irish territory, before disappearing into brothels as prostitutes.
13. Interview carried out at Doboj IPTF station on 23 January 2002.
14. Interview with K. D., Prijedor, 16 October 2001.
15. The author chose to review solely the most relevant international laws, as the BiH national law falls under three constitutions and falls short of being applied by the two national police forces, sharing four police codes.
16. Succession by BiH on 1 September 1993.
17. *Ibid.*
18. Not yet in force, ratification by BiH on 13 December 1996.
19. Succession by BiH on 1 September 1993.
20. *Ibid.*
21. IOM Press Briefing Notes – 7 May 2002 on http://www.iom.int/news/PBN070502.shtml; and http://www.uno.de/frieden/afghanistan/talks/agreement.htm.
22. Telephone interview with Jean Monet Professor Edward Moxon-Browne, University of Limerick.
23. Antonia Young, interviewed in Schtadtschlaining, Austria, on 20 May 2002.

6
Migrant Domestic Workers and Slavery[1]

Bridget Anderson

Migrant domestic workers in Europe

Paid domestic work is a feature of households all over the world, from Ecuador to Swaziland, from Spain to the Ivory Coast. In many countries it probably constitutes the single largest female employment sector (though its invisibility can make this difficult to document). It is work that is predominantly performed by women, usually managed by other women.

Domestic work is a key area of employment for women throughout the world. The demand for domestic workers in private households, both as carers and as cleaners, is marked throughout the European Union. There are many reasons why more and more domestic workers are needed: the elderly population, child-care problems, lack of welfare state, women entering the labour market and break-up of families.

Kalayaan was established in 1987, to support the rights of migrant domestic workers (MDWs) in the UK. We work hand in hand with a self-help organization for migrant domestic workers, UWA (previously known as Waling-Waling). Kalayaan and UWA have over 4,000 members from over 35 different countries, 90 per cent of them women, all of whom were undocumented when Kalayaan and UWA were formed. UWA was formed as a new type of migrants' organization, based not on country of origin/ethnicity, but first and foremost on legal status and type of employment, namely working as an undocumented migrant domestic worker. In this way, workers shared experiences across boundaries (of nationality, country of reception) with a view to identifying common problems.

Kalayaan also helped to form 'RESPECT' in 1996, which is a European network of migrant domestic workers' organizations, individuals, trade unions, NGOs and supporters that campaign for the rights of all non-EU citizens working in private households, both women and men, regardless of immigration status.

RESPECT supports the relevant campaigns of its members at a local, national, EU and international level. It facilitates the sharing of experiences and expertise in campaigning, organizing, lobbying and fundraising. It carries out research and disseminates information. We have also run four projects with the assistance of the Daphne Initiative from the European Commission. The projects have all looked at issues of violence surrounding MDWs' work and living.[2]

Why slavery?

So, why have MDWs often been described by the term 'slave'? We see the term used a lot journalistically: 'Slavery in Britain: servant makes midnight run to freedom', 'Five years for a couple with a slave nanny', 'London's domestic slavery'. Kalayaan is often contacted by journalists from a variety of media, all of whom want to expose the 'slave-like conditions' MDWs face in Britain (although preferably at the hands of Arab employers). So why are these sorts of terms, ostensibly supportive of (often) undocumented migrants and condemnatory of their oppressive conditions, used by a press that is not noted for its sympathetic analysis of migrants?

At the most obvious level, 'slavery' is often shorthand for long hours, no pay and imprisonment.[3] The power exercized over the migrant worker, and her corresponding lack of control over all aspects of herself, including vulnerability to physical, psychological and sexual violence, also provoke comparisons with slavery. Slave owners in the American South were clear that a slave must have no will, no opinion, and that they must be afraid of their owners. The following is a description, by a domestic worker in London: 'We were three Filipinas, she brought us into the room where her guests were, she made us kneel down and slapped each one of us across the face.' The casual, unpredictable nature of such violence demonstrates the power of the employer and is often a feature of the control of the worker. It is also, problematically for some feminist analyses, usually perpetrated by the female employer (Anderson, 2000b).

Status reproducers

Women working without papers, with no legal protection and isolated in private households are vulnerable to abuse. Their work as 'status reproducers' can be degrading; for example, cleaning cats' anuses, flushing employers' toilets, scrubbing the floor with a toothbrush three times a day or standing by the door in the same position for hours at a time. It is difficult to interpret such tasks as anything other than a manifestation of the employer's power and the worker's powerlessness.

Workers do not simply substitute for the work of their female employers. There is no total amount of domestic work that can be divided fairly between equal partners, or hived off to someone who is paid to do it. There is always more domestic work to be done. The divorcing of management from labour has consequences on the practical daily level: standards go up when one does not have to do the work oneself. The servicing of lifestyles and consumer goods that would be difficult, if not impossible, to sustain were the other household members to attempt to do the work themselves, and which, had the household members to do it themselves, they would probably not want to sustain, is an important component of paid domestic work:

> Every day I am cleaning for my madam, one riding shoes, two walking shoes, house shoes, that is every day, just for one person... plus the children, that is one rubber and one shoes for everyday school, that is another two. Fourteen shoes every day. My time is already finished...You will be wondering why she has so many bathrobes, one silk and two cotton. I say, 'Why madam has so many bathrobe?' Every day you have to hang up. Every day you have to press the back because it is crumpled.
>
> Filipina working in Paris

The confinement of tasks to those merely necessary for individual survival would enable most productive workers to service themselves. For domestic work is not only about 'caring', which is in that sense necessary work, it is also cleaning houses, washing up, ironing and so on. We do not have to live in tidy, dusted homes nor wear ironed clothes. Madam (the consumer) does not have to have so many bathrobes in the same sense in which Madam (the 'productive worker') maybe has to have her children cared for. Domestic work, mental, physical and emotional labour is reproductive work, and reproductive work is not confined to the maintenance of physical bodies, since people are social, cultural and ideological beings, not just units of labour. It is necessary work in that without domestic work humanity would not continue.

We need to accommodate the raising of children, the distribution and preparation of food, basic cleanliness and hygiene, in order to survive individually and as a species. But domestic work is also concerned with the reproduction of lifestyle and, crucially, of status: nobody has to have stripped pine floorboards, hand-wash only silk shirts or dust-gathering ornaments. These all create domestic work, yet they affirm the status of the household, its class, its access to resources of finance and personnel (Anderson, 2001).

Experiences of MDWs in the UK

Here I want to explain a bit about Kalayaan's work and the experiences of the MDWs who visit our centre. Kalayaan was set up for a specific purpose, namely to campaign for a change in the UK law. One main difficulty for migrant domestic workers in the UK was that of immigration status. Workers were dependent on the employer they entered with for their immigration status; they could not change employers legally, and if forced to run away (often without their passport) they could not work for anyone else. Moreover, once their original visa expired they would lose all right to be in the UK. This meant that, having escaped from one abusive situation, workers were very vulnerable to exploitation by secondary employers (usually British), who could take advantage of their immigration status with poor working conditions, low pay and always the threat of reporting the worker to the police should they not do what they were told.

Kalayaan lobbied the British government to get the status of MDWs regularized. In July 1998 the UK government finally announced publicly that they were going to give visas to future migrant domestic workers accompanying their employer which would allow them to change their employer. They would also regularize all those migrant domestic workers who had been living and working clandestinely (Anderson, 2000a).

Since the change in the law our work has not stopped! We still work to support and campaign for rights for migrant domestic workers. Immigration status is one issue of importance for migrant domestic workers, as it severely affects their rights, but there are many other issues which need to be focused on (employment rights, statutory rights and so on). Kalayaan keeps monthly figures detailing the kinds of difficulties faced by the workers we interview. These are more or less constant year to year.

Table 6.1   Abuse experienced by Kalayaan clients

Type of abuse experienced	August 2000[4] (percentage)	August 2001[5] (percentage)
Physical abuse	51.4	34
Psychological abuse	82.4	88
Locked in	40.5	62
Sexual abuse	5.4	3
Irregular food	51.4	31
Lack of room	60.8	not available
Lack of bed	47.3	45
Irregular pay	47.3	19
Paid less than £200/month	not available	90
Lack meal break	63.5	not available
Passport withheld	not available	68
No time off	not available	79

Note: August 2000, number of clients: 106; August 2001, number of clients: 90.

Slaves = victims

I am sure that all who know of these statistics rightly feel outraged that an employer could treat their employee in such a way and feel sympathy or pity for the victims. However, there is often a fetishization of victimhood. It is exacerbated by scrambles for funding, and by the eye of the media which exalts in a sort of pornography of oppression. Often, at meetings, supporters of domestic workers (not actually domestic workers themselves) have tried to surpass themselves in the dreadfulness of the situation of the people that they claim to represent. (You think it's hard in the UK being undocumented, you want to try in France, Germany...); (You think your clients have it badly, you should see x who endured y...); (At least your people haven't been forced into prostitution...); (Moroccans are much worse off than Filipinas...) – and so on.

In this looking-glass world, the most valuable are those who suffer most in the hierarchy of oppression. It is particularly easy to cast women in this role. On the one hand it is important to recognize that there are differences between migrant domestic workers and that these are sometimes associated with country of origin or religion in particular. This is exacerbated by the nature of their employment. Employers have a tendency to view migrant workers in terms of their nationality or ethnic origin rather than as individual workers. Different nationalities become defined by different traits and some groups are seen as more desirable to employ than others.[6] In London, for example, employers want Indians because they are docile, Filipinas because they are good with children and so on. This makes it difficult for African women in particular to find work. And when they do get jobs they tend to be lower paid, further from central London and longer hours than other people. While women from some countries have had to pay agencies, and therefore are more likely to be middle class, to have a level of education and to speak some English, women from other countries are more often from the rural poor. Lack of English again acts against them in the job market. The harder it is to find work the more likely you are to stay in an unsatisfactory, or even an abusive job. So migrant domestic worker does not signify a homogeneous group: while some workers are well paid and have, albeit in the face of great difficulties, negotiated reasonable conditions, others are abused and exploited and there are certain groups (national, economic, religious) who are more likely to have difficulties than others.

The problem with fetishizing victimhood is that by focusing on individual, dreadful cases of abuse and how benevolent and horrified supporters can 'help', it is too easy to think that the less dreadful cases do not matter. It is important to recognize that there are differences, not least because those who are in the stronger position, who speak English, who are better educated, have more days off, who live more centrally, and so on, will inevitably find it easier to participate and take lead organizational positions. So, unless we recognize such differences between workers, the organization risks leaving the most powerless behind. It is by raising the situation of the most powerless that all migrant domestic workers are empowered because, slave or happy family member, the mechanisms and structures that keep them doing the dirty work are shared.

And this is the problem with the rhetoric of slavery. Because one of the functions of the term 'slave' is that this is unacceptable. This is one reason why it is undoubtedly an effective campaigning tool, for it is a term that captures the moral high ground. 'We' cannot accept slavery. It is not 'civilized'. It is a word like 'genocide': we can never condone it. So, who is the villain in the slave trade? The traders and the slave masters. Who are the villains in the domestic worker industry? Evil and abusive employers. This focus enables a denial of the materialistic context, the structural forms of power that often allow the possibility of abuse in the first place. So structural adjustment, for example, or the immigration and asylum policy that drives migrants into risking their lives are completely ignored. For migrant domestic workers in the UK, who often accompany employers from the Middle East, the problem is often cast as one of evil Arabs 'importing' slavery. Maltreatment and abuse of workers was presented as a consequence of allowing people with no understanding of what constituted civilized behaviour to bring in their domestic servants. A frequent response to newspaper articles or television coverage are phone calls from viewers offering board and lodging in exchange for work, just to help the 'poor girls' out. These highly exploitative offers of employment (in a nice family) as a favour are made with kind intentions, for of course these readers/viewers are not at all like the evil employers they read about or see on the television. 'Don't be dependent on them, be dependent on us!' It is an active demonstration of kindness; the worker is a living illustration of her employer's charity. They are not slave mistresses; they have managed to transcend the exploitative relationships that are so exemplified in the lives of undocumented migrant women in Europe.

What can be done?

So, recognizing that MDWs are not a homogeneous group and that some MDWs suffer great hardship while others have managed to negotiate reasonable working conditions, what can be done to ensure that MDWs are not treated as *slaves* or *victims*?

1.   Domestic work needs to be recognized as work!

All too often domestic work is despised as *dirty work*. Work which is unskilled but necessary. It is not given the proper respect it deserves. Employers often describe their MDW not as workers but as *part of the family*, and not working but *helping out*. Many employers will expect the MDW to be on-call, to baby-sit in the evening (even if this is their time off), because this is *not really working*. Often employers calling Kalayaan looking for a domestic worker ask how many hours the worker is supposed to work every day and express surprise when we suggest a normal eight-hour day, with two days off. I think this is because the families who call us really do not see the worker as having a life outside of their house and that as *part of the family* they should want to do the extra tasks (just this once – clear up after the party, baby-sit tonight, do the extra washing up and so on). This undermines domestic work and does not treat the domestic worker as a worker.

2. Immigration rights

Immigration rights are absolutely crucial for MDWs. The immigration situation for migrant domestic workers is different across Europe. Different countries have different mechanisms for allowing migration to work in private households. It is not possible generally to get a visa for this kind of work. In Greece it is difficult to enter legally as a domestic worker, but it is tolerated if the worker is accompanying her employer.[7] The same system operates in France and Germany. In Germany, there are a large number of Polish immigrants who do not need visas to be in Germany, so they are usually present legally, but are often working illegally, in domestic work. In the Netherlands, domestic workers can only enter as au pairs. In those countries like Spain and Italy where you can get visas, you are tied to your employer and the numbers of visas applied for are far greater than the numbers that are given in their quota systems. In the UK, domestic workers can only enter the UK if their employer is entering the UK and the employer wishes their domestic staff to accompany them. They also have to be over 18 and to have worked for the employer for a minimum of one year. The RESPECT network campaigns for independent immigration status for MDWs across Europe. Lack of independent immigration status results in dependence on employers, the fear of deportation, threats from employers and so on.

3. The right to hold your passport

MDWs all over the world often are unable to hold onto their passports. Employers demand them from their workers as an effective means of control. As the statistics kept by Kalayaan show, on average around 60–65 per cent of the MDWs we see do not have their passports and often do not know what type of visa they have or for how long it has been given. The right to hold your passport is a fundamental right. As an Eritrean domestic worker said 'When somebody is holding your passport, where do you go? Your passport is your life.' Not having access to their passports results in innumerable difficulties for MDWs. They have to use a solicitor to discover what entry clearance was granted to them to enter the UK, they have to negotiate with their embassies for new passports, often costing large sums of money. Some embassies, such as the Indian Embassy, will not give new passports without a photocopy of the old passport and evidence of the right to stay in the UK. Others, like the Philippine Embassy are more lenient, recognizing that often MDWs are unable to have a photocopy of their passports. Some MDWs will have unintentionally overstayed their visa because of lack of access to their passports. Some employers will have told their workers that they have kept their visas renewed, but have not done so. Some employers will bring their workers to the UK on the wrong visas (for example tourist visas) which cause great difficulties to the individuals when the mistake is discovered. The police are reluctant to classify withholding passports as 'theft', so MDWs are forced to report their passports as 'lost' instead. Embassies are reluctant to demand their property back from unscrupulous employers.

Passport retention is an area that causes such distress and expense to workers that Kalayaan is hoping to start a major campaign focusing on this issue.[8]

4.   Countries need to sign up and abide by UN/ILO conventions

The Global Campaign for the Ratification of the International Convention for the Protection of the Rights of All Migrant Workers and members of Their Families continues.[9] The UN General Assembly approved the Migrant Convention on 18 December 1990 and by 10 December 2002 20 state parties have ratified the convention.[10] This will happen at the earliest on 1 May 2003. The UN Convention is very important because it extends fundamental human rights to all migrant workers, both documented and undocumented. It recognizes migrant workers are social entities with families and provides the right to family reunification.

There are two ILO conventions relevant to migrant workers: the Migration for Employment Convention (Revised), 1949 (No. 97) and the Migrant Workers (Supplementary provisions) Convention, 1975 (No. 143). Both have been ratified,[11] but extra pressure is needed to ensure that states abide by the recommendations and to encourage more states to ratify them.

5.   The right to join a trade union

The right to join a trade union is a crucial right for MDWs across Europe. In Greece, a union for domestic workers has been formed as part of the Athens Labour Centre and they will accept MDWs without papers. In Germany, most MDWs are not part of a union because most unions will not accept undocumented workers. In France, the main unions for MDWs are the CFDT or the SUD, which has close links with the Sans Papiers movement. In the Netherlands, although good co-operation is maintained with the FNV it is still unclear as to whether the FNV will accept undocumented migrants as members. In Spain, two trade unions are very active in campaigning for rights for MDWs, the UGT and

CCOO. In Italy the FILCAMS-CGIL has always respected MDW rights (RESPECT Network, April 2001).

Kalayaan's experience of working with the Transport and General Workers Union (TGWU) in the UK has been very positive. The TGWU accepted undocumented migrant domestic workers as members, gave them a reduced rate of membership, provided them with membership ID cards (a crucial ID when many migrant domestic workers leave their employers without their passports) and campaigned for a change in the law for migrant domestic workers to be given the right to change employers. Moreover, the right to belong to a trade union gives domestic workers a natural forum for organizing to protect themselves.

6. Employment rights

It is, in fact, employment rights that can potentially protect migrant domestic workers from many abuses. Domestic workers should have access to full and non-discriminatory employment rights and social protection, including the minimum wage, sickness and maternity pay and pension rights. In the UK, employees in the private household are explicitly exempted from coverage by the race and sex discrimination acts. This shocking fact means that employers could advertise for a worker with the proviso that 'no blacks need apply' and this would be legal. The ILO (2001) recognize that these employment and social rights need to be given to workers in the informal sector, and the trade unions could provide support in the necessary campaign and support work needed in these areas.

7.   Examine our attitudes

We need to recognize the effect using the term *slavery* has on those who use it and those it seeks to represent as *slaves*. We need to examine our own attitude towards *slaves* and *victims*. We need to treat MDWs as individuals, as workers and as people who are entitled to immigration and employment rights across Europe. And employers of MDWs need to consider the relationship they have with their worker, the expectations they have of her and the respect they treat her with.

8.   The Charter of Rights

Finally, RESPECT has drawn up with MDWs across Europe a Charter of Rights for MDWs. This charter can be endorsed by individuals and by organizations. The least we can all do is seriously consider our response to this charter and sign up to its principles.[12]

Notes

1. I would like to thank the editor of this book for inviting a chapter from Kalayaan and for the opportunity to write about migrant domestic workers and slavery.
2. Information about Kalayaan and RESPECT, including the results of some of our projects are available from Kalayaan, St Francis Centre, 13 Hippodrome Place, London, W11 4SF. Telephone: +44 (0)20 7243 2942; fax: +44 (0)20 7792 3060; e-mail: kalayaanuk@aol.com
3. Anti-Slavery International (ASI) defines a slave as someone:

   - forced to work – through mental or physical threat;
   - owned or controlled by an 'employer', usually through mental or physical abuse or threatened abuse;
   - dehumanized, treated as a commodity or bought and sold as 'property';
   - physically constrained or has restrictions placed on his/her freedom of movement.

   See ASI website http://www.antislavery.org/ for more information.
4. Of those 106 clients: 66 were from the Philippines, 26 from India, four from Nigeria, three from Indonesia, two from Ethiopia, two from Sri Lanka, one from Nepal, one from Botswana and one from Jordan.
5. Of those 90 clients: 52 were from the Philippines, 23 from India, five from Indonesia, four from Sri Lanka, one from Ethiopia, one from Tanzania, one from South Africa, one from Jamaica, one from Jordan and one from Slovakia.
6. Kalayaan operates a strict equal opportunities policy and will not allow an employer to specify nationality in their search for a worker.
7. For example, no work permit is given, but a tourist visa – although it is clear that the domestic worker is not part of the employers' family.
8. For more information contact Kalayaan.
9. For more information on the global campaign visit the December 18 website (www.december18.net) and the Migrants Rights website (www.migrantsrights.org).
10. State parties that have ratified the convention are: Azerbaijan, Belize, Bolivia, Bosnia and Herzegovina, Cape Verde, Colombia, Ecuador, Egypt, Ghana, Guinea, Mexico, Morocco, Philippines, Senegal, Seychelles, Sri Lanka, Tajikistan, Timor Leste, Uganda and Uruguay.
11. No. 97 has been ratified by 42 countries. It was adopted on 1 July 1949 and came into force on 22 January 1952. No. 143 has been ratified by 18 countries: Benin, Bosnia and Herzegovina, Burkina Faso, Cameroon, Cyprus, Guinea, Italy, Kenya, the former Yugoslav Republic of Macedonia, Norway, Portugal, San Marino, Slovenia, Sweden, Togo, Uganda, Venezuela and Yugoslavia. It was adopted on 24 June 1975 and came into force on 9 December 1978.
12. Copies available from Kalayaan or on the December 18 website (www.december18.net).

7
Bonded Labour in South Asia: India, Nepal and Pakistan

Krishna Upadhyaya

Introduction

In the 1926 UN Slavery Convention slavery was defined as: 'the status or condition of a person over whom any or all of the powers of the right of ownership are exercised'. That definition covered traditional forms of slavery, based on ownership, but it does not apply equally well to contemporary circumstances. Today, recognized forms of slavery include debt-bondage, serfdom, forced marriage in return for money and exploitation of children's labour. This chapter will focus on the forms of slavery that fall under the term bonded labour.

In the *UN Supplementary Convention on the Abolition of Slavery, the Slave Trade, and Institutions and Practices Similar to Slavery* of 1956, debt-bondage, known as bonded labour in South Asia, is defined as:

> where a debtor pledges his personal services or those of a person under his control as security for a debt, if the reasonable value of those services is not applied towards the payment of the debt or if the length and nature of these services are not limited and defined.

In 1999, it was estimated that there were 20 million bonded labourers, worldwide (Anti-Slavery International). There is no agreed estimate of bonded labourers in South Asia.

Bonded labour is a contemporary form of slavery (UNHCHR), where labourers are forced to accept exploitative conditions of work until the 'debt' is repaid. Debt is at the root of the system. This indebtedness distinguishes bonded labour from other forms of forced labour. The UN's 1956 convention and the ILO's Forced Labour Convention of 1930 provide a framework for combating this form of slavery. Although national laws exist in South Asia, they are either too broad, as in India, or are group or situation specific, as in Nepal. Indian legislation and Supreme Court interpretations incorporate all the situations that can be termed as 'forced labour'. Contrary to that, Nepalese legislation implies that '*kamaiya* labour' covers all types of 'bonded labour' although *kamaiya* is only one kind of the bonded labour among many other kinds present in Nepal.

In South Asia bonded labour exists in most economic sectors, such as agriculture, rural industry, the service sector, and also in the production of materials for industry or construction (hereafter primary source), such as quarries and brick kilns. Debt-bondage also occurs among victims of trafficking into prostitution, and migrant workers. Bonded labour is not exclusively an 'economic' phenomenon. There are also both sociological and political aspects. In addition to the poor, bonded labourers come from excluded groups, such as *dalits* or 'low-castes', as in India or Nepal (Robertson and Misra, 1997), or from minority religions and 'foreigners' as in Pakistan, or from ethnic minorities, who, historically, have been excluded. Often, workers from these groups borrow from their landlords for survival. The indebtedness often leads to bondage.

There is a cultural basis for the selection of *dalits* or 'low caste' workers for ploughing and other menial work: being excluded as members of the 'untouchable' caste, only they are considered fit for such work. Equally, they are vulnerable to exploitation by the 'high caste' landlords or moneyed class. The caste position of *dalits* and 'low castes' determines their class. This is the usual link of socio-cultural practice based on caste 'ideology of inequality', poverty and bondage. 'Tribal' (ethnic) groups, too, are excluded from the main caste groups.

British rule in India never intervened in the country's social systems, particularly the caste system, although a controversial decision for allocating electoral constituencies for *dalits* was made in 1935 (Haslam, 1999). The 1921 law for redistribution of land was not applied (ASI, 2002a). In Bangladesh, India and Pakistan, communities were forced out of their areas, based on laws connected with ownership and exploitation of forests. The indigenous communities were often seen as illegally occupying the forest. The 'land distribution' carried out after independence, particularly in India, brought little benefit (Menon, 1997). In Pakistan, many poor people were driven out of villages, because agriculture was mechanized (Bales, 1999). In Nepal, the Tharu suffered because 'only a small proportion of targeted land identified for redistribution passed into Tharu hands' (Robertson and Misra, 1997). The land distribution was seen as a political move to relocate hill people to districts bordering India. These social segregations, cultural practices, political moves and economic conditions reinforced and sustained bonded labour in the traditional agricultural economy. It is, therefore, very much a *system*. Nevertheless, it has not been static. The changes in labour practices have led to 'new', 'non-traditional' or 'emerging' forms of bonded labour, particularly in services, rural industries and primary sources, such as mining and quarrying. These changes can be attributed to the expanding foreign markets for Indian products like stone for gravestones and, in some cases, investments by multinational companies in industries like silk.

A final distinction to be made is the variation in the types of labour in use in different sectors and countries. They include family labour, migrant labour, child labour and individual male and female labour. Those working may be permanent or seasonal and locals or migrant.

Incidence of bondage in different sectors of the economy

Agriculture

Bonded labour was first reported in agriculture in the Indian state of Bihar in 1858. Bonded labourers were known as *kamauti*. Now, bonded labourers are known as *kaimaiya*, *kamiyah*, *haruwahi*, *kandh* in Bihar and *haliah* in Orissa, *harwashee* or *kamiya* in Madhya Pradesh, *hali* in Uttar Pradesh and in Maharastra (Robertson and Misra, 1997). *Naukari* is another name they are given in Maharastra, whereas it is *vatti* in Rajasthan. In South India, they are called *gothi*, *halia* or *jeetam* in Andhra Pradesh, and *jeeta* in Karnataka (Menon, 1997). All these terms, however, literally mean 'ploughman' or 'worker'.

Labourers are 'contracted' to work for their masters under the condition of bondage when they become indebted to them. This indebtedness can occur for different reasons, according to the time and place. In some places, the traditional system remains intact. Elsewhere, changes have taken place with time and changes in the rural economy. Usually, 'low caste' or *dalits*, who undertake 'polluted' work in the field, are easy victims of such a system.

A typical example of such a situation is Gujarat during the 1960s (ASI, 2002b). During this period, an extreme form of labour relationship between landlords and labourers existed in Gujarat villages. In the rural setting, only certain types of people were deployed for 'unclean' and 'polluted' work. The workers who, in many cases, eventually became bonded, were mainly *dalits* or other 'low caste' people. The caste rules played an important role in their selection. This indicates that bonded labour, also, has links with the hierarchy of social identity in South Asia. In addition to the labour relationship between *daniyama* ('the master' in Gujarati) and *halis* (workers), hierarchical caste relations maintained the caste behaviour of 'high caste' and 'low caste' – in most cases, this was exemplified in the practice of untouchability.

For many, the process of being trapped into indebtedness started with marriage. Male members of the *hali* class would take a loan to pay for their marriage, and so bondage would start. While the system starts with hiring men, due to the increasing debt, eventually their wives and children, too, work for the masters. The whole family, therefore, falls into bondage.

The debt increased if labourers were absent from work, or unable to work. Although the debt made them work like slaves, the masters usually would not admit that they were slaves. They maintained that the workers were like their children. Certainly, at times, they took care of them in many ways. If, however, the masters thought that labourers had acted against their interest, they could be very harsh. Seldom, however, did they show their cruelty in public. They tried to appear benevolent, by lending to the bonded labour families, on the grounds that it was a social system, rather than economic, being related more to prestige than profit. The system, therefore, sustained a patron–client relationship.

With greater commercialization in agriculture, less was invested in the labour force. Benevolence was replaced by the search for profit. The masters wanted a better return from the workers in whom they had invested, by making loans. This led to increased cruelty and brutality, with the masters being less concerned about their labourers' problems.

The social aspect of the system of bondage also changed with time. Changes in the rural economy contributed to altered lifestyles. Elite members of villages began to eat better food than their labourers, instead of everyone eating the same. Their lives had become much better than those of their labourers living in the same villages. As transport became more readily available, voluntary movement of labour became a reality. Villagers could travel elsewhere to obtain casual work, securing additional income and providing themselves with more bargaining power.

The mechanization in agriculture and the 1976 law against the bonded labour system resulted in at least some landlords refusing to provide loans in return for work from bonded labourers. Nevertheless, the old system of bonded labour is still very much in existence in most of the rural and interior parts of India. This includes most of the northern states, such as Bihar, Uttar Pradesh, Madya Pradesh and Punjab.

Although the traditional system disappeared in many places, due to the unequal development of different states and their economies, it still exists in a large part of the agrarian society of India. A specific example of this is *haliya* (*halvaha*) life in a village in Uttar Pradesh where *haliya* receive a small piece of land for their own use, while continuing to work for masters in respect of outstanding debts which, all too often, are transferred from generation to generation, with sons taking on the debts, and work, of their fathers (Bales, 1999).

For bonded labourers in agriculture, the chief characteristics are lack of freedom of movement, abuse and threat of violence, living in a level of poverty where nothing more than subsistence is available and dependence on a master for shelter. Bonded labourers may be agricultural labourers, or share-croppers, who are indebted to landowners and are forced to work. Or they may be agricultural labourers, indebted to landlords/landowners, who are allowed to go elsewhere for work during their master's off-seasons. However, they will be forced to return and work during certain periods of the year. Also, there is *begar*. This is unpaid labour mostly in return for 'shelter' and in line with the terms of the contract. Those are the main features, but there are variations in rural India, in relation to the loan, type of labour, methods of force and the mobility of labour. In addition, there are some visible changes, such as in Karnataka. Generally, in Karnataka it is only adult males and boys (and not the whole family) who work as *jeeta*, the Kannada word for bonded labourers (ASI, 2002c). As elsewhere, loans were the main reason for the bondage.

Apart from in indigenous areas, bonded labourers are chiefly *dalits*. This means that their relationships with their masters are long term, and few succeed in securing release by paying off their loans. Even if *dalits* are set free from bonded labour, their caste position implies they will do the lowest-paid or even unpaid jobs. A good example is the situation in Chakka Shandra village in Bangalore (ASI, 2002c). While the men were working as bonded labourers, the women worked as wage labourers, and earned R5 per day. Now, while the men are free, the women work as wage labourers, earning R25 per day. The men receive R50 per day without food, or R40 with food. This shows the vulnerability of women, and how, as the wives of men doing *jeeta*, they lose their bargaining power.

Coming from the *dalit* community, both men and women are involved in cleaning the village. This is unpaid work, and they receive only leftover food. The term 'cleaning' also includes the clearing of carcasses from the villages. This is usually undertaken by the male *dalits*.

Despite, therefore, having been freed from bondage, traditional caste relations continue, thus requiring workers to work as forced labour, as 'prescribed' by religio-cultural practices. This is enforced by the power of the upper caste moneyed section of the population. Effectively, therefore, labourers may simply move from debt-bondage to other forms of bondage.

Traditionally, in South Asia, a loan is not the liability of an individual, but of the whole family, chiefly because property is shared among the children of the household. In view of the children's filial duties towards their parents, a loan passes from one generation to the next. With enforcement by the higher caste and moneyed classes, the children, in turn, are entrapped into bondage. Muniappa, from Chakka Shandra village, is aged 45. He started *jeeta*, earning R15 per year at the age of seven. He does not know the size of the loan granted to his father by the landlords. His youngest son has continued as *jeeta*, replacing his father, while his other children work as *coolie* (wage labour). The eldest son is receiving training in connection with electric wiring, while the younger son, having recently been released, is taking up traditional work.

The use of males only, both adults and children, in Karnataka, rather than the whole family as in other areas, is seen as a change in the system. New and emerging non-traditional types of bondage exist in other sectors of the community, such as in brick kilns and gem-cutting. This is due to lack of work in the villages and significant movement among workers.

Seasonal debt also exists, mainly in sugar cane farming. Often such debts are repaid by labour, but not everyone achieves this, with the result that many remain indebted. A difference between the old form of bondage and the new and emerging forms is shown in the relationship between the master and his workers. The traditional relationship was feudal and personal. At the same time, it was very much an extreme form of exploitation. With the new types of bondage, there is much more of a business relationship between an employer and his workers. Often, this work is temporary, with the bonded labourers being migrant and seasonal.

Nobody knows how many bonded labourers work in agriculture in India, although there are estimates of the overall number of bonded labourers. Such estimates, however, vary, with significant differences in the numbers estimated by the government and by non-governmental organizations. The government of India maintained: 'as per reports received from state governments the total number of bonded labourers identified and freed was 256,000, of whom 223,000 have been rehabilitated' (ASI, 1997). However, a commission formed by the Supreme Court of India estimated that there were more than a million bonded labourers in the one state of Tamil Nadu. Another estimate puts the overall figure as being at least 10 million (ASI, 1997). Also, various states have denied the existence of bonded labour, in particular Punjab and Maharastra. According to a report, there are at least 15 million child bonded labourers in India (HRW, 1999).

In Pakistan, the route into debt-bondage is much the same as in India or elsewhere. Labourers are entrapped into bondage as the result of a loan advance. Such loans usually are taken simply for subsistence or for special expenditure, such as marriage, a festival, or medical costs for a member of the family. To this extent, the situation is very similar to that prevailing in India.

Most bonded labour in Pakistan exists in the agricultural sector. Other areas include brick kilns, domestic service, and the carpet and weaving industries. Also, there have been some reports of bonded labourers in mining and the fishing industry. According to the National Commission on Justice and Peace, of the estimated 6 million bonded labourers in Pakistan, approximately half belong to religious minorities – chiefly Christians and Hindus. According to the 1998 census, approximately 4.3 million belong to religious minorities.

Bonded labour, together with other forms of forced labour, is thought to exist mostly in Punjab and Sindh (Ercelawn and Nauman, 2001). Nevertheless, it is presumed that it exists also in the North-west Frontier provinces, although, so far, no study has been carried out in this area. Share-cropping is a widespread relationship between landlords and labourers in Punjab and Sindh. Labourers become involved through a loan advance taken in return for future work. Other forms of bondage also exist (Ercelawn and Nauman, 2001). Encouraging recent information suggests that there has been a decline in debt-bondage in Pakistan. It may be that the reduction in numbers is due to fewer landless tenants and also share-cropping.

In principle, with share-cropping, the harvest is shared equally between the workers and the landlords (*zamindars*). All too often, in practice, the *zamindars* take a greater share, partly as a repayment for the seeds supplied to provide the harvest. Sometimes, share-cropper tenants receive as little as one-third of the total proceeds from the harvest. The effect is that the loan and indebtedness operate in a subtle way. The share-croppers 'borrow' the seeds for sowing, and they borrow money for their daily needs. They are not, however, employed as 'labourers', but as 'free share-croppers'. Nevertheless, they are working for masters and remain indebted, as they scarcely manage to repay all that has been borrowed. Some may achieve this, but this leaves them short of food and cash for daily necessities. They are then forced back to *peshgi* – working for masters. The cycle of debt-bondage continues.

The masters, not surprisingly, deny that their share-croppers are bonded labourers. They argue that they are share-croppers and tenants. They are not, therefore, labourers, and certainly not bonded labourers. They argue that share-croppers take loans for their household needs, pay with crops or cash and, therefore, are not 'bonded'. One needs to see how the loan works in such a situation and the way in which it ties share-croppers to till the masters' lands, paying by means of whatever they produce.

The *zamindars* arbitrarily fix the price of the produce and decide which loan is to be repaid. This system provides a continuous labour force and indirectly compels them to work for the masters until the loan is cleared. They remain in debt for an indefinite period. The only benefit accrues to the masters: they do not need to manage the labourers and the land, and receive the yield without any hassle.

The bonded labourers in share-cropping in lower Sindh, known as *haris*, are minority Hindus and Bhills. Both are termed 'Indians' and are not registered as tenants. This makes them more vulnerable to exploitation, as they cannot claim tenancy over land. These bonded labourers are in a worse bargaining position in relation to the *zamindars* than Muslim share-croppers in other regions. In southern Punjab, share-croppers are mainly Muslim and the practice is not as abusive as in Sindh. Since a debt applies to a whole family, children are heavily involved in the work of share-cropping.

Agriculture in Nepal also involves bonded labour. Comparable to the situation in Sindh, bonded labour in agriculture exists in the five districts of western Nepal – Dang, Banke, Bardia, Kailali and Kanchanpur. The origins are in the Tharu practice of *kamaiya*. For generations, the traditional arrangement among rich and poor Tharu was a *patron–client* relationship, which was relatively non-abusive. It is said that initially this was practised among relations within Tharu households. The lender would agree with the person receiving the loan that the latter would repay the loan in the form of work. Often, the members of small land-holding families would enter into such a contract for a fixed period.

The change to that essentially social and non-abusive indigenous practice developed after the influx of hill communities to the western plains of Nepal during 1960s. More land was cleared, new settlements were created, and agriculture became a profit-making enterprise, rather than simply providing subsistence. This brought about a change in the *kamaiya* system.

While the *patron–client* relationship did not disappear altogether, often a more 'businesslike' contract was introduced. Traditionally, on New Year's Day, known as *maghi*, the Tharu would settle loans and the elders in villages would make plans for the forthcoming year. Also, labourers would 'contract' with the landlords to continue to work during the coming year, in return for an advance loan, popularly known as *saunki*. Sometimes, at this point, another landlord, in return for the *kamaiya* working for him during the coming year, will repay a loan. Indirectly, therefore, the labourer is bought. Usually, such loans are taken to meet medical expenses within the family, or the costs of a marriage or funeral, or festival. As in India and Pakistan, generally it is the labour of a whole family that is required. The wives of labourers, known as *bukarahi*, their unmarried daughters or sisters (*kamlari*) and children are employed in different ways. Typically, they are provided with a small hut (*bukura*) near the landlord's premises. They may ask for a further loan from time to time, increasing the total outstanding. In one survey, the amounts of loan taken ranged from R500 (nearly £5) to R91,000 (nearly £900). In many cases, the loan has been passed from one generation to another. Also, loans tended to grow with the worker's length of service. It appears that Tharu labourers who worked for non-Tharu landlords were in a worse position than the Tharus working for Tharu landlords. Often, the larger a landlord's holding of land, the greater would be the abuse to the workers. This was especially true in Bardia.

After the government announced he banning of *kamaiya* labour in Nepal in 2000, landlords have moved slowly towards other arrangements – mainly share-cropping. While there does not appear to be any loan involved, money is needed to meet the cost of bulls, tools and other resources. This may be taken as a loan, which is then deducted from the shared crop. While no study has yet been undertaken, it appears that part of the land remaining after share-cropping arrangements is tilled by the *kamaiya* families without any wage being paid. The system, therefore, appears to be changing into other forms of forced labour, but, at the moment, the situation is not entirely clear.

Apart from the *kamaiya* system, permanent debt-bondage is said to exist in the western districts of Rupandehi and Nawalparasi, although no comprehensive survey has been made. In the eastern plain, debt-bondage is mainly of a seasonal nature, and the labourers are low caste dalits. They are known as *haruwas* (meaning 'ploughmen'). Similar practices exist in the western hills of Nepal. Usually, the *dalits*, who are *haliya* (ploughmen), work to repay their loan. Debt-bondage in those areas, however, is not recognized by the government of Nepal. So far, non-governmental organizations have not carried out labour surveys among the dalits, preferring to concentrate their resources on other types of abuse and discrimination against dalits in general.

Rural industry

Among the major rural industries which employ bonded labour are plantations and industries allied to agriculture, such as rice mills, together with silk farming, carpet weaving and the processing of fish and seafood. Here, bonded labour is of the 'new' form, and looks more like a business relationship. Often, labourers are employed through contractors, with variations in the type of loan arrangement and the type of work undertaken.

In India, bonded labour is used in various fish-processing industries in states such as Andhra Pradesh, Gujarat, Karnataka, Maharastra and West Bengal (ASI, 2002b). It is chiefly single women who are employed in this way, and their vulnerability increases with time. Their freedom of movement is curtailed and the employers can control them more easily. They are forced to work, undermining labour standards and human rights such as leisure, working-hour provisions and minimum wage. Nationwide studies in such export-related and export-potential productions may reveal further issues of this nature. There has been plenty of controversy about the carpet industry in South Asia in connection with child labour and bonded labour. While, according to Rugmark Foundation, ethical trading initiatives, concerns of international communities and efforts to reduce child labour in the industry appear to have been successful, bonded labour continues to be practised – mainly in connection with goods for export. The bonded labourers are usually women and children, in Rajasthan, Bihar, Karnataka and Uttar Pradesh.

In much the same way, migrant and family bonded labourers are used in the production of *bidi* (cigarettes) and tobacco in Andhra Pradesh, Chattisgad, Maharastra and Tamilnadu. While the extent of the bonded labour is not known, these industries use considerable numbers of children. Vedika, a non-governmental organization, has documented cases of child bonded labour, drawn from local print publications in Kurnool District of Andhra Pradesh. They show that the children were brought to work to repay loans taken by their parents from a businessman. In the district headquarters of Kurnool District, Seenu, a nine-year-old boy, and Bhuvaneswari, a ten-year-old girl, were found working as *bidi* workers in a house. Their hands and legs were bound with iron chains. Their respective parents had taken loans of R2,000 (£20) and R4,000 (£40). Although the children had worked for more than eight months, the businessman claimed that the work had not even met the cost of the interest on the loans. The children had tried to escape several times, but were recaptured and iron chains and rods were used to restrict their movements. As a result, the children's legs and hands were wounded. It was claimed that the businessman was a government employee in the Collectorate. The *Vartha Daily* reported on the children's involvement in *bidi* work on 5 May 2000. It claimed that bribery is a major factor in the non-implementation of labour standards in the workplace.

Under labour law, it is the responsibility of management to ensure that workers receive minimum wages, identity cards, gratuity, insurance protection, medical facilities, housing, ration cards, and so on. The report claimed that there are more than 50,000 *bidi* workers, of whom only 5,000 are recorded and eligible for that protection. There are about 60 *bidi* factories in Kurnool. Although the workers are entitled to R40 for 1,000 *bidis*, only those 5,000 who are recognized receive R42, with the remainder receiving R32 for making 1,000 *bidis*. Most of the workers are *dalits*, and are Muslims. They suffer from tuberculosis, cancer, ulcers, skin diseases, etc., but are not offered any help. The workers find themselves forced to continue in this occupation, and they put their children into the same work.

Migrant family members, mostly male bonded labourers, work in rice mills in the states of Chattisgarh, Maharastra Punjab, Gujarat and Rajasthan. Many of the single men working in sugar cane plantations in Andhra Pradesh, Gujarat, Maharastra and Karnataka, also, are bonded.

Hybrid cotton seed production in Andhra uses children, mostly girls. The M. Venkatarangaiya Foundation says that the girls' health and education suffer. As elsewhere, the use of child labour makes it more difficult for adults to secure employment. The Foundation's study of the Telangana and Rayaseema regions of the state shows that the girls are employed under long-term contract, in return for loans advanced to their parents. It says that approximately 400,000 girls between the ages of seven and 14 are employed in hired cotton seed fields throughout India, with some 250,000 of them in Andhra Pradesh.

This industry is both capital and labour intensive. Local seed producers deal with large companies through middlemen. Pressure is exerted to increase productivity by controlling labour costs. This leads to the employment of children. Such children may be *dalits*, low castes, or come from indigenous communities. The majority of their families are landless or peasants working in subsistence agriculture. As a result, they take loans and advances from the seed producers, with their children acting as collateral for the loans. Some 95 per cent of the children working for local seed producers are doing so because of loans to their parents. Although any such loan generally is only for a year, 70 per cent of the children in the survey had been working for more than a year. Some 57.5 per cent were in their third year, and 12.5 per cent in their fifth year. It is said that the employers use girls for this work because they are considered more suitable than other family members.

Many of those producing salt from salt pans are bonded; typically single men in Gujarat and Rajasthan, and families in Tamilnadu. Bonded labour also is used in connection with both hand and power looms, with both single men and whole families being employed in this way in Maharastra, Orissa, Tamilnadu and Uttar Pradesh. The numbers involved are not known. Generally, the loan arrangements are made through middlemen.

The bonded labour situation has been studied in connection with silk weaving, particularly in Tamilnadu, which exports the silk products (ASI, 2002d). According to the Rural Institute for Development Education (RIDE), which is based in Kanchipuram, in its area about 75 per cent of the population work in the silk weaving industries. In addition to government co-operatives, there are about 200 private silk industries, employing nearly 15,000 people. RIDE claims that about 40 per cent of these workers are under the age of 16, and work 12 hours a day, without any breaks. Most of these child workers are in bondage as a result of loans, as the system of loans is so common in the weaving communities. The advances range from R1,500 to R3,500. Normally, the children's labour meets the interest on the loans.

In Pakistan, bonded labour practices have been observed in fisheries and the carpet industries, which produce mostly for exports. So far, there has been no intensive research. In fisheries and fish-processing work, it is mainly migrant labourers from Bangladesh and Burma who are employed, with many being bonded. In the carpet industries, it is mostly children, single men and women who are bonded. The workers in these industries live on the premises, which leads to increased vulnerability to extreme exploitation and abuse.

In Nepal, there used to be a considerable amount of child labour in the carpet industries, which exports more than 90 per cent of its products. The reduction which has been achieved can be attributed largely to mounting international pressure and the work of the Rugmark Foundation. No detailed study has been made of bonded labour in the industry. The General Federation of Nepalese Trade Unions (GEFONT) believes that indebtedness among the workers, especially those from the ethnic Tamang community, may have led them into debt-bondage (ASI, 2002b). Recently, Rugmark inspectors found 13 child weavers, one of whom had been working for nearly three years against a loan of less than £20 which his mother had taken from the employer. He never received any wages.

Primary source

In the Indian states of Andhra, Bihar, Delhi, Hariyana, Punjab, Madhya Pradesh and Tamilnadu, a significant proportion of workers in brick kilns are in debt-bondage. As in other sectors, there are variations in the types of labour and loan arrangements. In northern India, children and adults are living in slavery-like conditions; a study by the Institute of Development and Communication (IDC) revealed that children and their parents are bonded at brick kilns in Punjab. The study conducted for UNICEF and the Punjab State Human Rights Commission shows that the school drop-out rate of children at brick kilns is 89 per cent. Brick kilns chiefly employ migrant workers, with the largest numbers coming from Uttar Pradesh. Seventy-one per cent of child labourers are from the 'scheduled castes' – in other words, *dalits* and low castes.

Debt-bondage is also widespread in quarry and stone work. Local and migrant workers, including children, work in quarries, often in an exploitative environment; they are often bonded. The problem occurs in Andhra Pradesh and is repeated in many states in the north and the south. According to Vedika, an organization based in Andhra, children between the ages of ten and 14 work in quarries. Mostly, they work to repay loans taken from the stone businessmen during the off-season. Usually, they work from 8am to 4pm and receive between R20 and R30 per day (less than US 50 cents a day). Many children aged eight to 14 work in the cotton fields. The heavy work often is responsible for illnesses such as asthma, bronchitis and tuberculosis.

In the export-related gem-cutting industries in the states of Gujarat and Tamilnadu the workers are mainly men. They are paid in advance for this work, but generally less than the government minimum wage. Often, they are unable to repay the advance. This leads to bondage and vulnerability. In Tamilnadu, those bonded are mainly the male members of dalit families. According to Development Education for Women (DEW), the workers are entitled to the minimum wage, but may not receive as much. This results in continued indebtedness to the employers, and bondage.

In Pakistan brick kilns are the chief primary source industry where bonded labour is widespread. The practice is particularly marked in Punjab and North-west Frontier provinces. The workers generally are illiterate and landless people who are attracted to the prospect of an alternative livelihood instead of agriculture, and who are attracted by the loan advances. Since half of the wages earned are deducted to repay the loan advances, often additional loan advances have to be taken, which cannot then be repaid. In this way, loans often pass from one generation to another in a family. Sometimes, another brick kiln owner will repay a worker's loan, and take him on. In this way, the first employer, virtually, is selling the worker to the second employer (APFL, 1989).

Labourers preparing *katcha* (unbaked) bricks only receive credit for 1,000 out of every 1,200 bricks that they make. The owners, therefore, have 20,000 free bricks for every million produced (APFL, 1989). Currently, in Pakistan, some 700,000 men, women and children are thought to be in debt-bondage at nearly 4,000 brick kilns. Some labour organizations, including Pakistan Institute of Labour Education and Research (PILER) claim to have found bonded labourers at stone quarries and tanneries in Pakistan, but there are few details.

The brick kilns in Kathmandu and the plains of Nepal mostly use migrant workers (men and boys) from the Indian states of Bihar and Uttar Pradesh. Usually, middlemen contract them. They are said to be working against advances. Often, they are recruited in large numbers, and are held in the kiln areas. Child rights organizations say that nearly 50 per cent of the workers are under the age of 18. More research is needed.

The service sector

Throughout the Indian subcontinent, but especially in India, Pakistan and Nepal, women and children are employed in domestic work. In rural areas, they are part of the family labour employed by landlords and the moneyed class. Migrant domestic workers are more vulnerable than their rural counterparts, as they leave their homes and live in with their employers with the risk of being physically or sexually abused.

While more research into bondage among domestic workers in India is needed, it is clear that it exists. The Arunodaya Centre for working children, an organization working on child labour in Chennai, says that 'bondage among domestic workers remains invisible', since the workers are widely distributed within individual households. Nearly 80 per cent of the domestic workers are women (ASI, 2002d). It says that, in Tamilnadu, 29 per cent of the resident child domestic workers have taken advances for their work. There is also some bondage in construction work throughout India. Usually, men and boys are trapped into debt for such work, but details are scarce.

In Nepal, bonded workers in the domestic sector have been part and parcel of the *kamaiya* system. After the government announced that *kamaiya* bonded labourers would be freed, many landlords and their relations brought the children of former bonded labourers to Kathmandu and small townships such as Nepalganj and Dhangadi. Concerned Centre for Child Labour in Nepal (CWIN) provides details of violations of children's rights in published research (CWIN, 2002). Despite the freeing of *kamaiya* bonded labourers, many children from ethnic Tharu communities are still held in bondage in remote villages in five of the mid-western and far-western plain districts of Nepal.

Interventions

Intervention initiated internationally

The UN Supplementary Convention on Slavery in 1956 showed debt-bondage as a slavery issue which needed to be tackled. There have been other international instruments, particularly those from the ILO. Other organizations, also, have been involved. Anti-Slavery International, the world's oldest human rights organization, was the first to campaign against debt-bondage. Also, it had an important role in drafting the 1956 convention and in the creation of the UN Working Group on Contemporary Forms of Slavery. This has been a conduit for questioning governments about their efforts to eradicate slavery, including debt-bondage.

At the sub-regional level, the creation in the late 1980s of the South Asia Coalition against Child Servitude (SACCS) increased the pressure, and the organization played an important part in the global march against child labour. Through a number of public activities and campaigns in the countries in South Asia, SACCS has also resorted to interventions in the field and has rescued child bonded labourers in India and provided alternative livelihoods. The member organizations of SACCS became important players in different South Asian countries to help create Rugmark Foundations.

Intervention initiated nationally

Work against the system of bondage in South Asia started at a national level in the mid-1970s, and in India the campaign became a movement in the 1980s. The Bonded Labour Liberation Front, under the leadership of Swami Agnivesh, created awareness in the political arena and among the judiciary. Cases of bonded labour were taken to the Indian courts and court verdicts have played an important part in the fight against the system. In 1975, Indira Gandhi's government included the eradication of bonded labour in its 20-point programme, which was announced during the State of Emergency. This resulted in legislation. It was powerful, authorizing local officials to prosecute those employing bonded labourers. It also provided for the identification, release and rehabilitation of bonded labourers. In many states during the mid-1980s, bonded labourers were released and rehabilitated, although corruption, misappropriation and manipulation were reported in Madhya Pradesh and elsewhere.

After the 1980s, there was little progress with the identification and release process. Very few bonded labourers were released in the 1990s. Nevertheless, organizations working for bonded labourers continued their efforts. Often, they met with resistance from the employers and indifference from the law enforcement authorities including Vigilance Committees, which, under Indian law, are obliged to identify bonded labourers. Membership of the Vigilance Committees is drawn mostly from the moneyed and industrial classes, who could be said to have a vested interest. Another factor to which the slowdown was attributed, was that some organizations converted from engendering a movement to running small projects.

Recently, the Supreme Court of India assigned all cases relating to bonded labour to the National Human Rights Commission. It has been actively engaged in settling cases and recommending governments to act when instances are identified. Unfortunately, the actions of most government agencies seem to be perfunctory. While some governments in the southern states are taking some action, northern governments, including Punjab, seem reluctant to recognize the existence of bonded labour. The government of Tamilnadu is creating a database of bonded labourers, using reports from various organizations.

It has been said that released bonded labourers could expect help in connection with rehabilitation for up to three years. The government of Karnataka has taken the same line as the government of Punjab in saying that all were rehabilitated in the 1980s. There were denials of the existence of bonded labourers, until 2000 – when five bonded labourers were found in iron chains. The government then undertook various surveys. While many were supposedly released, in most cases this was not followed up with the required rehabilitation.

A number of organizations, including Volunteers for Social Justice, Punjab, JEEVIKA, the Bonded Labour Liberation Front and SACCS, use the law and campaigning methods to release bonded labourers. A problem is that, with insufficient arrangements for rehabilitation, there is a very real risk that those who have been released will once again become entrapped. Efforts are being made to secure improvements. Volunteers for Social Justice, Punjab, for instance, has filed cases in courts on behalf of nearly 8,000 bonded labourers. Also, the National Human Rights Commission has been used successfully by Swami Agnivesh and Vivek Pandit, who secured the release of 202 people, including 42 child workers, in Madhya Pradesh in 2000. The Bonded Labour Liberation Front, with Swami Agnivesh, is continuing to work on the problem. In January 2003, it secured the release of a number of bonded labourers from quarries in Guragaon, in Hariyana.

In Pakistan, the government passed legislation in 1992 very similar to that applying in India. Organizations such as the Bonded Labour Liberation Front (Pakistan), the Human Rights Commission of Pakistan and the Pakistan Institute of Labour Education and Research have helped the situation by running campaigns, undertaking research and using the courts.

In the 1980s and early 1990s, the Bonded Labour Liberation Front worked hard in connection with bonded labour in brick kilns and the carpet industry. The Human Rights Commission of Pakistan has helped to create awareness, intervening in cases of bonded labour in agriculture, and bringing cases to court, especially in Sindh province. In 2002, the Special Task Force of Sindh constituted by the Human Rights Commission of Pakistan took cases to the Supreme Court, and won. However, the Task Force lost the case in Sindh High Court, which gave the verdict that the *haris* (tenants), on whose behalf it filed the case, were tenants and therefore their problems should be seen in relation to the Sindh Tenancy Act, rather than the Bonded Labour (Abolition) Act.

As in India, the problem of bonded labour continues, more being needed than symbolic reactions. A National Plan of Action for Bonded Labourers was introduced in 2002. But, so far, it has not been implemented, and so there has been no change. This again is attributed by many to the vested interests of the authorities, most of whom are landed and moneyed class people.

In Nepal, it was only in 1991 that intervention started, following the formation of the multiparty democracy. Research conducted by a national human rights organization, Informal Sector Service Centre (INSEC) brought the subject into the open. This was followed by intervention, together with Backward Society Education (BASE), another Tharu-based organization. That action led to the formation of Kamaiya

Concern Group, a coalition of governmental, non-governmental and intergovernmental agencies. Their wide-ranging interventions at national and local levels, through projects and campaigns, together with the organization of bonded labour, resulted, in 2000, in the government announcing a ban on *kamaiya* bonded labour in Nepal. While those efforts brought about freedom, the government left those freed without the necessary support and care. International and national organizations were faced with the need to provide temporary help. Government support was very slow to materialize. The government has more recently provided certification and some land – although not enough – to help with rehabilitation.

Success has been only partial. It appears that nearly 50 per cent have not been freed and are still in the clutches of the landlords. And, of those who have been freed, it is estimated that about 40 per cent are still without support. Various agencies, such as the ILO and charities, continue to support the children's education and well-being.

Conclusions and recommendations

The problems surrounding bonded labour in South Asia are not attributable to the activities of multinational companies. This is primarily a domestic difficulty. Culture, tradition and feudal or semi-feudal relationships have provided the underlying support for bonded labour and other exploitative and forced labour practices. Nevertheless, multinational companies and increased foreign investment and trade due to globalization have brought about changes in the system, resulting from their financial interest in silk and also tea and other plantation crops. However, here, a labourer's contract generally is with contractors, and the trading company in question may not be known or directly involved.

At the same time, 'globalization' has resulted in much more being known about bonded labour, and more action being taken, with organizations applying international pressure on national governments. Links between local and international NGOs have enabled the local NGOs to raise the issues in international human rights forums and so put more pressure on their own governments to take effective action.

There has been increasing interest in 'ethical' trading. Customers on the other side of the world often are happy to pay more for goods in the knowledge that their production has been free from any form of slavery or forced labour. Some carpets, tea, footballs and clothes are now sold on that basis. Similar action could be taken with the silk and artificial gem industries. While that is a step in the right direction, the vast majority of bonded labourers are providing goods and services for *local* consumers. *Bidi*, bricks and agricultural produce, for instance, normally are for local consumption, and international ethical trade codes are unlikely to help the labourers involved.

Apart, therefore, from the liberation and rehabilitation of bonded labourers, greater awareness needs to be created among local people and consumers. International organizations and solidarity networks can encourage and help governments and local authorities to implement the international labour and human rights standards which, generally, already have been ratified.

At the national level, many programmes of governmental and non-governmental organizations have been concentrating on individual bonded labourers. That is good, as far as it goes. It does, however, leave the root causes of forced and bonded labour untouched. The whole system must be tackled. Implementation of the law and initiation of punitive actions against those employing bonded labourers can achieve this. Punitive actions often receive publicity, and have the effect of spreading the message. In addition, programmes should address the widespread discrimination against certain sectors of the population, whether it be due to caste, ethnic origins or religious beliefs. The cross-cutting issues like gender should be included in all activities at different levels. Children should be targeted as a priority. Any development programme designed to help bonded labourers must have a human rights component to allow them, eventually, to claim, assert and enjoy their human rights. A rights-based approach in analyzing the situations of the bonded labourers, especially identifying the rights violated and the perpetrators and corresponding duty holders, must help in devising programmes to provide effective support for bonded labour communities and in ending the abuse.

To succeed, the release and rehabilitation of bonded labourers must be monitored by a competent and independent authority. Without such monitoring in the past, corruption and mismanagement in the distribution of rehabilitation packages have been reported in both India and Nepal. Bonded labourers must be supported, so as to enable them to work and use the skills they have already acquired. Meanwhile, awareness-raising at local level, particularly training law-enforcement officials, and advocacy work at international and local level must be continued. To ensure continued freedom, bonded labourers or ex-bonded labourers should be unionized.

8

Child Labour in Latin America: Issues and Policies in Honduras

Rachel Nizan

Introduction

Child labour is a topic worth studying as for many children and their families in Latin America and elsewhere it is a day-to-day reality and a means of survival.[1] Child labour can have a detrimental impact on various aspects of children's health and can deny them the right to education.[2] In this way, child labour sets a pattern for the reproduction of poverty in that it stunts the physical and intellectual development of a whole generation of workers, who as adults will be forced to work in low-paid and low-skilled jobs. At the same time, there is the inherent possibility of child labour being exploitative, as economic necessity forces children to work and lets employers take advantage of their situation. The worst forms of child labour are often carried out under slave-like conditions, under the threat of violence and for no or little pay, with long hours and heavy and hazardous duties. This puts the worst forms of child labour in the realm of contemporary slavery. It is important to see that child labour and other forms of contemporary slavery – as pointed out throughout this book – are related through common causal factors, such as poverty and the negative effects of globalization. Yet, in order to combat successfully different forms of slavery, different sets of actions are required.

The aim of this chapter is to identify the specificities of the worst forms of child labour as a form of contemporary slavery by giving an overview of child labour issues and policies at both the global and the local level.

The first part of the chapter will evaluate whether the present international human rights regime on children's rights is biased towards a Western conception of childhood. This is particularly important, since

137

our understanding of childhood will determine how we think of the relationship of children and work, and hence, how we perceive of child labour. In this respect the chapter will briefly examine how the *UN Convention on the Rights of the Child* (CRC) emerged as a paradigm of international human rights, focusing on the child as a subject of international regulation within an international rights regime.

The second part of the chapter will assess child labour issues in more detail. The complexity of the subject matter will be highlighted by analyzing the reasons why children work and how our understanding of child labour is formed and has shifted over time.

The third part will look at the case study of Honduras, which, due to its endemic poverty, illustrates well one of the main reasons why children work. After looking at the social issues, the relevant policies and legislation in Honduras pertaining to child labour and children's rights will be evaluated. An appraisal of the interplay between international and national legislation will be made, drawing out areas that conflict. Here the shift in thinking on child labour will be analyzed and an assessment will be made of the extent to which this shift has brought about changes in policies as carried out by the different agents combating child labour issues in Honduras – the state, international organizations and NGOs – and how these have impacted on the actual number of working children.

The concluding part points out the broad difficulties of implementing policies and legislation on child labour in Honduras, what successes have nevertheless been attained, and what remains to be done in order for the worst forms of child labour not to persist. The conclusion also engages with the question to what degree the persistence of child labour is linked to the context of globalization and the changes this triggered in the trade and labour environment, as well as a possible change in the nature of poverty and what this means for child labour. Or whether child labour is simply endemic to the region as a consequence of poverty and a means of survival, keeping in mind that child labour is not a new phenomenon.

The chapter takes the stance that, ideally, the causes leading to all forms of child labour should be eliminated. Realizing that this is a long-term and hard-to-achieve goal, the chapter agrees with Convention 182 that the worst or most unacceptable forms of child labour (including slavery-like practices) should be eradicated, while working conditions for the non-exploitative forms of work should be improved. Furthermore, action should be taken to progress towards an 'ideal' situation, where child labour will no longer be necessary.

Childhood

According to the CRC, a child is defined as 'every human being under the age of 18 years unless, under the law applicable to the child, majority is attained earlier' (CRC, Article 1, as cited in Hart, 1997, p. 10). This definition, however, has a number of limitations. First, the definition is very broad and therefore problems might arise from jumbling together different age groups, since a five-year-old and 15-year-old are quite different. It might therefore be more useful to use sub-categories such as infant, child and adolescent,[3] although these categories do not necessarily reflect differences in experience for children in different contexts adequately. Some very young children who need to work are perfectly competent to make their own decisions, whereas children in other situations might need more guidance. It thus seems that chronological age alone is not sufficient to define the concept of *child*. '[C]ultural and social factors [and the degree of] social responsibility have to be taken into account, too' (Rodgers and Standing, 1981, as cited in Grootaert and Patrinos, 1999, p. 2).

It looks like the concepts of the child and of childhood as used in international conventions are defined from a Western perspective.[4] Furthermore, children were not always perceived as helpless creatures needy of adults in the West either; any rights they had were very limited. In short, childhood is a fairly new and problematic concept, emanating from 'liberal-democracies and industrial societies' (Ennew and Milne, 1989, p. 12).

This concept of childhood leaves little room for the realities of life in Less Developed Countries (LDCs), where children often have to work to support themselves and their families and have to take on responsibilities from an early age, which are not acknowledged in the CRC or LDC country legislation. It might be useful to have a minimum standard in the context of age for purposes of analysis, and also with regards to labour legislation and so forth. Yet, if this does not take into account regional variations and differing needs, it becomes problematic, as our Western views are readily imposed on others, which Burman (1996, p. 46) points out might 'map uneasily on to Southern settings'. This merits a closer examination, especially since the 'Western' views on childhood form the basis of the CRC, which has been widely ratified and is seen by some as 'rapidly approaching the status of the world's first universal law' (Green, 1998, p. 202).[5] The generalized concept of childhood is crucial to our understanding of the relationship of children and work and how we think about child labour. Children should be playing and should not have to work, as work is considered an adult activity and according to the 'universal' or global view of childhood, it is separate from adulthood. Since the West maintains the incompatibility of childhood and work, while LDCs (in practice at least) do not, 'the assertion that there is a universal standard prohibiting child labour betrays [an] ethnocentric inspiration' (De Feyter, 1996, p. 439). Despite differences in experience, there should be a 'minimal standard of decent behaviour'.[6] This means that certain cultural ideas and practices are simply not acceptable, since a move towards complete cultural relativism would not allow for a stance against abuses of children's rights.

In this sense the CRC should be understood as 'providing a flexible framework that brings cultures together around children's welfare rather than an instrument of censure endorsing a single model of childhood' (Boyden, 1997, p. 224). The CRC, thus, forms the basis to work from and to put children's rights on the agenda, while ensuring a 'minimal standard of decent behaviour' and at the same time taking into account local factors.

The CRC is important with regard to child labour, as it formalized the shift in thinking on children and children's rights in general. This shift was from the perception of the child as a passive recipient and object of rights to an active participant and subject of rights[7] (Bartell, 2001).

Child labour

Child labour is by no means a new phenomenon. 'In different parts of the world, at different stages of history, the labouring child has been a part of economic life' such as was the case during the Industrial Revolution in Europe and the United States when children were employed in factories and mines (Basu, 1999, p. 1083). Nowadays child labour is mainly to be found in LDCs. In more recent years, especially since the adoption of the CRC, child labour has re-emerged as an issue of broad public concern and debate, which in turn has lead to 'a global campaign to eradicate [its worst forms]'.[8] It is now more encompassing in that it includes not only children's work in factories, but also work in the informal sector and work in illegal activities such as bonded labour, slavery and prostitution (Bachman, 2000, p. 31).

Defining child labour can be tricky as it involves value judgements, in that our understanding of childhood will determine how we think of the relationship of children and work. According to Myers defining child labour 'is essentially political [as it poses] an emotionally charged choice of social values and objectives [as well as having to chose] the social problem that should be eliminated' (Myers, 1999, p. 22). Is it child labour that should be eliminated, or rather the causes leading to it? Furthermore, it might not do justice to all the issues involved in the debate, for example, the reasons why children work, which can differ according to local factors,[9] or the reasons for wanting to eliminate child labour, for example, protectionist agendas. Such agendas are particularly important in the context of increasingly globalized economies, where LDC economies are supposed to be open to international trade, yet at the same time international standards on child labour are used to the detriment of LDC exports. An often cited example is the Harkin Bill[10] which calls for the boycott of goods produced with child labour (Basu, 1999).

Reasons why children work

In order to be able to combat at least the worst forms of child labour, it is important to understand why children work. The main – and most frequently mentioned – reason for child labour is poverty and the lack of alternatives for children from poor families, especially where education and the ensuing investment in human capital are concerned.[11]

As with income distribution, access to education is very unequal in Latin America, although primary education is constitutionally guaranteed in the region.[12] For many children and their families good-quality and affordable education is not available. In addition, there are hidden costs, such as school uniforms, books, transport, and most importantly the loss of the child's income (Ennew, 1994). The child's salary might be needed to support family income or to pay for its education. To combat this problem the International Programme for the Eradication of Child Labour (IPEC)[13] developed the Bolsa Escola programme in the Federal District of Brazil, which compensates families who send their children to school (López-Calva, 2001). As parents do not incur extra costs or losses by sending their children to school, the programme has been very successful in increasing the rate of children in primary education and in combating child labour.[14]

Other important factors concerning child labour are the lack of awareness, indifference and cultural traditions. In many societies and cultures child labour is perfectly acceptable, regarded as having a socializing and educative function. In this sense it is understood as a valued and meaningful activity which prepares children for adult life.

Work, however, becomes a problem when it is hazardous and exploitative. A further problem is the ignorance and lack of political will to tackle the problem, although this has slowly been changing (Boyden and Rialp, 1995, p. 183; Lansky, 1997, p. 241). This is demonstrated by the international concerted efforts that have been undertaken – at least in theory – to combat the worst forms of child labour. Since poverty is cited time and again as the main reason why children work, the link between the two merits a closer examination.[15] Poverty and child labour are linked in that child labour is a response to poverty; children have to work to support themselves and their families.[16] However, the ILO argues that child labour perpetuates poverty in that it generates poorly skilled adults who will only be able to work in low-wage labour and it might also stunt the physical and intellectual development of the new generation of workers. This is referred to as the 'life-cycle poverty trap' (ILO, 1997).

Relationship between children and work

Two main views on the relationship between children and work emerge from the literature. The first view, which has determined much of the discourse on child labour, holds that childhood and work are incompatible. The second view, which is more progressive than the first, holds that children have a right to work, while work is understood as a valued and meaningful activity which gives children 'a status within society' (Renteln, as cited in De Feyter, 1996, p. 439). Indeed, Salazar argues that traditionally child labour was perceived as 'an essentially socializing activity intended to impart skills [for every-day life]'. This was particularly important in the rural sector, where families often rely on subsistence farming and the whole family is expected to contribute (Salazar, 2001, p. 175).[17] These skills would basically prepare children for adulthood, which was seen much more as a gradual process and not a complete separation of childhood and adulthood, as it often is perceived of in the West (although the West is slowly moving back towards including work experience in education). Furthermore, many Western children grow up doing the shopping, washing the car or helping out on the family farm during summer holidays. These skills develop the child's sense of belonging and a sense of responsibility both for him or herself and for the wider family unit. Child labour is acceptable, as long as the child is not subjected to hazardous and exploitative forms of work. This becomes more problematic in an economic context where there has been a shift in the purpose of the child's work away from a socializing and educative function to that of earning a wage (Salazar, 2001). The changes brought about by globalization in the trade and labour environment clearly have changed the context of child labour, emphasizing the need to earn a wage.

A frequent classification of child labour is the division into the categories of child work, which is usually perceived as being more benign and being of educational value, and child labour which usually takes place outside of the home and is seen as being exploitative and detrimental to the child (Green, 1998; Basu,1999). A further category is child slavery, which forms part of the worst forms of child labour.[18] Despite this differentiation, 'work' and 'labour' are often used interchangeably, such as by Basu (1999), whereas other authors prefer to speak only about child work and not child labour, such as Green (1998).[19] Blagbrough suggests that child labour should be looked at in a 'continuum', that is 'certain conditions turning work into child labour and child labour into the worst forms of child labour' (personal communication). Crawford's argument that 'it is not necessarily the type of work that is hazardous, but the conditions under which it is carried out' (2000, p. 13) points in the same direction and again shows that the categorization of child work, child labour and child slavery is not a neat one. If we accept that some forms of work are not harmful for the child and might even be helpful in its education process, it then becomes important to define when work does become harmful and therefore unacceptable. Children's work becomes unacceptable when it precludes children from going to school and when it is detrimental to the child's physical, mental and moral development (International Institute for Labour Studies, 1993, p. 14). This is where a shift in thinking on child labour has taken place. The ILO together with IPEC and other organizations working in the field of child labour – such as UNICEF, Save the Children and Anti-Slavery International – have moved away from the all-out abolition of child labour. Arguably, it was the NGOs that influenced the thinking of governmental organizations. This solution was based on the 'Western' idea that children should not work, as well as the fear that child labour would bring down adult wages and 'exacerbate adult unemployment' (Boyden and Rialp, 1995, p. 212). The abolitionist view also has a protectionist component. That is, the belief that countries using child labour have a competitive advantage over those not using child labour due to cheaper production costs. The most recent example is the Harkin Bill calling for the boycott of goods produced with child labour. This argument does not consider, however, that boycotts are mainly applicable to the export sector where only circa 5% of all children work (UNICEF, 1997, p. 21; Bachman, 2000, p. 38). This figure would probably be slightly higher if one were to include outsourced labour in the form of family production lines in the informal sector. In the increasingly globalized trading system, firms are coming to rely more and more on such production systems (SCF, 2001; ILO, 1997). In conclusion, not all work is harmful for children. At times they can learn from it and often their family's subsistence relies on it. This shift in thinking is born out in Convention 182 of the ILO. It sees the eradication of the worst forms of child labour as a priority for action.

Honduras

The third part of this chapter examines the issues and policies of child labour in the context of the case study of Honduras. This is of particular interest since the topic of child labour in this country has been underresearched. Furthermore, the Honduran case illustrates one of the main reasons why children work, namely endemic poverty, which was exacerbated by Hurricane Mitch and the ensuing social problems. Moreover, Honduras is signatory to the relevant international legislation on child labour and to the CRC.

First, a brief overview of the country will be given by placing it in the Latin American context. Then the extent of the problem in Honduras will be assessed. In a further step, the policies to combat the problem will be outlined and evaluated, which will shed light on where the debate on child labour stands in Honduras, what has been achieved and what remains to be done.

Social panorama

Latin American economies have most recently been characterized by the debt crisis of the 1980s and the structural adjustment programmes (SAPs) which were introduced to correct the structural imbalances. These, in turn, had a detrimental impact on the region's social indicators, since social expenditure was the first to be cut back in an effort to streamline countries' budgets and economies. This resulted in increased poverty, with higher child labour and school drop-out rates (Raman, 1998, p. 6).[20] Latin America has a number of very specific characteristics such as a fairly high degree of urbanization, income inequality and unequal access to means of production, poverty, dependence on primary commodity exports, and a large proportion of the population being under the age of 18. The latter point means that a high percentage of the poverty burden is born by children under the age of 15 (60 per cent) (Bartell, 2001, p. xxi). According to the Inter-American Development Bank (IDB) around 33 per cent of the Latin American population fall below the $2 a day poverty line, which is regarded as the minimum needed to cover basic consumption needs (IDB, 1998, p. 22).

Honduras 'has traditionally been the poorest country in Central America, depending on banana and coffee exports to bring in foreign exchange' (Green, 1995, p. 229). In comparison to its conflictual neighbours El Salvador, Guatemala and Nicaragua, it has been fairly peaceful. However, Honduras did have a bout of military dictatorship, which put severe restrictions on civil and political liberties and perpetrated gross human rights violations.[21]

Honduras and its neighbours are characterized as having the worst levels of social exclusion and inequality and the highest percentage of households suffering from poverty or extreme poverty in the region. Consequences of this poverty are very weak social indicators, such as life expectancy, infant mortality, sanitation and access to safe water and a high degree of indebtedness (Caballero, 2000, p. 113; IMF, 1999, p. 5). Factors contributing to poverty in Honduras are 'slow economic growth; the unequal distribution of income; the low level of education; and the weakness of local governments' (Groves, 2003, p. 1).[22]

As is the case for Latin America in general, a substantial number (43 per cent) of the Honduran poor are children under 15 years of age (IMF, 2001, p. 16). This indicates a life-cycle poverty trap, as under these circumstances child labour becomes a necessary means for survival. But at the same time it perpetuates poverty, in that it precludes the children from becoming skilled adults, who will work in low-paid jobs. Indeed, the average level of schooling in Honduras is second grade. A study by the Honduran Institute of Childhood and Family (IHNFA) found that 24 per cent of children aged seven to 13 do not attend school, while only 43 per cent of children registered in primary school actually end their primary education. The prospects for higher education look even bleaker with 30 per cent (of the initial 43 per cent) graduating from secondary school and only 8 per cent graduating from university (IHNFA, 1998, p. 6, as cited in Caballero, 2000, p. 17). The Honduran economy was growing at 3 per cent in 1998, but Hurricane Mitch hit the region in late October of that year. As a result of the dreadful effects of Mitch, Honduras was classified as a heavily indebted poor country (HIPC) by the IMF and the World Bank (WB).[23] In order to qualify for HIPC status and receive partial debt cancellation, Honduras had to complete a poverty reduction strategy paper (PRSP). This paper outlines the strategies proposed to combat poverty. What makes the PRSP interesting is the strong involvement of civic groups, as well as the inclusion of a strategy to combat child labour in the report.[24] Nevertheless, levels of poverty were already very high before the hurricane. '47% of the population lived on less than US$1 a day, and about 75% lived on less than US$2 a day' (IMF, 1999, p. 5).

Just as levels of poverty increased after the passing of the hurricane, so did the levels of children incorporated into the economically active population (EAP). The number of child labourers aged between ten and 14 increased by 41,957 in one single year, according to figures quoted in the Honduran *Plan de Acción Nacional* (National Action Plan, PAN).[25]

Extent of the problem in Honduras

In order to assess the extent of child labour in Honduras and how the figures have changed with the adoption of the CRC and most recently of ILO Convention 182,[26] statistics for various years will be examined. In this context the impact of SAPs and social policies will be considered.

In addition to general problems of data collection and the probability of not comparing like with like,[27] there are some specific problems and limitations in assessing child labour statistics. The literature points out that there is a scarcity of available data on child labour and an uncertainty as to the accuracy of the figures given. This is due to 'practical difficulties involved in the design and implementation of child surveys [especially in the informal sector]', and the absence of a clear-cut methodology to obtain and analyze data on how many children work (ILO, 1996, p. 7; Save the Children, 2001, p. 34). Another more obvious problem, as pointed out by Lansky, is that

> [f]ew countries keep specific statistics on child labour – not least because children are legally not supposed to be at work. There is indeed a strong disincentive to keeping statistics that would expose a gap between official policy and actual practice and risk attracting unwanted international attention.
>
> 1997, p. 241

With the implementation of ILO Convention 182 and its recommendation this is, however, slowly changing. Recommendation 190 specifically calls on states to keep up-to-date statistics on child labour. The Honduran PAN mentions several figures on child labour. It points out that there was a steady increase in child labour from 1990–8, with a yearly incorporation of 1,335 children aged between ten and 14. As SAPs were in place during this period and the economy only started to pick up as of 1996, it can be deduced that there was an increase in child labour due to the policies that were implemented under the umbrella of globalization.[28] It should also be noted that the economic situation did improve as of 1996, but that the rates of child labour, nevertheless increased.

Furthermore, it is very difficult to gather information on children working in the informal sector, in illegal activities or in rural areas. The magnitude of the problem is shown with an estimated 49 per cent of child labour taking place in the rural sector (Ministerio de Trabajo, 1998). Adding other informal sector work – for which statistics are not yet readily available – this number would increase.[29] Green points out that statistics show far more boys working than girls which is an indication of the hidden character of girls' work, both in the house and in domestic service (Green, 1998, p. 33). The problem with the hidden nature of children's work is that it is not obvious and society, the government and the labour unions therefore do not readily act on it (Salazar, 2001, p. 173). But with the ratification of ILO Convention 182 and the increase in children's work following the devastating consequences of Hurricane Mitch, there has been a high level of political commitment to reduce child labour (Groves, 2003, p. 2). The increased sense of urgency to act on child labour has also been influenced by the international attention the problem has gained in the last few years, especially since the almost universal ratification of the CRC.

Policy issues and legislation

As a result of growing importance of children's rights, including protection from the worst forms of child labour, on the international development agenda, policies on child labour in different countries are becoming more alike without completely eliminating local cultural differences. An illustration of this argument in the context of child labour, is given by both Crawford and White, who point out that the definition of the worst forms of child labour and of harmful or hazardous work given by Convention 182 leaves enough scope for countries to define it according to their national laws and regulations (Crawford, 2000, p. 6; White, 1999, p. 141).

The international policy instruments for combating child labour are mainly to be found in the field of legislation. Legislation is a powerful instrument for the elimination of child labour (Cuadrao, 1999, p. 100). The most relevant parts of international law to implement through legislation are ILO Convention 138, the CRC and ILO Convention 182.

Other important policies are awareness-raising and advocacy work to ensure that child labour issues are given priority treatment on the policy agenda. It is also important to raise awareness within civil society, which in turn can put pressure for action on its government and can influence local employers of children through specific campaigns and normative pressure. Furthermore, engagement with the causes making child labour necessary, such as poverty and its consequences, is crucial.

Activity to combat child labour in Honduras has increased in recent years, in line with the shift in international thinking on child labour. Although Honduras ratified ILO Convention 138 on minimum admission to work in 1980, the point of departure for a more serious commitment to child labour was the ratification of the CRC in 1990. In this context the Code on Children and Adolescents[30] and, most recently, the framework for ratifying and implementing ILO Convention 182 came about. The current debate on child labour in Honduras, again, much in line with the international debate, is that a solution for the worst forms of child labour should be found immediately, leaving space for a more gradual and progressive eradication of child labour in general. This approach is suggested by the PAN.[31] This action plan sets the guidelines for combating child labour and outlines the most recent policies in this field, as well as providing a framework for the ratification and implementation of Convention 182. The PAN's main aim is to significantly reduce child labour over the five-year period 2001–6. The PAN was prepared by the National Commission for the Gradual and Progressive Eradication of Child Labour (Comisión Nacional) which was set up by Presidential Decree 17–98.[32] This process ensured that a framework for both the ratification and implementation of the new ILO Convention on the worst forms of child labour would be in place. An important element of the PAN has been research, which helps to determine the scope of the problem and to decide what action should be taken. Two important studies in this regard, are maps indicating where the worst forms of child labour occur and which sectors need to be given priority for action. These studies, commissioned by IPEC and Save the Children UK, were used for debating the PAN and represent the areas of investigation and action of these organizations.[33]

Research also forms the basis for the *Diagnostico General* (National Diagnosis), which is based on the latest household surveys of 1999 (Comisión Nacional, 2000b). This diagnosis highlights the findings, discussions, proposals and recommendations on the child labour debate in Honduras and provides the framework for action taken under the

PAN. The diagnosis identifies both poverty alleviation and education as important policies for the improvement of the child labour situation. To this end it includes a poverty reduction strategy and a proposal for educational reform.[34] The key areas of action of the poverty reduction strategy which are important for the amelioration of the situation of child labour are the reduction of rural and urban poverty, human capital investment, and strengthening the social protection of vulnerable groups. This is to be achieved through accelerated equitable and sustainable economic growth, which should ensure the continuity of the strategy (Comisión Nacional, 2000b, p. 99). In the context of rural poverty, equitable access to land is important, as it allows for 'income improvement and food security for rural families' (IMF, 2001, p. v). The Honduran Social Investment Fund (FHIS) – together with the World Bank – is carrying out such projects and IPEC Honduras includes a micro-credit component in its programmes to help rural families (personal communication). In urban areas micro-credits are provided for 'the development of small and medium-size enterprises, as a source of generating employment [opportunities for adults] and income for poor families' (IMF, 2001, p. v). Investment in human capital, especially in the form of education, is important. This is to be achieved through 'greater coverage, quality, efficiency and equity [at all levels of schooling], thus, guaranteeing a better-quality work force and greater efficiency of higher and non-formal education' (IMF, 2001, p. v). The FHIS supports community-based education projects and educational reform projects.[35] The success of programmes such as IPEC's Bolsa Escola in Brazil in increasing the rate of children in primary education and combating child labour would indicate the scope for replication in other countries. Especially as such programmes provide a real and more viable alternative to banning child labour (López-Calva, 2001).

All these measures would – if successful – work towards lessening the need for child labour. 'Work-study programmes' as outlined by Boyden and Rialp, provide another possible solution to the child labour problem (Boyden and Rialp, 1995, p. 212). These programmes build on the educational factor work can provide while ensuring a certain level of education for the workforce, which is paramount in the neo-liberal market economy (Salazar, 2001, p. 171).

The strengthening of the protection of vulnerable social groups includes the project for the 'Gradual and Progressive Eradication of Child Labour', which hopes to help 20,000 working children per year (Comisión Nacional, 2000b, p. 99). The problems and limitations of the poverty reduction strategy, as well as of the PRSP, is their high cost. Their financing is dependent on a substantial increase in social expenditure. This not only requires commitment on the part of the government and taxpayers to social spending, but also economic growth to finance these measures. With debt cancellation under the HIPC initiative only constituting approximately one-quarter of the actual debt[36] and the global economic climate looking less than rosy, it remains to be seen what can be achieved.

Institution building and awareness-raising

Another important policy element is institutional strengthening and capacity building. Good institutions with well-trained staff are crucial to providing an effective framework for action on child labour.[37] In this context, a key institution is the Ministry of Labour, which also oversees the work of the National Commission.[38] The Secretary of Labour is assigned several functions and duties by national legislation. These are, the issuing of work permits for children over 14 years of age,[39] inspection of working conditions, managing complaints and reports of infringements, as well as enforcement measures such as imposing sanctions on employers defying legislation on the protection of children (Comisión Nacional, 2000b). Labour inspectors are crucial to the work of the Labour Secretary. As resources are limited, and access to rural areas – where a large part of child labour occurs – is difficult, awareness-raising among civil society in general, and child workers and their parents more specifically, is important.[40] Through this, it is hoped that children and adults will denounce infringements of children's protection and the worst forms of child labour (Groves, 2003, p. 4). This in turn would lessen the workload of the labour inspectors, while ensuring that employers do not get away with having children work in particularly exploitative and slavery-like conditions.[41]

To this end, Save the Children UK together with the Ministry of Labour developed a project aimed at strengthening 'the capacity of the regional technical sub-councils,[42] ... [as well as raising] awareness amongst civil society to advocate against the worst forms of child labour and monitor the implementation of Convention 182' (Groves, 2003, p. 4). This project has been instrumental to further awareness-raising activities in regional areas. Groves points out that '[p]rior to the project ... [such] activities were limited and primarily focused on legislators and other Tegucigalpa based institutions' (Groves, 2003, p. 4). The project also fulfils the crucial function of linking the various actors involved in the implementation process, from the children themselves, their families and their employers to local, regional and national organizations, as well as NGOs. This is important as it creates a sense of ownership of the implementation process among the Honduran people, although, arguably, it is imposed from the outside and in a top-down manner. Despite broad support for the Convention's ratification – largely due to worldwide awareness-raising campaigns of NGOs, IPEC and UNICEF[43] – the ratification and implementation processes have been carried out 'by a small number of politically powerful individuals' (Groves, 2003, p. 8). Creating a sense of ownership is important, as it will also determine the level of the project's success.

Policy evaluation

It is as yet early days to evaluate most of the policies undertaken under the framework of the PAN. Nevertheless, some observations can be made. No figures on child labour more recent than 1999 are currently available for Honduras, which makes it hard to determine if the policies so far have been successful in reducing child labour. An assessment of the effect of the policies for child labour reduction will probably yield the best results after the termination of the PAN's initial five-year project period in 2006. Despite fears that the new government would not commit to the PAN,[44] it was fully adopted and in July 2002 the Commission was sworn in (personal communication).

Some of the research undertaken has been translated into intervention projects. IPEC Honduras is currently working on projects in the coffee and melon sectors, for which agreements were signed in July 2002. The project on diving in the Mosquitia was supposed to go ahead at the beginning of October 2002. Intervention projects are planned for domestic work, sexual exploitation and scavenging.

Awareness-raising and advocacy work, as well as institutional strengthening are extremely important. The Save the Children UK / Ministry of Labour project has shown that these are areas where, with fairly limited financial resources and plenty of human input, a lot can be achieved. Nonetheless, cuts in ministerial budgets of 17 per cent undertaken by the new government, present some practical limitations, such as the 'government['s] capacity to implement the PAN and wider poverty reduction initiatives'. The change in government also entailed 'replacing old staff with new political appointments' which resulted in a loss of 'institutional learning' (Groves, 2003, p. 10). This emphasizes the need for institution building and learning as an ongoing priority.

Problems and limitations of legislation

Several difficulties present themselves in the implementation process of Convention 182. These are mainly contradictions and gaps within national legislation. One of the central problems is the lack of consensus within national legislation as to the minimum age for the admission to work. This is problematic, especially in that the Constitution sets 16 years as the basic age for admission to work, whereas the Children's Code sets it at 14 (Comisión Nacional, 2000b, p. 92).In order for the implementation process of Convention 182 to go ahead, a consensus on minimum age will have to be found.

The PAN points out some limitations as to the application of the pertinent legislation. It specifically refers to the Children's Code and the fairly limited competence of the institutions in charge of monitoring child labour and applying sanctions. The PAN stresses that the general institutional limitation is especially marked in the informal sector and the Worst Forms of Child Labour (WFCL).[45] This situation is exacerbated by a lack of training programmes as well as instruments and institutions for denouncing the exploitation of child labour, which in turn limit the implementation process of Convention 182 (personal communication). Therefore, the policies undertaken for institutional strengthening and capacity building are extremely important and it is certainly a point that needs to be developed more strongly.

In conclusion it can be said that legislation is undoubtedly important in setting the policy framework for action on child labour. But it has to be kept in mind that legislation alone is not enough to combat the complex problem of child labour. It will have to be attacked at more than one level. It has been argued that legislation was only a supporting factor in the eradication of child labour in Europe. The main factor was economic growth and progress, which called for better-skilled labour and made child labour unnecessary (Basu, 1999).

Conclusion

This chapter aimed to give an overview of child labour issues and policies in Honduras. Child labour is a very complex problem, which is accentuated by difficulties in defining it. The two most prominent positions are first, that childhood and work are incompatible, and second, that due to the realities in LDCs many children have to work to support themselves and their families. There has been a shift in thinking from the first to the second view, which made a categorization of acceptable and harmful and exploitative work necessary. This was reflected in the launching of the process of Convention 182, which focuses on the eradication of the worst forms of child labour as a priority for action.

Although the CRC is based on a Western concept of childhood there is a need for a 'minimal standard of decent behaviour' (Alston, 1994) which ensures against abuse of children's rights. This view is reflected in the near universal ratification of the CRC.

Several problems pertaining to implementation policies on child labour and the relevant legislation have been pointed out. Child labour has only fairly recently evolved as a topic that is broadly being engaged with. It will, therefore, take time for measures adopted at international level to translate to the national and local level. In this context, it has been shown that awareness-raising on all levels of civil society and government is important. This will help to create a sense of ownership of the policies, as well as a sense of urgency to take action on the worst forms of child labour and their most intolerable forms. Furthermore, cuts in budgets impose practical limitations. This is particularly problematic in the case of labour inspectors, who were already lacking funds prior to the budget cuts. Consequently, they focus their monitoring activities mainly on urban and formal sector employment, as it is more easily accessible, at the detriment of the informal sector, where the majority of child labour takes place. The question then arises: why does child labour persist? Child labour is not a new phenomenon, but concrete actions to manage it are fairly recent. With the increase of globalization and the changes this triggered in the trade and labour environment, the rates of poverty, and as a consequence thereof also of child labour, have increased. Furthermore, the complexity of the issues involved in child labour – and the fact that most of them need to be addressed by solutions that will bear fruit only in the long term – unfortunately indicates that child labour will persist in the short and the medium term. Therefore, it is important to make sure that Honduras concentrates on action to eradicate the worst forms of child labour through the implementation of ILO Convention 182 and the policies foreseen by the National Action Plan (PAN). Feasible alternatives are required for children to be removed from exploitative and slavery-like working conditions. In the international field action should be taken to progress towards an 'ideal' situation, where child labour will no longer be necessary.

Table 8.1   Child labour in Honduras, 1990–8, prior to Hurricane Mitch, in proportion to EAP

	1990	1992	1994	1996	1998	1999
Total EAP	1,605,917	1,652,348	1,852,438	2,074,205	2,222,658	
EAP Children (10–14)	89,532	69,351	79,614	96,862	100,213	142,170
EAP Adolescents (14–18)	193,601	201,188	223,528	265,722	279,309	

Source: *Informe Sobre Desarrollo Humano*, Honduras, 1999; PNUD (Baer *et al.*, 2000, p. 19, Table 2); (Comisión Nacional, 2000a, p. 5).

Notes

1. According to ILO estimates Latin America alone is home to about 8 per cent of the world's 211 million child labourers. This is the latest estimate on child labour and slightly differs from the widely quoted 1995 estimate of 250 million. For differences in data gathering see ILO 2002 *A Future Without Child Labour* (ILO, 2002, pp. 19, 15).
2. For a more detailed catalogue of rights refer to the UN Convention of the Rights of the Child, mainly Article 32.
3. Infants and children are the age group up to 12 years old, adolescents from puberty (12–14) up to 18 years of age (Mireilla Carbajar UNICEF Education Programme (personal communication).
4. A key text relating to childhood being a Western constructed concept, cited widely in the literature on childhood and children's rights, is Ariès, 1962.
5. To date all countries apart from the US and Somalia ratified the CRC, which makes it nearly universal.
6. This phrase is attributable to Alston, 1994, p. 17.
7. A good example regarding children's participation was the Global March 1998, which was also important for raising awareness for the new child labour convention.
8. In this regard see also Groves, 2003, p. 1.
9. See Salazar, 2001, p. 179. Also refer to Chapter 9 in this volume for a view on the reasons why children work in the Ghanaian cocoa industry.
10. The Harkin Bill or Child Labor Deterence Act in the US outlaws imports that have been produced with the use of child labour (ILO, 1997).
11. Education is an important investment in human capital, as it can have a direct impact on health, birth rates and standards of living. In addition it also plays out on economic progress, meaning that investment in education would lead to a better-educated workforce capable of using more advanced forms of technology (IDB, 1998, p. 53).
12. In countries such as Brazil the degree of inequality in education can make a difference of up to nine years (IDB, 1998, p. 17).

13. IPEC, launched in 1991, carries out work and studies in the field of child labour in partnership with local organizations and develops plans for action. At the same time, it helps raise awareness of the problems of child labour, as well as assisting 'countries strengthen legislation and enforcement and monitoring capacities'. The work of the IPEC – local alliance is based on a 'Memorandum of Understanding between the [local] government and the ILO, detailing areas of cooperation' (UNICEF, 1997, p. 22).

14. The compensation for families with school-age children is a grant of approximately the 'equivalent to the monthly minimum wage' (www.hri.ca, Bolsa Escola).

15. This chapter uses the IMF's definition of poverty. In this sense poverty can be understood simply as lacking the necessary income to cover one's basic needs (IMF, 2001, p. 9).

16. Salazar points out that the economic contribution of children varies from country to country and region to region. It varies from 'insignificant' in Colombia to 15 per cent in Guatemala and even more significant in Brazil (2001, p. 180). This is arguably also why the Bolsa Escola programme is successful in Brazil.

17. See also Crawford, 2000, p. 7.

18. Neither literature nor practitioners so far speak about child slavery in the Honduran context, but some forms of child labour and the conditions in which they are carried out might point in that direction.

19. The chapter refers to child labour and to unacceptable forms of child labour as the WFCL (worst forms of child labour), as defined by Convention 182. The chapter agrees with the basic premise that it is the element of exploitation, which makes child labour unacceptable and calls for its eradication.

20. Raman refers to Cornia, Jolly and Stewart 1987.

21. See, for example, Becerra, 1999.

22. Page numbers for Groves refer to the unpublished version of the paper.

23. The HIPC initiative was set up by the IMF and the WB in 1996. The idea was to offer 'a comprehensive approach to reduce the external debt of the world's poorest, most heavily indebted countries...[while] placing debt relief within an overall framework of poverty reduction' (World Bank, http://www. worldbank.org/hipc/about/hipcbr/hipcbr.htm [accessed 17 August 2002]).

24. In this regard see http://www.imf.org/external/np/prsp/2001/hnd/01/ 083101.pdf. For a more critical view on the HIPC initiative and the PRSP see the Press Release, August 2002 of the Social Forum of External Debt and Development of Honduras (FOSDEH). See also Groves, 2003, p. 4.

25. The total number of child labourers in 1999 was 491,740 (ten to 17 years). This figure includes children who work at home and do not go to school (Comisión Nacional, 2000a, p. 5).

26. It is too early to see what kind of impact the adoption of Convention 182 has had on child labour. However, the implementation process includes a project on 'the Gradual and Progressive Eradication of Child Labour', which aims to reduce child labour by 20,000 children per year.

27. Problems arise, for example, when referring to age groups; one statistic may refer to ten to 13 year olds, while the other one refers to ten to 14 year olds. At the same time there is no agreement on the exact number of children working, as different reports give different figures.

28. This deduction could be made with more confidence if statistics for the 1980s were available. See Table 8.1.
29. This work also includes domestic service, which is carried out mainly by girls and is classified as a WFCL, often carried out under slavery-like conditions. Salazar points out that '[h]undreds of thousands of very young girls [in Latin America] are concentrated in...domestic service' (2001, p. 173). IPEC Honduras estimates that there are about 100,000 minors working in domestic service in Tegucigalpa alone (personal communication).
30. This code interprets children's rights in the Honduran context in the light of the CRC. Article 114 specifically calls for state action for the gradual eradication of child labour.
31. National Plan for Action for the Gradual and Progressive Eradication of Child Labour in Honduras (Plan de Acción Nacional).
32. The President (Flores Facusé) issued this decree in 1998 as a response to advocacy work undertaken by NGOs, which helped make child labour a priority for action.
33. For more information see IPEC Honduras (www.eltrabajoinfantil.com/english/investigacion.htm) and Aguilar, 2000. Some areas of research of the two maps overlap, such as melon and coffee plantations, as well as scavenging.
34. The poverty reduction strategy is also reflected in the PRSP, which was conducted in order to qualify for the HIPC initiative.
35. For detailed information on these programmes see www.fhis.hn and http://www4.worldbank.org/sprojects/Results.asp?Coun = HN&Sec = All&Lend = All&sYr = All&eYr = All&Env = All&Stat = All&display = 10&sOpt = Country&st = DetSrc&x = 16&y = 7.
36. World Bank and IMF Support Debt Relief for Honduras http://wbln0018.worldbank.org/news/pressrelease.nsf/673fa6c5a2d50a67852565e200692a79/bccf5311bb2bbb118525691800511858?OpenDocument.
37. IPEC is instrumental in the field of training of both NGOs and governmental organizations. It has also drawn up a manual for the training of labour inspectors. This helps to strengthen the monitoring mechanisms on child labour (www.eltrabajoinfantil.com/english/conozca1.htm).
38. The Commission, responsible for setting up the PAN and responsible for its implementation, does not include working children, which is seen as a limitation of the Commission and of the PAN more generally (personal communication).
39. Work permits are 'a prerequisite for entering employment' (ILO, 1996, p. 82). Needless to say, such permits are only granted for work which is acceptable by its nature and the conditions it is carried out in. Consequently, they do not cover the informal sector where most of the WFCL occur.
40. For a more comprehensive view on enforcement problems and labour inspection see ILO, 1996, p. 91.
41. The demand side of child labour shows that children are employed precisely because they are children: that is for the fact that they provide cheap labour and are 'acquiescent' (Boyden and Rialp, 1995, p. 186).
42. These sub-councils are responsible for the implementation of the PAN at the regional level.
43. An important campaign in this regard was the Global March against Child Labour, which was centred on children's participation. For more information

see www.globalmarch.org and http://www.casa-alianza.org/EN/human-rights/labor-exploit/global-march/.
44. Honduras elected a new president (Ricardo Maduro) and government in November 2001, which came to power in January 2002.
45. The PAN indicates prostitution and drug trafficking as two of the WFCL in Honduras (Comisión Nacional, 2000a, p. 43). For a more general view on the limitations of legislation in the informal sector see Save the Children, 2001, p. 34.

9

Child Labour, Education and Child Rights Among Cocoa Producers in Ghana

Amanda Berlan

Introduction

The International Labour Organization (ILO) reports that 246 million children aged five to 17 worldwide are involved in child labour, that nearly three-quarters of these are exposed to the worst forms of child labour, and that 73 million working children worldwide are under the age of ten. This last figure alone is greater than the entire UK population. The highest proportion of working children is in Sub-Saharan Africa where nearly one-third of children age 14 and under (48 million children) are in some form of employment. Seventy per cent work in the agricultural sector such as on farms or in cattle herding. Although children in the agricultural sector vastly outnumber children stitching footballs or weaving carpets in sweatshops, they have received much less attention (Human Rights Watch, 2002a). The case of children working on cocoa farms in rural Ghana (and on cocoa farms across West Africa in general) have been a notable exception to this lack of attention. The interest in labour conditions of cocoa growers was sparked by the discovery in April 2001 of a ship in the Gulf of Guinea, which was initially erroneously thought to be taking trafficked children to work on cocoa farms in one of the West African countries. Although it later emerged that the children were more likely to be used as domestic servants or head-load carriers, the case triggered a wave of concern about labour conditions in the cocoa industry in West Africa, particularly in relation to children. Embarrassed chocolate manufacturers were accused of endorsing slave-like practices and suddenly found themselves trying to explain labour standards on the cocoa farms. Anti-globalization campaigners seized on this case as a further illustration of the abusive power of multinationals and renewed their calls for corporate social responsibility (CSR) and Fair Trade. A new round of tug-of-war between multinational companies and the socially conscious had begun, and the debate has raged on ever since. Accusations concerning poor labour practices and the exploitation of children still abound and Ghana is often cited as a country where such abuses are common. In this chapter I outline certain common misconceptions about the cocoa industry in Ghana and I highlight the importance of local factors in understanding certain forms of child labour and contemporary slavery. I illustrate how academic research can make a useful contribution to the world of policy-making and advocacy by reviewing a rights-based, prescriptive approach in the light of evidence I have gathered during 12 months of fieldwork among cocoa producers in Ghana. More specifically I investigate the role of education in combating child labour and the need to adopt a holistic approach to child rights in this context.

Myths surrounding the cocoa industry in Ghana

Much of the general concern surrounding globalization has rightly been the seemingly unstoppable power of the multinationals and the low prices on the world market of basic commodities. A lot of attention has been given by campaigning groups to the meagre returns given to Third World producers, which, combined with increased awareness about the plight of children in sweatshops or in other forms of abusive labour, has created a lot of sympathy for and interest in Fair Trade. In the case of cocoa growers in Ghana, the concern that labourers, and children in particular, are slaving away on Western-owned plantations is somewhat misplaced. Expatriate land ownership was outlawed in 1957 following independence and Kwame Nkrumah (the first president of the Republic of Ghana) took drastic steps to place the agricultural sector firmly back into Ghanaian hands. There are still many legal restrictions on foreign land ownership or the setting up of large-scale plantations, and cocoa is typically grown on family-owned farms, which on average do not exceed ten acres. Following independence, the cocoa industry was reorganized and the government established a complete monopoly over it by taking over every aspect of cocoa from the purchase of beans from the farmers to agricultural extension services or foreign export. Licenses for foreign cocoa buyers were outlawed and the government became the sole channel for buying cocoa from farmers and selling it to foreign buyers on the international market. Part of this absolute monopoly remains today as the Ghana Cocoa Board (Cocobod); it is still the main institution allowed to sell cocoa for export. The cocoa industry was partially liberalized in 1993 and this enabled the creation of private Ghanaian cocoa-buying companies, which buy from the farmers and sell the cocoa to the government. Technically, these private companies are allowed to sell up to 30 per cent of their cocoa purchases for export, although most companies do not use this facility (for reasons of credit access), and the government remains the main cocoa exporter.

Thus the cocoa chain can be summarized in the following manner: the farmer sells his or her cocoa to a local cocoa-buying company, which sells it to the government cocoa board, which sells it on the world market to chocolate manufacturers such as Cadbury or Nestlé. It is a myth that unscrupulous foreign buyers buy directly from the farmers; the 'man from Del Monte' of advertising campaigns, does not have a Ghanaian counterpart calling on cocoa farmers and offering them lamentable returns for their hard work. Even Fair Trade organizations, some of which claim to be buying directly from farmers, have to go through the channels described above. Direct purchasing from cocoa farmers for export is standard practice in countries such as Cameroon and Nigeria, but it is not common in the case of Ghana, where Cocobod mediates most of the cocoa purchases. The only difference between the Fair Trade chocolate manufacturers and others is that they only buy cocoa that has been sold to the government by Kuapa Kokoo, a cocoa-buying company that satisfies Fair Trade criteria. This arrangement is strictly monitored to ensure that only cocoa produced by farmers who are members of the Kuapa Kokoo co-operative can be sold as Fair Trade.

Another myth is that the cocoa farmers in Ghana are poor and therefore reliant on their children's labour because of unpredictable world market fluctuations and low commodity prices. Historically, the price of cocoa in the global market has not been the same as the local price given to producers in Ghana. Following independence, in order to address the volatility of prices in the post-war period and to stabilize prices paid to farmers, the government instituted a fixed-price policy based on the former colonial model. This means that the price of cocoa to be given to farmers by cocoa-buying companies is set annually by the government, independently of price fluctuations on the world market. For example, following a military uprising in the Ivory Coast in September 2002 and general political instability in the region, the price of cocoa on the world market reached a 16-year high. This did not affect the price paid to farmers, for whom the price of cocoa for that year had already been agreed. However, independently of this, the price was reviewed shortly after, and the government raised the price to 531,250 Cedis[1] per bag, which represented a considerable price increase from the previous main season price of 274,000 Cedis per bag.[2] As Ghana has a fixed-price policy for cocoa the producers are not directly exposed to the surges and slumps of the world market, although the state is, of course, more likely to offer farmers an attractive price if the world price is high.

Given the complexity of the issues described above, most of which are specific to Ghana, a certain amount of confusion is understandable. This confusion is unfortunately only reinforced by campaigning organizations making claims such as:

> The Ghanaian government used to set the purchase price for cocoa, and it varied according to the international market. When prices went down, the cocoa farmers in Kumasi earned less, and often struggled to support their families. Now the farmers have got round this problem by selling their cocoa to Fair Trade organizations around the world.
>
> Fair Trade buyers pay the farmers promptly and give them a guaranteed price usually higher than the market rate – known as the Fair Trade premium – making their way of life more sustainable.[3]

Farmers who are members of this Fair Trade co-operative do *not* receive a significantly better price than the government-set market rate, as the $150 for Fair Trade chocolate is invested in a fund to be spent on community projects such as the installation of piped water. Cocoa farmers who are members of Kuapa Kokoo co-operative only receive a very small amount (normally 1,000 Cedis) above what other farmers receive. It is also worth noting that Kuapa Kokoo is not the only cocoa-buying company offering rewards to its farmers and that most companies donate farming equipment or provide valuable services to the farmers such as training in farming methods. However, Kuapa Kokoo is unique for being based on values such as participatory democracy and gender equality, and arguably offers more regular and generous returns.

The real pricing issue for cocoa farmers in Ghana, which is linked to good governance rather than market forces, is what percentage of the world market price the government has granted them. In this respect, the farmers have been badly treated, as historically their share of the world price has been very low. In 1983–4, for example, the price given to cocoa producers by their government represented as little as 21 per cent of the world market price. In 2000, prior to a change in government, the farmers were still only receiving 57.5 per cent of the world market value for their cocoa beans (Oxford Policy Management, 2000). In countries such as Indonesia, Malaysia and Nigeria farmers receive between 80 and 85 per cent of the world price for cocoa (International Cocoa Organization, 1999). While the difference between world price and producer price enabled the government to make considerable profits, which could be used to run the country, most of the revenues were invested in urban rather than the poorer rural areas and this has caused a lot of resentment among rural dwellers. The price review from 274,000 Cedis to 531,250 Cedis detailed above is in accordance with the government policy to gradually increase the share of the world market price that producers receive until it reaches 70 per cent in the 2004–5 season. This is part of a broader government initiative to alleviate rural poverty and to curb the long-established smuggling of cocoa into the Ivory Coast, which represents an enormous annual loss of revenue for the state and is fuelled by the higher price of cocoa in that country. In addition to receiving an adequate share of the world market price, it is important that farmers are given a price commensurate with rates of inflation in order to increase their purchasing power. Unfortunately further significant increases in the price of cocoa will be necessary in 2003 to compensate for the huge increase in living costs caused by the loss of subsidies on fuel since the last cocoa price adjustment.

Under pressure from international financial institutions such as the World Bank, Ghana may fully liberalize its cocoa industry in the foreseeable future, which would mean an end to its fixed-price policy and enable foreign cocoa buyers to buy directly from farmers. This would give producers a higher share of the world market price but would also signify a much greater exposure to world market volatility, and the loss of market intermediaries (such as private cocoa-buying companies or the Cocoa Board's Quality Control Division), which often provide valuable services to the farmers.[4] The full advantages and disadvantages of these changes are unfortunately too complex to investigate further in this chapter, and the effect these may have on labour conditions would be speculative at this stage.

While issues such as pricing or the structure of the cocoa industry may seem far removed from child rights, it is necessary to understand that they are the complex local economic matrix in which labour relations evolve. Globally the power of multinationals and low commodity prices *are* matters of concern, but I hope to have illustrated that Third World farmers suffer as a result of many different economic and political parameters which extend beyond these factors, such as domestic marketing arrangements or government policy. In the case of children on cocoa farms in Ghana, the blank position held by many advocates of social justice that children work because big corporations exploit them and world prices are low, is both untenable and damaging to the overall cause. I am not arguing that chocolate manufacturers can be exonerated from trying to improve labour standards on cocoa farms because of the structure of the cocoa industry in Ghana. Instead, I am arguing that pressure on big multinationals to adopt the notion of CSR must be tailored to individual cases in order to produce optimal social benefits for producers, and this requires an in-depth knowledge and under-standing of the context in question. In the case of Ghana, chocolate manufacturers have limited power to monitor labour standards on every individual cocoa farm, and are constrained by market regulations as to how far they can trade directly with producers. This does not render the concept of CSR useless in this context, but means that invest-ment in the producer communities will have to go through particular channels and the Fair Trade organizations have shown this is entirely possible.

Child labour and child trafficking on cocoa farms in Ghana

Levels of child participation in activities on cocoa farms in Ghana are high. My personal estimate is that 95 per cent of children in farming households work on their parents' or their relatives' farms, although their involvement varies considerably in time and intensity. The termi-nology used to describe their activities can be misleading as the use of terms such as child labour or child work imply exploitation or greed and in some contexts these are not predominant causal factors. The estimate that 95 per cent of children of cocoa farmers work on the farms includes children who are in full-time education and only carry out duties often described as 'light duties', which are not exclusive to cocoa farming, such as weeding or fetching water. Often their involvement is limited to after-school hours, weekends and school holidays. Such involvement does not fall within the scope of ILO Convention 182, which defines the worst forms of child labour as comprising:

- forms of slavery or practices similar to slavery, such as the sale and trafficking of children, debt-bondage, and serfdom and forced compulsory recruitment of children for use in armed conflict;
- the use, procuring or offering of a child for prostitution, for the production of pornography or for pornographic performances;

- the use, procuring or offering of a child for illicit activities, in particular for the production and trafficking of drugs as defined in the relevant international treaties;
- work, which, by its nature or the circumstances in which it is carried out, is likely to harm the health, safety or morals of children.

Child rights activists and organizations such as the ILO place a clear emphasis on the elimination of the worst forms of child labour as described above. Some clear-cut cases of abuse exist in Ghana, although they are by no means as widespread as certain activists suggest. During the entire course of my research I have encountered child trafficking in only one cocoa village. I was not able to interview the children in question and the information was given to me by a local farmer who is a member of the Kuapa Kokoo Fair Trade co-operative, and had been sensitized to the problem of child trafficking at one of their gatherings. A small number of children from the north of Ghana had been brought to the village by local farmers to work full-time on cocoa farms. They worked the same hours and performed exactly the same duties as adult labourers and received no financial reward (although I was told the children's families had received a one-off payment). Such practices are clearly in breach of Convention 182 and the farmer who gave me the information intended to act on this matter, initially by trying to resolve it at village level, or by reporting it to the relevant authorities if this was not successful.

I cannot make any categorical claims as to how widespread child trafficking on cocoa farms is and I am hesitant to make any claims that could be taken out of context and further tarnish an image Ghana has undeservingly acquired. However, I am very confident that child trafficking on cocoa farms in Ghana is very limited, and particularly disproportionate to the coverage it has received. There is a definite paucity of hard facts and reliable information on this issue, although there is no shortage of speculation. Most sources alleging there is slavery on Ghanaian cocoa farms cite 'research carried out' or make passive statements such as 'such practices have been uncovered in Ghana' but fail to give sources, references, dates, or anything that could give any substance to their claim (*The Independent on Sunday*, 19 May 2002). My personal suspicion is that many of these findings are based on desk research rather than resulting from any reliable field-based investigation. Certainly my own research does not support the claim that the Ghanaian cocoa industry is rife with trafficked children working in conditions akin to slavery. However, I agree that some serious breaches in children's rights occur, and that any child trafficking on cocoa farms – however limited – must be stamped out. More broadly, child trafficking from the north of Ghana to more affluent towns in the south such as Accra or Kumasi, is an increasing problem (African Centre for Human Development, 2002). Most of the trafficked children are taken to work as kitchen staff, domestic servants, head-load carriers or traders, and never return to their families. Therefore my recommendation to policy-makers and campaigning groups would be to focus on the wider problem of child trafficking in Ghana, and not let the limited child trafficking on cocoa farms overshadow child trafficking in other sectors.

The other category of work defined in ILO Convention 182, which applies to cocoa farming in Ghana, is 'work, which, by its nature or the circumstances in which it is carried out, is likely to harm the health, safety or morals of children'. This is open to interpretation as it relies on a context-based rather than globally formulated definition of risk and danger. Each country, after consulting with employers' and workers' organizations and other interested parties, is expected to determine what constitutes such work, although some guidance is given in ILO Recommendation 190. The recommendation suggests paying special attention to work that exposes children to physical, psychological or sexual abuse, or work in an unhealthy environment which may, for example, expose children to hazardous substances. In the case of cocoa farming in Ghana dangerous work could consist of exposure to pesticides, inadequate protective clothing (such as rubber boots), insufficient nourishment or access to drinking water, actual or threatened physical violence, long hours, or children working away from close kin (such as a farmer taking in a child from a poor acquaintance and making him or her work in exchange for food and shelter). Such types of abuse are largely poverty-driven, and more common in isolated villages with low levels of investment and with weak infrastructure, such as villages with no school or difficult road access. Poor, isolated villages are less likely to attract adult migrant labourers from the north in the labour-intensive season and to suffer from a shortage of manpower due to urban migration, therefore making them more reliant on child labour.

Child labour in this context makes intervention and policy-making extremely problematic. As outlined in Chapter 1 of this volume, different kinds of action are required for combating different abuses such as child labour or enslavement. Child trafficking along set routes by networks of traffickers is a relatively recent phenomenon (compared to child work), and is likely to increase unless deterrents such as tough legislation and means of implementation are put in place. In contrast, child labour fuelled by poverty cannot be tackled effectively in isolation from its root causes. Monitoring and law-enforcement have practical limitations in remote villages with little legal infrastructure. In many cases outlawing all child labour would only exacerbate the difficulties facing farmers for whom it is often the best choice given the constraints they face. Using their own children rather than a paid labourer is, in some cases, the only way they can save enough money to pay for education for those children. Other factors to take into consideration include whether the local school is worth the financial sacrifices it entails. Some schools record a zero per cent success rate in final examinations and there is widespread dissatisfaction with schools in rural areas. One farmer told me that he intended to use his profits from the cocoa season to open a small provisions store. He said he refused to carry on paying school fees and sending his children to school as they had attended school for many years and were still almost illiterate. The difficult issue of schools in the rural sector will be further expanded on later in the chapter.

Reconciling culture, policy and child rights

Development and campaigning organizations stressing children's rights to education and freedom from abusive labour are presenting a long-term agenda that, given the magnitude of the problem, will take time to benefit the children in question. When assessing what is in the best interest of a child in an immediate sense, a balance has to be struck and local conditions have to be taken into consideration. In certain cases it may be better for a child to be acquiring valuable experience on a farm they will later inherit than to be pushed into a poor-quality school where they will learn little and be taking away most of the family income. This may leave the family unable to pay for basic things such as health care. Often there are no jobs available even for school leavers, as an education is by no means a passport to employment in many struggling Third World economies with high rates of unemployment. The country paper on India, presented at the Fourth World Conference on Women in Beijing, states that:

> Poverty cannot be stamped out so easily; it has many dimensions to it. Low earnings and low level of skill earning ability, lack of assets and access to training or education are accompanied by poor health, malnutrition, absence of shelter and food insecurity. The characteristics associated with poverty thus extend well beyond low incomes.
>
> Government of India, 1994

Although this was written to illustrate a particular point relating to India, it equally applies to the case of Ghana: acute, long-term poverty is not a purely financial question at the household level. Its manifest-ation in problems such as child labour requires sustained, long-term state investment and international support to improve education, road building and telecommunications, which would stimulate economic growth and reduce endemic poverty.

The conditions described above make the implementation of the rights-based approach particularly thorny. Asserting a child's right to freedom from slavery and their right to quality education is laudable, but hard for policy-makers to implement in very poor communities where the problem of child labour is more acute, and not a matter of choice. The gap between policy, advocacy and practice was further illustrated at the World Day Against Child Labour held on 12 June 2002. This was marked in Ghana by a big press conference in Accra which was led by representatives from key advocacy organizations such as the ILO, UNICEF and Children in Need Ghana (CING). The information packs distributed included a list of 'The Things Children Can Do To End the Worst Forms of Child Labour', stating:

1. Say no to work that is harmful and degrading to you.
2. Speak with people in your community about the problem and what can be done.
3. Report cases of child exploitation to the authorities concerned.
4. Learn more about child labour and the laws against it.
5. Ask your government to ratify and fully implement the Convention on the Worst Forms of Child Labour.
6. Write letters to the editors calling for immediate action to end the worst forms of child labour.
7. Tell businesses that you will buy nothing from them if they exploit children.
8. Call your friends together and form a group united against the problem.
9. Volunteer your time and support for organizations working to protect children.
10. Pledge to continue your efforts until every child enjoys their right to a childhood.

I have yet to meet a child working in the rural sector in Ghana – which makes up over 70 per cent of all working children – who would be able to take any of these steps. The assumption that a child would be sufficiently literate, have a sound working knowledge of international conventions on children's rights, and would want to make a passionate commitment to this cause, betrays a certain naiveté on the part of the advocacy groups who compiled this list. It is also strikingly at odds with the mindset and cultural environment of most working children. In Ghana considerable emphasis is placed from an early age on values such as obedience, respect for parental or adult authority and hard work. Children are strongly reprimanded if they contradict or stand up to an adult; they have to take part in the household chores such as cooking, cleaning, doing laundry, shopping or looking after younger children. The *Environmental Studies* textbook used by children at primary level in class two (seven to eight year olds) details 'Our responsibilities'. It states: 'We have responsibilities. Our responsibilities are our **duties**. Our duties are the things we have to do everyday as children. It is when we do our duties well that we can **enjoy** our full rights. We have duties to perform in the home, at school and in the community ... Our first duty as children is to **respect** and **obey** our parents' (bold in original). The textbook then lists some of the children's duties in the home, which include making the family happy, taking care of younger siblings, fetching water, keeping rooms and serving plates clean, and doing homework everyday, and goes onto state: 'It is our duty to help our younger brothers and sisters to learn. Our Parents have the rights to punish us if we fail to do household duties.'[5] Similarly, duties to be performed in school include sweeping and dusting the classroom and the compound as well as weeding the school grounds if necessary. It is worth noting that children's tasks are generally more physically demanding in rural areas where children are likely to have to walk longer distances to fetch water or have additional duties such as gathering firewood. Most Ghanaian children perform tasks many European adults would find challenging such as carrying heavy buckets of water or killing a chicken and fully preparing it for consumption. Almost all Ghanaian children I have met have been hardworking, polite and even keen to perform tasks that they see as part of their duty. Ghanaians believe it is important to socialize children in this manner in order for them to grow up to become useful and responsible members of society. Laziness is widely despised and a popular inscription on the back of cars or buses is 'Lazy man no chop' – that is, you will not receive your daily bread unless you have worked for it (chop is a local word for eating). Encouraging children to participate in household affairs, serve and help elders is an integral part of family life in Ghana. I am frequently told the importance of serving parents in return for them having taken care of you and the need to help siblings as 'you never know when you might need them'. The average Ghanaian child – particularly one raised in a village – bears little resemblance to the dream child of Western development campaigns, who is a free-thinking, highly opinionated agent, fully engaging in the freedom from child labour by practising his or her right to play and socialize. In this cultural context the rights-based approach may be slow to gain popular acceptance. Child rights organizations will only find a sympathetic audience to their cause if their agenda is carefully formulated to balance local beliefs with global concerns. For example, asserting a child's right to play over his or her duty to contribute to the household income may be less fruitful than sensitizing people to the way in which child labour interferes with education (which will be expanded on in the later part of this chapter), or to the growing problem of the commercial exploitation of children.

The Ghanaian culture of reciprocity and work, and the concern for family cohesiveness lend support to child work in the family context. Broadly speaking, cocoa producers justify the presence of their children on cocoa farms in such terms. Children need to participate in household affairs to gain maturity and become responsible; it is also necessary for them to work hard and help their parents. However, within this perspective the children's actual role may vary immensely between different farms and different areas. As illustrated above, factors affecting the degree of their involvement include whether there is a satisfactory school nearby, or poverty levels. Other variations include the age of the child or even the time of year, as some seasons are more labour intensive than others. I gained further insight into the farmers' attitudes towards child labour following the Kuapa Kokoo AGM held in July 2002. The co-operative Kuapa Kokoo, which supplies the cocoa for Fair Trade chocolate, frequently addresses the farmers on the problem of child labour and it was raised once more during the course of this meeting. One group of farmers discussed the issue further when they returned to the village. Their overall feeling was that child exploitation is a bad thing and they would therefore not employ children to work on their farms on the same terms as adult labourers. Yet most of their children attended school and they saw it as fitting and appropriate to involve their children in farm work when they were not in school. This attitude is reinforced by the lack of realistic alternatives to child work in rural areas. Indeed it is hard to argue against child labour when the alternative is inactivity and boredom. In this respect, child work on cocoa farms in Ghana must be understood as an alternative to doing nothing rather than an alternative to going to school or taking part in any other productive occupation. In keeping with their strong work ethos, most farmers believe inactivity leads to frustration and laziness, or could lead a child to move to the city in search of a job and end up involved in crime or prostitution.

The need to understand global and local factors, and the need for policy-makers and activists to be knowledgeable about specific cases, is not solely an issue in advocacy or policy, but also in research. In Chapter 3 of this volume, Nizan already draws attention to the difficulties of analyzing data on child labour due to practical problems such as lack of comparable statistics or of appropriate methodology. The complex case of child work in the cocoa industry in Ghana provides a good illustration of the need for research to be carried out in a qualitative and holistic manner rather than based on strict, pre-defined global criteria. The International Institute of Tropical Agriculture (IITA) report, published under the auspices of USAID/USDOL/ILO, was commissioned in 2001 to determine the extent of child labour and slavery on cocoa farms in Ghana, Cameroon, the Ivory Coast and Nigeria. In the case of Ghana, the initial findings were compiled on the basis of interviews with heads of households only; no children were interviewed. Perhaps not surprisingly, none of the farmers interviewed reported employing children to work full-time on their farms. However, they did concede that children were involved in weeding of the farm and breaking pods (and used cutlasses for both these tasks) and 0.96 per cent of farmers reported using children in pesticide application (although this may just involve fetching water to mix chemicals). These activities were deemed to be potentially dangerous by the researchers and thus fitting the description of hazardous work given in ILO Convention 182. However, tasks such as farm clearing and using cutlasses are not exclusive to cocoa farming and are performed daily by children all over Ghana. Weeding can even form part of school duties. Using a cutlass to break pods is much more efficient and less physically exhausting for a child than alternative methods, especially as the children are very accustomed to using them. I am not arguing that there are no significant dangers inherent to cocoa farming or that children do not suffer as a result of their work on the farm, as there are, of course, always risks associated with using cutlasses or farm clearance. However, tasks common in cocoa farming have largely been taken out of context and labelled abusive without sufficient understanding of the local context. For the purpose of comparison, a child working in a stone quarry in Accra would be much more likely to injure themselves with a hammer used to break stones, especially as the children in stone quarries are recruited at a much younger age. No cocoa farmer would contemplate hiring a child below the age of seven (and most full-time working children are over 14 years old), whereas owners of stone quarries even 'employ' toddlers to sit in the dirt in the scorching heat for up to ten hours a day. Sadly, children in this form of slavery receive very little international attention and child rights organizations should be cautious not to let the sensationalism surrounding child labour or slavery in the cocoa industry in West Africa bias their research findings and detract from other needy cases.

The effectiveness of field-based investigations (and subsequent policy formulation) may be further undermined by the methodology used in researching the problem. In the case of children in cocoa farming, short-term, quantitative surveys asking children questions such as 'Do you go to school?' 'What equipment do you use on the farm?' or asking farmers 'Would you hire a child to work full-time on your farm?' 'Do your children apply pesticides?' have serious limitations. A child who is enrolled in school and not involved in high-risk tasks is likely to be perceived as being less 'damaged' by child labour, and a farmer whose children only participate in farm work outside school hours is not seen as significantly interfering with the child's education. While there is no guarantee that a farmer or a child are answering the questions truthfully anyway, the focus on risks associated with farming, or the use of school enrolment as a measure of success against child labour, overshadows the real damage being caused by child labour and the need for intervention. Such a focus reveals a very narrow perception of child rights as it does not reveal long-term effects such as the physical damage caused by exhaustion, malnutrition, or by carrying heavy loads, or the effects of child labour on a child's right to obtain a *quality* education. A quantitative approach and short-term surveys only provide a partial body of information on which to formulate policy, and often result in too much attention being paid to the wrong issues, such as whether or not a child is using a cutlass to open a cocoa pod. Therefore my recommendation to development organizations and policy-makers would be to avoid relying exclusively on short-term, quantitative surveys using pre-established definitions and to recognize the value of a more qualitative approach. The integration of qualitative and quantitative data is central to effective child-related policy and campaigning, as well as a key strategy for targeting the rise of contemporary slavery identified in this volume. I shall now expand on some of the more long-term effects of child labour, and use the conditions in rural schools in Ghana to illustrate the need to take a holistic view of children's rights on the issue.

Child labour and learning achievement in the rural sector

Campaigners and policy-makers often see education and child labour as mutually exclusive. However, figures for Ghana indicate that both school enrolment and the number of working children are relatively high (Ghana Living Standards Survey 1991/1992). Addison *et al.* (1997, quoted in Heady, 2000) even report that for some groups of children there is a positive correlation between labour force participation and school attendance. Heady (2000) points out that almost three in four Ghanaian children who work on the household farm also attend school. During my fieldwork I noticed that a majority of children in cocoa-producing communities are in school, and that their parents are emphatically in favour of education. Indeed most cocoa farmers no longer see cocoa farming as a lucrative activity and education is (sometimes to an unrealistic extent) thought to be a panacea as they believe it is the way out of cocoa production for their children. This enthusiasm is in sharp contrast with the often depressing reality of the schools.

Recent statistics reveal that 60 per cent of pupils in primary schools have not acquired basic literacy skills (*Daily Graphic*, 10 October 2001) and that 652 schools all over Ghana are short of teachers (*Daily Graphic*, 19 October 2002). Although Ghana spends 24.3 per cent of total government expenditure on education and 29 per cent of the total expenditure on education is spent on primary education, over 90 per cent of these funds is spent on salaries alone (*Daily Graphic*, 10 October 2001). In such an underresourced environment it is no surprise that many schools, especially in rural areas, record high drop-out rates or even a zero per cent success rate in end of year examinations. In spite of such unsatisfactory conditions and although most working children are already in school, development organizations and pressure groups continue to campaign for greater school enrolment. Heady (2000) reacts against the conventional view that high levels of child labour will result in low school enrolment and argues that the negative impact of child labour is more reliably determined by measuring academic performance. Comparisons of the performances in easy and advanced reading and mathematical tests of working and non-working children revealed that working children did not perform as well as non-working children. Heady found that working could be expected to reduce the score of the typical child by the equivalent of nearly two years of schooling. Possible reasons given for these results include exhaustion and no time to do homework, which could considerably reduce the children's interest in academic study and capacity to learn. Examining the nutritional intake of working and non-working children may further explain the low educational achievement of working children. Many of the children who work on cocoa farms eat very little or not at all before going to work on the farm or to school. The contribution of low food intake and physical effort is likely to exacerbate their exhaustion and affect concentration and learning ability. This idea is supported by a survey carried out in the Abura Asebu Kwamankese District of the Ghana Education Service, which found that virtually all pupils in the district went to school on an empty stomach, and that this impaired their capacity to pay attention during lessons (*Daily Graphic*, 30 May 2001). In addition, the heavy loads carried by children to or from the farm (generally on their heads) are a cause of muscular strain, headaches and injuries, which can also hinder academic progress. The conditions described above practically illustrate how child labour can perpetuate poverty by undermining the effectiveness of education and thus form part of the 'life-cycle poverty trap' identified in Chapter 3.

A further factor contributing to low educational achievement and lack of interest in school is the use of English as the teaching language at secondary level, which is a source of difficulty in rural areas where local languages are spoken much more commonly. Most children in villages have not acquired a satisfactory level of English by the time they enter secondary school. However, teaching children in their own language at secondary level would be impossible for a variety of reasons such as the lack of appropriate terminology in local languages for certain subjects. A fuller discussion on the use of English at secondary level, which is both an extremely complex and controversial topic in Ghana, is unfortunately beyond the scope of the present chapter.

The issue of corporal punishment, generally in the form of caning, also does little to stimulate the children's interest in school. While corporal punishment is common in Ghana, in my experience there is a marked difference between the way it is carried out in the home and in school. In the home offences likely to incur it include disobedience to parents, laziness or theft and I have not witnessed a child being beaten without having committed some kind of offence. Some children have even admitted to me later that their parents were right to punish them and that they had misbehaved. In the context of school physical punishment has much more ill-defined boundaries. The justification given by teachers and parents for corporal punishment is that it helps maintain order and discipline and motivates the children to work hard. While it may achieve these aims, confusion and resentment arises in the minds of children due to a number of factors. First, not all teachers cane children, as certain teachers believe this is not in the best interest of the child. This means that offences such as lateness will incur physical punishment in some classes and not others. As a result caning can become associated with individuals rather than individual offences in the minds of the children. Second, they can be beaten if they fail to answer a question correctly even in cases of genuine ignorance. This may be better illustrated by the following example: one of the teachers in the school of the village where I was based asked the children in class the definition of technology, which they had learnt the day before. As none of the children were able to recall it accurately the teacher caned every child in the class. Many children see caning as part of school life in the same way as learning to read or write and never question this practice because they have grown accustomed to it. However, some of them recognize that such punishment is much more arbitrary than punishment in the home context and feel it is unfair. An American volunteer who worked in a nearby village told me the story of a little girl who had to be coaxed to school by her mother who even gave her small sums of money not to cry and to remain at her desk. My American friend summarized the girl's aversion to school in the following manner: 'Why would she think school is a good place? She comes there, she probably has no prospect of moving up, she is forced to sit in a chair while teachers lecture and yell at her in English which she probably doesn't understand and when they realize she doesn't understand she probably gets caned.' While many campaigners and policy-makers rightly encourage education and literacy, and many children in Third World countries long to be in school, the experience of children in rural Ghana indicates a need to remain pragmatic when promoting school attendance. It also reinforces the need to improve conditions in deprived schools in order to make education a real alternative to child labour.

In addition to the problems identified above, frustration and disillusionment are common among teachers in the rural sector due to low salaries and meagre job rewards, which can result in poor-quality teaching, lack of commitment and even poor attendance in school. The majority of teachers I have interviewed during my research have had other means of income such as farming or trading, and do not feel they could survive without this extra source of revenue given the low salaries in the teaching profession. Newly qualified, young teachers resent being posted to small village schools lacking decent road access, phone lines or electricity. Many school headmasters have long lost interest in tracing up children from poorer families who are working full-time and are not in school, as part of their salary is deducted for every child enrolled at the school who has not paid school fees. Therefore they turn a blind eye to children from poorer backgrounds who are sent to farm rather than school in the knowledge that they may struggle to collect school fees from them. The description of school conditions demonstrates that although putting children in school is hailed as a victory for child rights and the key to ending child labour, the poor-quality education in schools may actually be driving children to work. It is also wrong to assume that child labour is less harmful to children who attend school than to children who do not as there is evidence to show that their performance suffers considerably. More fundamentally, one could question whether the school environment is such an ideal one. While issues such as language or caning taken in isolation cannot account for high drop-out rates or low rates of success in exams, cumulatively they make school a deeply unattractive environment for a child, especially when combined with other factors such as child labour and malnutrition. Many children who work full-time on a cocoa farm and do not attend school have chosen to drop out, as they prefer the conditions of working on the farm to being in school. The implication for policy-makers is that any strategy on child labour has to include provisions for improving quality of education, and school enrolment alone does not necessarily constitute an improvement in child rights, or mean that child labour is being effectively tackled.

Macro-level solutions to the problem of child labour and the role of government

While it will take many years to significantly improve education in rural areas, the government is taking significant steps to combat child labour and promote child rights. Over the past decade or so, the government took a host of key measures. For example, Ghana was the first country in the world to ratify the *United Nations Convention on the Rights of the Child* in 1991. It ratified Convention 182 for the Elimination of the Worst Forms of Child Labour in 1999. The Ghana National Commission on Children (GNCC) was established in 1991 and constitutional provisions on the rights and protection of the child were made in 1992. The Children's Act was passed in 1998. This set of laws deals specifically with issues such as child labour, protection from degrading treatment, or right to refuse marriage and betrothal. Although new laws are presently being drawn up specifically to deal with child trafficking, there is already sufficient provision in existing legislation to prosecute any offender. The Women and Juvenile Unit of the Police Department (WAJU) was set up especially for the reporting of violence or forms of abuse such as child labour or rape. Following an agreement between the government of Ghana and ILO/IPEC, the IPEC programme was launched in March 2000 with the support of the Ministry of Labour. The Statistical Information and Monitoring Programme on Child Labour (SIMPOC) was commissioned in order to determine the magnitude of the problem of child labour and child trafficking in Ghana. The Child Labour Unit has been set up within the Ministry of Labour to provide legislation and strategy against child labour. A National Plan of Action to combat Child Labour was developed in November 2000. And finally, the Ministry of Women and Children was set up in January 2001.

Although there are no explicit targets to reduce child labour in the cocoa industry at present, the government has also taken a number of measures specifically to improve conditions and living standards among cocoa farmers, which will indirectly affect child labour. These include raising the main season producer price from 217,000 Cedis in 2000 under the old government to 531,250 Cedis in 2002. This is a considerable increase for the producers and represents a much higher percentage of the world market price (although there are concerns that this may still be inadequate in view of the present high rates of inflation). The government is taking serious steps to combat the smuggling of cocoa into the Ivory Coast and is heavily investing in chocolate manufacturing facilities to add value to the cocoa beans and create employment. It has also reintroduced the farm-spraying initiative whereby all cocoa farms are sprayed with pesticide and insecticide free of charge. Although this scheme still requires improvement and has suffered many practical setbacks, mass spraying has already considerably reduced farmers' expenditure on the farm in certain areas. It will also reduce the damage caused by cocoa pests and disease, thus improving production. Through boosting cocoa yields and increasing the farmers' disposable income, education or health care are made more affordable. The long-established Cocoa Marketing Board Scholarships for children of cocoa farmers remains ongoing, and roads in the major cocoa producing areas are being rehabilitated in an investment of over 6.5 billion Cedis (*Daily Graphic*, 14 March 2002). A better road network will facilitate cocoa sales and boost investment in rural areas. This can contribute to stemming the rural exodus and make rural areas more attractive to teachers or health care professionals.

During my first visit to Ghana in 2000, there was a climate of despair among cocoa farmers for whom the partial liberalization of the industry and the SAP had meant the loss of precious subsidies for input on cocoa cultivation. For example, the price per litre of cocoa insecticide had increased from 1,500 Cedis to 20,000 Cedis (while the half-season price for cocoa at the time was only 141,000 Cedis per bag). In these circumstances, many farmers simply had no other choice but to make their children work on the farm full-time as school fees had become completely unaffordable. Although the SAP aimed to assist poor producers, it had a negative effect on farmers' livelihoods and this strongly impacted on child rights. More positively, a change of government and new policies have seen an improvement in living standards and given the flagging cocoa industry a new impetus. Such changes are central to promoting sustainable and responsible farming practices and, combined with increased awareness and campaigning on the issue of children's rights all over Ghana, create an environment in which child labour can be more effectively tackled.

Conclusion

The aim of this chapter was to present some of the complexities surrounding the problem of child labour on cocoa farms in Ghana in a way that could make a practical contribution to policy-making and advocacy. The field data I have used are by no means exhaustive and only convey the reality of village life as I have experienced it. In this respect, I make no claim to absolute objectivity in my research findings. Issues such as the socialization of children, corporal punishment or the quality of rural schools can vary and are also to some extent subject to individual interpretation. On such complex and often sensitive issues there is always much more to be said and further questions need to be asked. When writing about development issues from an anthropological perspective, one must also manage a sometimes uneasy balance between ethnography and advocacy. By making my recommendations to policy-makers and campaigners (as distinct from sociological analysis) as explicit as possible, I hope the distinction between these two positions has emerged clearly to the reader.

There are numerous paradoxes associated with the particular case of children and cocoa in Ghana. First, although globalization has brought a new sense of familiarity with Third World problems, it has not necessarily led to a better understanding of them. Because of the domestic structures of the cocoa industry in Ghana, there is a need to think broadly about child labour in this context, and to dissociate our thinking from the stereotypes of rogue farmers and rapacious multinationals often presented to us in the media. In-depth knowledge and understanding of domestic structures are prerequisite to advocating corporate social responsibility in the chocolate industry. Second, much of the marketing of Fair Trade in the UK (especially in relation to Fair Trade cocoa from Ghana) involves stressing the need to remove market intermediaries and the benefits of trading directly with producer groups. This support for free trade is in conflict with these same groups' rejection of free trade on the grounds that trade liberalization leaves farmers exposed to powerful multinational companies and to the volatility of world market prices (as discussed in Chapter 12 in this volume).

Similar tensions emerge when assessing child rights in this context. The quest to promote education and freedom from child labour focuses on the removal of children from cocoa farms and on school enrolment. However, field-based evidence suggests that school enrolment is not a straightforward answer to child labour, as the two are closely interconnected in the vicious cycle of poverty, and that quantitative assessments should not be an exclusive measure of the need for intervention. A more holistic appraisal of the children's lives reveals that the difficulties they face vary greatly, and gives substance to the view that campaigners and policy-makers tend to limit their interest to particular issues. I do not wish to undermine the valuable work carried out by such groups. I am simply stating a need to pay attention to the more complex and nuanced reality of children's lives and to steer away from preconceived ideas concerning the needs of children in Ghana in order to make intervention more effective. What is perhaps the greatest paradox in this case is that the children's own perspectives (or even that of the communities they belong to) are often ignored in the process of trying to find solutions. While this is by no means a new phenomenon, it continues to plague the world of child rights and is a greater obstacle to change than any of the issues identified above.

Notes

1. In January 2003 the exchange rate stood at £1 = 13,800 Cedis.
2. There are two prices each year, the main season price (when most sales take place) and the half-season price. The half-season price for 2002 was 387,500 Cedis.
3. http://www.oxfam.org.uk/programme/secure3.html.
4. The loss of market intermediaries following the liberalization of the cocoa industry in Nigeria and Cameroon, for example, resulted in a decline in the quality of cocoa beans and reduced contract reliability (International Cocoa Organization, 1999).
5. *Environmental Studies for Primary Schools, Pupil's Book 2* (Badu, 2000).

Part III

Strategies and Frameworks for Change

10
The Global Framework for Development: Instrumentality or Contested Ethical Space?

Nigel Dower

Introduction

The main purpose of this paper is to advocate a wide agenda for development ethics which includes the global framework for development to do with international relations, globalization and the role of individuals, as a framework in which many ethically contested issues arise. The way we think of the ethical challenges of economic slavery is partly dependent on these issues, both because it is itself a manifestation of bad development and because it is a cause of economic poverty. The standard 'neo-westphalian' paradigm, descriptive and normative, in which states and international institutions are the primary determinants of what happens globally, the global economy is viewed as the engine of development, and individuals in global civil society play a small part, is challenged. Various ethical issues to do with the ends and means in this paradigm are raised. The responses to these issues affect the ways in which the extent to which a central goal of development – the alleviation of extreme poverty – is achieved and therefore are part of development ethics. This thesis is illustrated with brief discussions of the cosmopolitan challenges to standard 'internationalist' assumptions in international relations, a critique of foreign aid and its relation to the rest of foreign policy, the impact of globalization and the ethical dynamics of the global economy, the diverse responses to September 11th, and the increasing role of individuals in global civil society.

Perspective

On the account developed here development ethics is an aspect of cosmopolitan or global ethics. Development ethics is the ethical assessment of the ends and means of development at all levels – local, national and global. In all these cases a common global framework of values is assumed, along with a common framework of transnational responsibility to promote these values or to combat what mars and undermines them. The focus of this chapter is on these more general issues of development; it is included in this volume because its wider theme, it is argued, is of vital importance to the issues of new slavery, as will be illustrated from time to time in the course of the argument. Thus, anyone interested in tackling the evils of new slavery needs to recognize that progress with this goal partly depends on our engaging in an ethical critique of the basis of international relations and of our understanding of the individual in her global context.

I shall take it (without further argument here) that extreme poverty is an evil because it involves pain and suffering, and malnutrition and disease, it is life-shortening, and it undermines human dignity, partly because it is disempowering.[1] I also take it that economic slavery is inherently bad because it involves labour and ways of living which are forced on people through violence and the threat of violence. Generally where there is forced labour, there is extreme poverty for those so forced. Forced labour is not only evil in itself but it is also the *cause* of the multiple evils of poverty – general lack of empowerment through lack of sufficient resources to exercise any real autonomy, a cause of ill health and disease and so on. Equally the causal relation exists in the opposite direction: extreme poverty and lack of opportunities are among the factors that lead people into becoming enslaved (willingly, semi-willingly or through deception), so that apart from the inherent evils of extreme poverty there is added negative value of its being instrumental in leading people into the further evils of being enslaved.

Thus if one of the goals of development is to remove that which undermines human dignity and fulfilment, the removal of new slavery and the conditions of its continuation should be seen as a key element of the goal. The question might, however, be raised whether economic slavery is a necessary condition of development – an evil to be accepted or promoted, either because it is the lesser of two evils facing poor people themselves (for example, child labour in some economic circumstances) or because economic growth requires an underclass doing menial but necessary jobs including some working under coercive conditions? While I dispute these claimed necessities, the point I wish to stress here is that, even if one accepted them, they represent a degree of imperfection or failure in that stage of development – a serious cost in the balance sheet of development as a mixture of benefits and costs – a cost that is standardly not taken seriously enough. This is a reflection of a more general point about many standard views of development – even if it is legitimate to accept that development generally involves some winners and some losers (and so cannot be Pareto-optimal), the costs of economic growth to the poor, if acknowledged at all, are not acknowledged enough.

This leads me to my major theme. What are the consequences of our taking seriously the evil of poverty – including the evils of economic slavery as itself a manifestation of bad development and as a cause of economic poverty – and treating that as a global ethical priority? In what follows I try to show that the standard ethical consensus about goals and about the international framework of institutions and practices is simply inadequate. Issues are far more ethically complex than is often supposed – and this is so even if we focus our attention on poverty alleviation as the central concern of development ethics.

Challenge of the dominant model

The following is a simplified model of how the world is understood by many of those who are in positions of influence, especially in governments and business companies.

Goals

There is general consensus about the goals to be pursued: development as the general improvement in conditions of life for all countries but especially poorer countries, within which some priority is given to reducing extreme poverty; protecting the environment; maintaining or seeking the conditions of peace, including now security from terrorism; protecting and promoting human rights; and promoting and maintaining transparent and democratic forms of governance. Underlying this is the premise that all human beings are in some fundamentally ethical sense equal: all human beings matter and matter equally.

Means

The ways these goals are achieved and are to be achieved are primarily through a strong and stable system of states, supported mainly by the global economy and marginally by global civil society. States are the primary determinants of the life-conditions of people – their citizens – including the pursuit of and support for development. Through international co-operation, states achieve international security, develop international laws (for example, to protect the environment), and singly or collectively provide various forms of intervention such as development aid or military protection of rights. The global market – international trade and investment by companies large and small – is the chief engine of economic growth in all countries, and thus plays a significant role in reducing extreme poverty (through the spreading of general wealth – 'a rising tide lifts all ships'). One of the chief elements in this engine of change is technology, since technological innovations continue to be, as they have been for several hundred years, what enable us to extract the conditions of human well-being from the raw materials of the world – only now it has to be done in sustainable ways so that future generations have access to these goods as well. There may be disagreements about what technologies work best, but these disagreements are largely empirical disputes about causality. A third significant factor, much more apparent in the last 30 years than before, though still a very small factor compared with the other two, is the influence of ordinary human beings – not in governments or business – acting in the voluntary sectors in NGOs and in other more informal networks of global civil society. Their activities make a little difference at the edges – the goals are certainly achieved a little more because of them – but states, acting individually or collectively, together with the agencies of the global economy are still the real determinants of how things are for the world, and how far the goals are achieved.

Neo-westphalianism

This may be called the neo-westphalian model. I call it this because it does acknowledge that things have changed from the heyday of the westphalian model of a world dominated and shaped by sovereign states, which, by a mixture of conflict and co-operation according to a limited set of rules, determined how things went in the world. Globalization has made some difference but not all that much: international institutions, for example the UN, are more extensive than before; the economic non-state actors – especially the larger companies and banks – have become much more powerful and challenge the freedom of manoeuvre of states, especially weaker ones; far more individual human beings are directly involved with organizations which have global goals and remits. But that said, states are still the dominant reality. We are not yet at the stage of a 'post-westphalian' world (Linklater, 1998) nor is it something we should be trying to move towards. This leads to the third set of points.

Normative assumptions

The picture described in the paragraph entitled 'Means' is not merely meant to be a description of how things work, but to provide a normative account of how the key agents are meant to behave. States belong to a society of states, within which they legitimately pursue their national interests within a framework of respecting the sovereignty of other states, upholding international law and being willing to intervene in other parts of the world – traditionally giving aid, more recently intervening to protect human rights. Those involved in the economy are likewise entitled to pursue the maximizing of profit, but within a certain framework of norms of fair dealing and complying with such laws – like environmental or labour laws – as are applicable. Individuals are entitled to pursue their own 'life projects' or conceptions of the good (including devotion to particular others and/or to particular associations/groups, such as a church) within a framework of respect for others and duties of justice, including a *limited* obligation of general benevolence towards others. NGOs give expression to a sense of wider responsibility that some individuals feel, though this sense of responsibility and membership of such bodies are both to be seen as optional and voluntary.

A further common assumption then is made that insofar as the world is clearly not a place in which the goals I specified are fully realized – I need not rehearse the shortfalls – it is not because there is anything wrong with the model. The key actors have their allotted roles; the normative profiles are perfectly satisfactory. What is wrong is that actors, either as individuals or acting within their institutional roles, simply do not live up to the norms – possibly by: indifference to others and/or an idea of selfishness that denies even limited benevolence; bias and prejudice in cases of racism, sexism and religious bigotry; willingness to do what is known to be wrong or unjust, as in the cases of nepotism, bribery and many other forms of corruption; or by practising or conniving at institutional slavery (often made acceptable and widespread by the prevailing culture).

There is a fair degree of ethical consensus in the above model. It is not that ethical values are denied or regarded as irrelevant (though a few years ago this was more common in International Relations thinking and the corporate world). They are rather assumed to be fairly self-evident. Policy disagreements are taken to be mainly over institutional and technical issues about what works and so on – hence the global framework of international order and co-operation according to agreed norms is seen as an instrumentality or a means towards agreed ends. There is, however, little place for ethics as a critical intellectual enquiry into the ethical bases of these practices or into the justification of policies in the light of rival ethical positions. There's no need since there's broad agreement anyway: ethical enquiry is only necessary if there is controversy or challenge. This complacency, however, is precisely what I want to dispute. The field is rife with ethical issues (not just technical 'means' issues), for which self-conscious ethical enquiry or ethics is necessary.

Failures in the model

I shall argue that this model is seriously defective in at least three respects. First, the goals of poverty reduction, development, peace, environmental protection and human rights observance are far more controversial than is often assumed. It is not that people disagree that these are indeed core goals, rather they disagree about the interpretations of what they really are, and why they are valuable. The assertion that failures in the world are due to individual or institutional failure to follow agreed norms underestimates the existence of real differences of norms or at least interpretations of them; for instance, do certain kinds of 'payment' really constitute 'corruption', especially if they are seen as the oil of, rather than the impediment to, development? Under what conditions does 'consent' effectively transform into 'being coerced', if the work that is offered turns out to be different or done under different circumstances from what had been envisaged? This means that there have to be core ethical debates about such questions, the answers to which matter since some answers are better than others. Second, among these disagreements will be disagreements about the relative priority of different norms (or values to be promoted). Does poverty alleviation really have significant priority over economic prosperity in general? Just how much should a country or individual regard self- or national interest as trumping humanitarian concerns? Does sovereignty trump human rights concerns when issues of intervention come up? How important is the reduction of economic slavery within the wider framework of poverty reduction? It follows from these kinds of issues that the normative assumptions above about what the key actors should do needs itself to be seriously questioned or at least shown to be inadequate, since they fail to bring out the complexity of the dilemmas of an ethical kind that can arise. Third, the model is empirically inadequate, since the dynamics of the world are more complex than is suggested. The neo-westphalian model may indeed have to give way to a post-westphalian model, especially in respect to the increasing role of individuals acting in a global arena – as global citizens, as many would now say (see Dower, 2000, p. 2003).

Dimensions of development ethics

My interests here are very general, but they have a particular bearing on the subject matter of development ethics. This is because the model and its critique are relevant to the concerns of development ethics, both in regard to the goal of poverty reduction, but also in regard to the general policies of development, especially in poorer countries.

The range of questions relevant to development ethics

A central focus of development ethics has been an ethical critique of the two key goals: poverty reduction and development itself. A better understanding of just what makes poverty an evil will give us a more sophisticated understanding of what kinds of measures will really reduce poverty. If, for instance, poverty is evil because of the undermining of autonomy as well as or as much as lack of food or health, then measures that really empower the poor are more deeply satisfactory than measures that merely provide food or medicine (O'Neill, 1989). Likewise measures which reduce or remove economic slavery as a particularly acute form of disempowerment or undermining of autonomy will be given a good rationale for being included in poverty reduction strategies. A better understanding of what the processes of development are really about in terms of an adequate characterization of the criteria of flourishing and progress will lead to more sophisticated models of development than economic growth or even growth with equity (Sen, 1999). Thus, we have the great debate between neo-Aristotelians, Kantians, human rights thinkers and welfarists (Aman, 1991).

Development ethics has also attended, though less vigorously, to other questions. For example, if environmental values matter too, how can we integrate these with development values into a coherent ethical package? How important is the 'process' value of participation, not only as effective means to other goals but as a development goal itself? If corruption is an impediment to development – as the fair distribution of increasing benefits or more basically as economic growth itself – how can we best understand it and the values which can effectively limit it and counter its corrosive effects? What is the ethical basis of aid, whether it is given by individuals or by governments? Looking more generally at the economic relations between countries, what are the ethical guidelines for these? Is economic liberty adequate? If not, what principles of social justice should inform the market or the ways states co-operate with one another?

That these and many other ethical questions are relevant to development ethics and ought to be accorded more attention is one of the points I want to stress in this chapter. Even if we took the primary rationale of development ethics to be the goal of poverty reduction – a narrowness of subject matter I would personally resist – any ethical question the answer to which affects the extent to which and the manner in which poverty reduction occurs is an ethical question for development ethics. Wherever there are differences of view about what is to be done which reflect differences of values and norms (not just differences of factual belief, for example about effective means), we have the appropriate subject matter for development ethics. The issues of new slavery or corruption, for instance, reflect an important ethical dimension to effective development – often not sufficiently recognized in more idealized discussions of development. However, my own focus will be on analogous failures – both in practical implementation and in theoretical conception – in the global framework within which all development efforts take place.

The complexity of development ethics

The complexity of development ethics is confirmed if we make explicit two further assumptions generally shared by critics of conventional development including most self-styled development ethicists. The first assumption is that what we are not required to do is maximize some good output. I mean by 'not maximizing' at least two distinct things.

First (and this is something defenders of conventional development would agree with, too), we should not think that the whole of ethics is about producing the best balance of good over bad, however defined. I take it that if something like this were accepted, we would have a revolution in ethics along the lines implied by Singer's famous argument that we ought to prevent all the preventable evils we can (Singer, 1972). Apart from distorting and flattening the ethical life, this would turn all justification of action into just a matter of working out what works – essentially questions of causality.

But second, more specifically, even if we did not accept a *general* maximizing principle, we should also resist a *targeted* maximizing approach towards the development goal of reducing poverty. By this I mean that if an individual or a government has for whatever reasons (itself a matter of ethical controversy) decided to use certain resources for the alleviation of poverty, it then prioritizes the question of efficiency: how can she or we use this resource most efficiently, that is by maximizing the good outcomes? In these days of managerialist thinking it may seem perverse to question this latter objective. My point is not that one should deliberately not be efficient, rather that deciding whom to help and in what ways is a more complex matter than working out what works or is causally effective. The question of how we help raises various issues:

given pre-existing ethical customs and sensitivities, the manner of helping needs to both respect and take account of these. The manner in which the process occurs – whether it is democratic and participatory – is also an important consideration because these values (which are themselves moral values) are important. Another way of putting this is to say that there is an ethics of the means. Means have ethical content both in respect to values independent of the goal pursued and also in respect to the values implicit in the goal. Gandhi said: 'the means are the ends in the making' (Gruzalski, 2001). In both respects the ethical content of the means is not simply a function of the causal relation of bringing about an end. Maximizing a desired outcome or promoting it efficiently tends to assume the latter relation as the key determinant of its justification (or else lets in complexity through the back door by making moral values an outcome).

The second common assumption is that the acceptance of ethics at all assumes that a person, organization or state is not simply entitled to promote their own best interests regardless of others. At the least we are required to adhere to rules constraining our behaviour so that we do not unnecessarily harm others or frustrate their interests. The majority view includes assisting others who need our help by means of furthering justice and combating injustice, whether institutional or perpetrated by individuals.

But the implications of accepting these two assumptions are not generally noted. Since we can neither do everything nor nothing, how much to do and in what ways to respond to the wider world become open questions. As these are immensely complex issues to do with what does and does not count as legitimate pursuit of interests in the face of the impact our actions have on others (or what is and what is not justifiable interference in others' lives) and about the extent and manner of helping, ethical issues to do with development issues abound. In summary, there is a rich middle ground between an unacceptable 'maximizing' approach and moral indifference, a middle ground in which questions about what helping and furthering justice (including combating injustice) means, how much to engage and in what ways arise. (It is worth noting that in some contexts the duty to 'help' may be seen as distinct from duties of justice, including duties to further justice, and certainly charity and justice need to be distinguished; on the other hand, in regard to what individuals ought to do to further justice, they may correctly be described as helping to promote justice or oppose injustice, and the moral motivations for such acts may be a complex mixture of benevolence and a sense of justice.)

Development ethics as global ethics

If our goal then is the alleviation of extreme poverty, all the above questions are relevant at all levels and in all areas. They apply to all kinds of agents: individuals and organizations in rich countries, individuals and organizations in poor countries, rich governments, poor governments, NGOs, business companies, international organizations. This is because the way in which people make their decisions in terms of the ethical criteria involved make some difference to what happens directly or indirectly *vis à vis* extreme poverty. Development ethics needs to focus more than it has on some of these questions.

I focus on one or two of these questions, without attempting to cover the whole field. My suspicion is that a disproportionate amount of intellectual energy has actually been poured into the debate about the right theory of value underlying development – the debate between neo-Aristotelians, Kantians, human rights thinkers and so on. This debate is important, and in some cases adopting one approach as opposed to another may result in different policy recommendations.

But these differences are little compared with the general differences between these positions and a conventional approach to development, which is more dominated by economic growth assumptions. Critiques of the latter can be mounted from any of the ethically enriched positions. A similar issue exists in connection with environmental ethics: much intellectual energy is expended on the debates between biocentrists, ecocentrists and enlightened anthropocentrists (who accept the de facto ecological limits), though all of them have powerful arguments against the conventional and shallow anthropocentrism of mainstream thinking.

For me the crucial challenge is the construction of an adequate global ethic for the twenty-first century – a global ethic which both informs what individuals do and how they perceive themselves, and also informs our understanding of international relations and the norms that should guide states and economic actors, and reflects the changing realities of our increasingly globalized world. These concerns may seem far away from the concerns of poverty alleviation, and yet like a boomerang, the way they are thought through and the conclusions reached have, or could have, powerful impacts on the prospects of the poor – possibly more than the outcomes of ethical debates about the good in development itself. This is relevant to the challenge of economic slavery since in many ways the key issues are about: the extent to which ethical constraints on international trade including trafficking are taken seriously; the extent to which there is or is not a relativistic acceptance of practices elsewhere (like child labour); and the extent to which people or governments in one part of the world care about what happens elsewhere – all issues in global ethics.

Illustrations of wider global issues relevant to development ethics

The internationalist paradigm

I start with international relations and how states behave and justify their behaviour. Although few are now attracted to old-style Hobbesian realism, which denies that there can be ethical relations between states, mainstream thinking about the ethics of international relations is still a long way off being really cosmopolitan in approach (see, for example, Dower, 1998). It assumes a world order maintained by a society of states whose primary objective is to maintain national interests within a limited moral framework of respect for sovereignty and a commitment to international law and such other agreements as they come to accept through co-operation. Traditionally this internationalist model supported a fairly minimalist approach towards what happened internally in other countries such as poverty or economic backwardness, but in recent years, particularly in the second half of the twentieth century, it has come to encompass more concern – though not from the point of view of many cosmopolitans *enough* concern – for such problems, along with other problems to do with environmental destruction and human rights violations (Williams, 2002).

At one level this is a function of a perception of shared global problems and, with increasing knowledge and technological power, an increasing acceptance among both the governed and those who govern them of some responsibility to do something about distant disasters and evils. At another level this is a function of agreements and laws which countries, for whatever reason, come to accept in the international arena. Such things as the agreement by rich countries at the beginning of the 1970s to give 0.7 per cent of GNP in official aid, or the commitment to halve world poverty by 2015 at the 1995 Copenhagen summit, while not of course hard law, provide a background normative pressure which countries now, in principle, accept.

There has been something of a shift within the internationalist paradigm from a minimalist position to one in which there is some concern for what happens elsewhere. It is, in a way, parallel with the shift in thinking that has occurred over the functions of government, which were once seen to be primarily about external security and internal law and order but now include managing the economy and providing many positive forms of social support. This is not a uniform shift. Indeed part of what is exciting within even mainstream International Relations is a wide-ranging debate on just what the responsibilities of states are – their nature and extent – *vis à vis* one another, in the areas of development, environmental protection, intervention for the sake of human rights and so on. The outcome of these debates, which are really about how the international society now conceives itself, will make a big difference as to how well or badly development for the poor really goes. Development ethicists need to be in there, informing those policy debates with the leaven of cosmopolitan ideas. Since the internationalist approach is not necessarily averse to cosmopolitan ideas – in many formulations it is seen as the best way to advance these ideas in the real world (Bull, 1977; Navari, 2000) – the cosmopolitan needs to emphasise this consideration in the formation of national polices and international agreements. This has a bearing on the role of individuals; I return to this point later.

Someone who adopts a thorough-going cosmopolitan approach to international issues like world poverty will generally recognize that adjustments within mainstream thinking about these issues has not gone far enough and that a more radical critique is also needed – a critique more in the mode of discomforting prophets (not negotiators or reconcilers) or working against the grain (rather than working with the grain). This critique should not replace engagement by other development ethicists in the negotiation of new consensuses but should exist alongside it, since different people should do different things. Its goal is change in the medium or long term, not the short term. The critique may focus on the failure to get priorities right, that is on the normative dimension of policy, or it may focus on the assumptions of the international order itself – that states are and have a right to be the key players in the international arena. Let us take these in turn. I shall start with two examples relating to the priorities issue – policies on aid, and responses to September 11th 2001.

Critique of foreign aid

Have rich countries really got their priorities right in respect to the levels of aid that they give, bilaterally or multilaterally? Quite apart from any moral issue connected with failing to reach the 0.7 per cent target rich countries actually agreed on in the 1970s, the more basic question is: should countries be willing to make contributions which might actually affect negatively the level of wealth within them? Such a suggestion might seem to be wrong because it conflicts with any country's right to protect its economic interests. This right might seem self-evident if interpreted modestly, but as a strong claim to being an overriding factor, it is problematic. But does the latter right mean that a rich country should not be required to share its wealth, only part of its incremental wealth – that is, part of its growth? But why should we accept this restriction? Are rich people morally entitled to keep all their wealth? Are countries any different? Perhaps they are, it may be said, because a government has a duty to its citizens not to pursue policies which lead to some of its citizens being forced to have a worse standard of living, for example through unemployment. But this cannot be right. Most policies (perhaps all or at least all that are actually justifiable), especially those of the neo-liberal, have the consequence of there being winners and losers. The question is: is the distribution of winners and losers socially acceptable or justified? If the problematic distributions are those which involve the very poor being impoverished further, then the response should be: 'have national policies that protect the poor', not 'resist all forms of aid that might weaken the overall GNP of a country'. In any case if it is an appeal to the position of the very poor that is made in justifying national policies, that same appeal is precisely the basis for a vigorous aid policy, too. If on cosmopolitan assumptions (which we take it here the defender of national interests accepts in principle) all people matter equally, then all poverty matters equally.

This point is reinforced if we press home the problem of consistency in foreign policy. An ethical foreign policy should be a consistent foreign policy. There is something paradoxical about a policy of foreign aid sitting side-by-side with a policy on debt-servicing if poor countries are having to pay in debt-servicing considerably more than they receive in aid grants. There is something morally disturbing about a policy on aid – however well meaning – being accepted by a government which at the same time uses its economic power to determine terms of trade favourable to itself, to set up trade barriers, to preside over the development of patent laws especially in the field of biotechnology, in order to maintain its economic superiority over struggling poorer countries, or maintains economic relations with those who practice economic slavery. Again rich countries take with one hand and give back a fraction with the other hand. There is also, arguably, something morally incoherent about pursuing a generous policy on aid while adopting a very tough policy on refugees, especially of an economic status. If we are willing to share some of our wealth (perhaps only incremental wealth) by giving aid, why not do likewise by providing a source of support or livelihood in the place where one is? Our cosmopolitan commitments are well tested by attitudes towards immigration (Beitz, 1983). (The issue is debatable of course: am I morally inconsistent if I give to or support measures to help the homeless in my own country, but refuse to let them into my house? If not, and my country is not like my house, then a moral difference can be found. Certainly the house/country parallel seems to be somewhat misguided.)

Of course, all these claims are highly controversial and not fully defended here. They may be controversial among development ethicists as well as between development ethicists and defenders of national policies. That is the point. These are highly controversial ethical debates, and the ways they get resolved in policies make an immense difference as to how far and in what ways poverty is addressed in the world.

September 11th 2001

Another area of controversy is over the appropriate responses to international terrorism after September 11th. Apart from any special concerns about the rightness of the kind of military responses following the autumn of 2001, I wish to flag the wider issues to do with both the privileging of the 'security against international terrorism' agenda and the interpretations of this privileged status in terms of what has to be done (Dower, 2002). How we think countries should respond to those events makes an immense difference to the fate of the poor in the world. It is a vast topic. Let me focus on a couple of aspects.

First, by making this security agenda a priority, a downgrading of other international goals is signalled, conceptually and empirically – conceptually by, for instance, giving security a very narrow focus; empirically by devoting vast resources to combating terrorism which realistically leaves less to be spent on other agendas. If security is taken in the broadest sense to cover environmental security, economic security, health security and so on – aspects of security that are far more important and pressing for the vast majority of people in the world than the faint possibility of being the victim of a terrorist attack – then policies for the world based on security alone – let alone other core values – would be very different from those in place now.

Second, more effective policies to combat terrorism which included a serious attempt to reduce the root causes of terrorism such as global inequalities or a militarized world fed by the arms trade, again make a difference to the fate of the world's poor. How far the world is really changing after September 11th is an open question, as much a matter of decision as a matter of prediction. How we understand and justify a 'new world order' must be a key question for development ethics – even if the latter focuses only on world poverty. This is even more so if we think of development as about change in any country as a whole or, increasingly, the world as a whole.

Globalization

In many ways, 'development of the world as a whole' has now become an agenda issue. Globalization itself can be seen as part of the developmental process. Although globalization is, like development, a process of social change that some welcome and others decry, it may be thought that there is one crucial difference: development is generally seen as something pursued and as an object of public policy, whereas globalization is perceived rather as a large-scale effect of or summations of myriads of transactions taking place in deterritorialized social spaces (Scholte, 2000). This contrast is overdrawn in both directions. Certainly some agents see globalization as something to be welcomed and worked for; since globalization takes many different forms, we can make choices which affect the forms it takes.

One dimension of globalization, namely cultural globalization or globalization of community, involves the emergence of global civil society. This is the pattern of formal organizations and informal networks of individuals, many of whom have active concerns about the world (though not necessarily in agreement with one another about what is to be done). The point about the emergence of this form of transnational agency is that people both engage in issues to do with things like world poverty and debt and expect to be heard and to make a difference. This phenomenon is a challenge to the existing internationalist paradigm discussed earlier precisely because it is premised on the belief that individual agents have a legitimate role to play and that states ought to listen to them. The older paradigm of individuals acting as citizens within states but not beyond and of states dealing with global issues through relations with one another is being challenged (Held and McGrew, 2000).

In other respects the world is changing too. Even the international system is changing itself, in terms of the relative power of member states and the power which international bodies exert. How international organizations function, how far their decision procedures are democratic and in what ways, what their ground rules are, are key questions in an increasingly active debate – in part an ethical debate – about the nature of global governance (Commission on Global Governance, 1995). How that is developed will make big differences to the fate of the poor.

Perhaps even more significant is the emergence of the power of corporations, large and small, that make up the global economy. This aspect of globalization – the globalization of production – is often seen as globalization itself and is precisely what makes it a bad thing! But an attitude of total rejection is unwise; we need to find ways in which the process of economic globalization can be humanized from within (Scholte, 2000).

First, the development of the global economy does not have to be based on neo-liberal values of the free market with minimum regulation. Global capitalism could be more regulated by rules safeguarding labour conditions – including, in particular, conditions of economic slavery and exploitation – or the environment, and could be subject to more or new taxation (such as the proposed Tobin tax on international money trans-actions), and still be capitalism (see Chapter 11 in this volume). This is exactly what we have within some economically advanced countries.

Second, precisely because of the great global power of corporations operating somewhat independently of the international system of states, there is an increasing recognition, even within such organizations, of a framework of ethical accountability. It is no accident that with increased power, the whole idea of the 'stakeholder' as opposed to the shareholder has gained significance. This idea is important because it recognizes a wide constituency of groups of people who may be affected negatively by the activities of a company. How wide the constituency is, is a key contested issue. Furthermore, there is an immense increase in interest in what is known as 'corporate social responsibility' and even 'corporate global citizenship'. In saying this I am not overlooking the fact that there is a long way to go; in the meantime, the general impact of the corporate world on the poor of the South is, on balance, either bad or much worse than it could be if only more responsible attitudes were adopted. But there are growth points within the corporate world for ethical critique and these need to be fostered and built upon. Some development ethicists may actually feel it is right to consort with the enemy camp. For the global economy to work more humanely for the benefit of the poor, a transformation is needed from within – aided of course by those outside willing to engage in constructive dialogue with those within who are interested in it.

Third, there is a great danger that we objectify the global economy as though it has little to do with ordinary people. In fact it has everything to do with them, especially in their role as global consumers and investors. Almost all who are well-off are part of this vast economic process, as are the very poor; but the well-off are beneficiaries of it in a way the very poor are not. I say this not to induce guilt but to remind the well-off that they are caught up in the global web of imperfections. They can just accept it and benefit (so perhaps they might feel guilty about that) or they can do their bit to make the world better, not least by examining their own patterns of consumption and investment. Thus they can become ethical consumers and ethical investors, if they are willing to critique the sources of the goods they acquire, for example whether they are produced in conditions of economic slavery/exploitation like the production of carpets or trainers by children. They can become ethical investors if they invest in companies with better track records or look into where their banks and pension schemes do *their* investing. If enough people did these things, businesses would have to change their policies in order to sell their products or have more resources for new investment.

Role of individuals

This leads me to the final point – the roles of individuals. In a way the crucial roles of individuals have already been outlined: government polices on aid will be partly a function of what their electorates want; businesses will respond to the consumer preference of people; most significantly, individuals can become directly involved in global civil society and seek at a global level actively to influence what governments, international bodies and business corporations do. If the life-conditions of the very poor depend partly on what these bodies do, then what individuals do, in turn, makes a great difference. The ethical task then at this point is to engage in dialogue, debate and discussion about the nature and scope of global responsibility. One way into this is to raise the question: are we global citizens? This is a surprisingly controversial question and for that reason is an important one to ask.

Nussbaum expresses well the need for cosmopolitan education in her lead piece 'Patriotism and Cosmopolitanism' in *For Love of Country* (Nussbaum, in Cohen, 1996), but the controversial nature of her proposal is well brought out in many of the replies in that book. Almost everyone nowadays accepts in the abstract the idea of universal human values, now often thought of as universal human rights, but what is not a matter of universal agreement is the idea of significant responsibilities which are global in scope. Unless or until the latter idea is widely accepted and the communitarian resistances to it fully dealt with, countries, companies and individuals will preach the evils of poverty but do relatively little about it. There is an immense ethical challenge here. It is the challenge of a robust global ethic.

I shall close with an illustration of this based on a conversation I had with Charles Beitz, a person for whom I have immense respect as a key player in putting international ethics on the map. He put forward a robust theory of international justice – liberal cosmopolitanism – which proposed radical redistribution of wealth from rich countries to poor countries with appropriate international institutions to achieve this (Beitz, 1979). In the course of the exposition he remarked as an aside that this proposal did not entail a commitment to world government or to world citizenship. The latter point about global citizenship puzzled me and I suggested that if a world based on such admirable redistributive policies were ever to be possible it would require the active engagement of people exercising global responsibility as global citizens – both in putting political pressure on governments to agree to set up such mechanisms, in being willing to live the values they advocate and be personally generous in helping to bring about a just global order, and, I now would add, in being willing publicly to welcome possible reductions of standards of living as a result of such redistribution. He dismissed this line of argument on the grounds that we had to 'insulate' the individual from too much pressure from the world. Here indeed is the challenge.

Relevance of development ethics to new slavery

What then is the relevance of development ethics for new slavery? Can critical enquiry into the ethical basis of development help to combat its occurrence? New slavery occurs because of the combination of two factors: (a) there are those who are willing to enslave others: they may do this knowing it to be wrong or believing in some twisted moral account that 'justifies' it as not really coercion or deception or as being acceptable anyway; (b) there are those who allow themselves to become enslaved because they themselves or those in authority over them, like parents, feel that what is proposed is the lesser of two evils or because they are misled into thinking that what is proposed is not slavery. Generally the motivation in both variations is economic hardship not to say desperation. What then is needed to reduce these practices? First, what is needed is a legal, institutional and cultural framework which makes it more difficulty for enslavers to do what they do, such as effective legislation, and a public moral culture deeply antithetical to it (naming and shaming; ostracism and so on). What, on the other hand, is needed to reduce the likelihood of victims getting enslaved is a reduction in the conditions of extreme poverty.

Development ethics, as I have indicated in the course of the discussion, contributes significantly to these changes in the following ways. First, it involves sustained ethical reflection on the *bases* for the rejection of new slavery. No doubt most people would agree that such slavery is seriously wrong, but ethical reflection on *why* it is wrong which is embedded in answers to the wider questions 'what makes extreme poverty an evil?' and 'what makes it the priority for public policies, nationally and internationally, in regard to development?' should strengthen the recognition that new slavery is a priority issue. Furthermore, development ethics helps to embed such discussion in a recognition that the right to be free from slavery is not an isolated right but one of a range of universally recognized rights which development ethics seeks to integrate into an overall ethical framework.

Second, this ethical framework provides the basis for both a solid justification for policies, laws and institutions, but also for effective development practice. Clearly ethics has a key bearing on the formulation of development policies (concerning its goals and chief means) and in the development of a regulatory framework of rules and laws. But it is also vital to the motivation of all ordinary agents both to uphold and to further those policies and laws. This is not merely a matter of people being willing to go along with policies and to obey rules and laws. It is rather a matter of there being an ethical culture in which agents are generally motivated to further policies (beyond mere compliance to law) and to encourage others to comply with law, to further policies and oppose those who thwart policies or break laws.

This is particularly important in respect to new slavery, since the evils generally occur because the law is not effectively enforced. Those opposed to this have many kinds of things they can do – raising awareness among others (like this book), being vigilant about the existence of such practices, taking care not to be unwitting beneficiaries of them (like buying goods which are the product of sweated labour). These are all aspects of active moral responsibility. The ethics of development is partly about the forming of the ethical culture of responsibility – including, significantly, a culture of corporate ethical or social responsibility in the corporate world. This is particularly pertinent in areas in which bad development occurs because of such factors as new slavery and corruption. The development of this culture is crucially dependent upon the development of appropriate NGOs that campaign on issues like new slavery, and are a vital part of the emerging global civil society. A critical ethical passion drives many in such organizations – and it is the approach of development ethics which provides the critical tools for effective ethical passion.

But we should not just look at the challenge of reducing the incidence of active enslaving. There is the challenge of reducing the incidence of those drawn into being enslaved – and that is the ethical challenge of addressing extreme poverty. The nature and extent of our responsibility is very broad indeed. The challenge is precisely (going back to the issue I raised with Beitz) to reduce the layers of insulation which normally protect us from the world. If development ethics can help us be more morally exposed to the realities of the world, then it will help us tackle one of the root causes of new slavery, namely extreme poverty itself – which is itself for many of us reason enough to act anyway.

While I have never advocated a Singer-like account of relentless obligation, I do think it is precisely openness to the world and acceptance of a global dimension of personal moral responsibility that are needed. Though many ethical challenges – like economic exploitation, including economic slavery, and corruption – face development in poor (and rich) countries themselves, changes in the global framework within which development occurs are also vitally important. These will not take place without the input of individuals everywhere. Those of us who are privileged to think and talk about these issues as academics from the security of affluence need to remember this – and act as well.

Note

1. See for example N. Dower, 'Poverty', in Singer, 1991; on the aspect of disempowerment see O'Neill, 1989.

11
Strategies for Change: The Tobin Tax

Emma Dowling

Targeting contemporary forms of slavery requires an analysis of the conditions that allow for such dehumanizing practices to occur. Poverty and economic disempowerment are central to the proliferation of slavery. In this chapter I draw out some possible links between the present global economic system and contemporary slavery. I focus in particular on financial markets and more specifically on currency speculation in order to show what impact such practices have on the lives of human beings, especially the world's poor. I then outline existing proposals for a currency transaction tax, known as the Tobin tax, and discuss the ideological debate that underpins it. My intention is to draw attention to the systemic problems of processes of globalization and our inter-pretations of it, the complexities of which are highlighted in Chapter 1 in this volume. I argue that change is possible, if we are willing to deconstruct and reconceptualize our perceptions of the globalized world to put a concern for human beings rather than profit at the heart of the system and engage in debate about the kind of world we would rather live in.

Currency speculation is one aspect of international trade and finance that destabilizes vulnerable national currencies, consequently endan-gering the livelihoods of a country's citizens. It is not only the weaker developing countries that are affected by the consequences of currency speculation. Currency crises triggered by global financial speculation and subsequent forced currency devaluation have occurred in Latin America, Russia and Asia as well as Africa, with immense social consequences. However, increasingly it is not only financial elites or big businesses that engage in currency speculation, but the ordinary, overwhelmingly middle-class individual, who is encouraged to profit from this market. The Global Forex[1] website explains that

> now the foreign exchange [forex] market has been opened up to individual investors...unlike the sums of money previously required by the banks and brokerage firms, comparatively low margin requirements are finally available that now allow virtually any individual to trade along with the professionals and institutions.
>
> Global Forex

The language of this website reflects an appeal to people's desire for thrill: 'because of the advantages of sheer volume and daily volatility, excitement of this market is unparalleled' (Global Forex). The detrimental effects of currency speculation on the lives of real people are not mentioned and the fact that this market is only minimally regulated is heralded. This shows the underlying neo-liberal stance, which prioritizes market freedom over human well-being.

This chapter assesses the state of the debate surrounding the Tobin tax. It makes the argument that the tax poses a workable mechanism to decrease the volatility of financial markets and yields resources to fund global solutions to global problems enhanced by poverty, such as contemporary slavery. The chapter draws attention to the structural disadvantages of the vast number of disempowered people who are at the mercy of a global economy with no means of controlling their own welfare within it. Furthermore, the argument seeks to overcome the conceptual resistance to social justice movements by unpacking the political and economic interests behind theories that are portrayed as common-sensical within conventional notions of economic theory and trust in the freedom of the market. This dominant ideology of neo-liberalism, which emphasizes the priority of economics over politics by calling for less intervention in economic processes, is questioned. Whereas unregulated financial markets are proposed as a way to maximize profit for the benefit of all, in reality such a policy operates only for the benefit of those that are already at a structural advantage within the system. In other words, a just distribution of power and wealth, based upon notions of equality, is disregarded. For this reason, arguments against a Tobin tax are unpacked to expose them for what they are; namely arguments in favour of maintaining a status quo in which human exploitation can thrive.

Detrimental effects of currency speculation

Since the breakdown of the Bretton Woods system in 1972, exchange rates are no longer fixed but can be defined as the 'relative prices of national currencies...determined by the interplay of supply and demand in foreign exchange markets' (OECD, 1995, cited in Patterson, 2002). This has led to the development of a market in which financial actors, such as individuals, companies, governments and international organizations can speculate on the value of a currency. Speculation is 'the act of buying and selling with the aim of benefiting from price movements, rather than to finance international trade, or to acquire interest-bearing assets' (Hayward, 1999, p. 1). Here lies the first problem: 95 per cent of currency transactions today have no connection with trade in real goods and services. Over 40 per cent are conducted within three days and 80 per cent within a week. Over 60 per cent take place between foreign exchange dealers (Patterson, 2002, p. 2). Worldwide daily currency turnovers have risen from $70 billion in 1970 to $1.5 trillion in 2001, which is an increase of more than 2,000 per cent (Wahl and Waldow, 2001, p. 5). These figures highlight the extent of currency speculation in today's financial markets.

Speculative operations involve, in particular, short-term 'round-trips', whereby tiny currency fluctuations are exploited in order to make profits from buying a currency and selling it again very quickly, often within a day. If devaluation of a currency is deemed probable, local and foreign investors will borrow local currency and then convert the loan into a stronger currency. If the devaluation occurs, the speculator will be able to buy back enough local currency to repay the loan and still make a profit. The problem is that such 'betting' actually turns into a self-fulfilling prophecy and the currency devalues as an increase in the demand for a certain currency depresses the value of the local currency. Consequently, markets are destabilized. The human costs are great as currency devaluations inevitably have an effect on national economies, especially those of developing countries as they are already more likely to be less stable. Economic indicators such as the gross domestic product (GDP) often help to further disguise the problem as they do not reflect how many people are actually thrust into poverty due to such activity (Hayward, 1999, p. 2).

Examples of the human costs of currency speculation can be found in particular in South-east Asia, Latin America and Russia. The 1992–3 currency crisis within the European Monetary Union, the banking and financial crisis in Asia in 1997 and the current debt-servicing crisis in Argentina are often quoted as resulting from such activity (Patterson, 2002, p. 3). Financial crises in South-east Asia, Russia and Latin America have led to increased unemployment and inflation as businesses came under pressure. In attempts to stabilize the economy, national governments were forced to reduce their spending. Health care and the provision of education were the inevitable casualties and there have been considerable increases in child labour, prostitution and malnutrition. In particular women, who form already the majority of those in precarious forms of low-paid employment, were more often than not the first to be laid off due to the traditional notion of women's wages as the second income of a household. Furthermore, because of the conventional conception of the woman as the nurturer or carer, it is the woman who has had to assume the traditional burdens that surface as a result of the reduction in state services. In Mexico, following the devaluation of the peso in 1994, wages fell by 30 per cent and 2.2 million people were forced into unacceptable living conditions, raising the number of Mexico's poor to 40 million. The devaluation of the Russian rouble in 1998 led to the doubling of living costs, thrusting 22 million people into poverty (Hayward, 1999, p. 2). Neighbouring countries also felt the detrimental effects of financial crises through their economic and political links. Additionally, the increased levels of public debt meant that the foreign ownership of these economies was increased. Even if these economies begin to make recoveries, as is seen now in Asia, social conditions will lag behind for a considerable period as it takes far longer for social infrastructure to recover from such shocks.

Before continuing, however, I would like to stress that currency speculation is not the root of all evil; many domestic fiscal policies and other political factors affect the value of currencies in a way that speculation does not bring about and a tax cannot remedy (Wahl and Waldow, 2001, p. 10). Contemporary slavery has many complex origins and modelling single causal links can lead to an oversimplification of the issue. Nevertheless, I would argue that speculative activity does not help to prevent any of these processes either and more often than not might even intensify the problem. Likewise, an analysis of how poverty is increased and sustained within the global economic system can help us identify desirable solutions to it.

Characteristics of the Tobin tax

The prestigious American economist James Tobin first proposed the Tobin tax in 1972. Any Tobin-style tax is an *ad valorem* charge on the

gross sum of any foreign exchange transaction; any speculative operation would therefore incur the tax twice, once when bought and again
when sold. Originally, Tobin proposed a percentage between 0.5 and
1 per cent; however, more recent proposals have argued for a lower percentage within the realms of 0.01 and 0.1 per cent for fear of deterring
actual beneficial activity. The Tobin tax can be said to have five main
objectives,[2] which I shall discuss in turn in order to shed light upon its
feasibility.

Encouraging investment

Any currency transaction tax seeks to encourage investment instead
of speculation. Most short-term speculation is carried out for profit
purposes only. Although some short-term transactions are closely linked
with real economic activity, such as hedging trade and investment
against exchange rate risk, and some are part of a short-term (rollover)
financing strategy of long-term investment, it would be confusing to go
into too much detail here. In the event of an implementation of the tax,
traders can still find enough opportunities for hedging risks. Short-term
speculation is rendered more profitable than long-term investment in
the sense that it yields immediate profit resulting from small profit
margins, yet it has drastic destabilizing effects. Mainstream neo-liberal
thinking neglects such problems.

However, recent studies show that short-term investment behaviour
leads to irrational economic behaviour such as short-term thinking.
Such thinking means that there is an increased asymmetry of information and results, which makes investment impossible. Also, extreme risks
are taken. Private investors have more capital than central banks and
therefore more control over the market, which they exploit in favour of
profit. Furthermore, due to such short-term fluctuations, central banks
and supervisory agencies have much less time in which to detect a crisis
and react by buying a currency under pressure. Daily speculation leads
to the build up of speculative bubbles, which eventually have to burst
and more often than not cause crises as values are so far removed from
reality: despite the fact that speculative business of banks and funds has
been detached from the real economy, financial crises have not (Wahl
and Waldow, 2001, p. 7). The tax is said to be able to curb speculation and
encourage investment, since even a small tax would render short-term
activity unprofitable (the only reason speculators make such profits is
because of the huge sums they employ) but would have far less effect
on long-term investment;[3] 'Undesired hot money is held back but the
liquidity needed for real economic activity can pass through...this is

what the well-known slogan refers to: "throwing sand in the wheels without bringing the wheels to a halt"' (Wahl and Waldow, 2001, p. 10).

Reducing exchange rate volatility

This has repercussions for the second objective of the Tobin tax, namely to reduce exchange rate volatility. It can be argued that at a tax rate of 0.25 per cent there would be a 33 per cent decline in short-term speculation that would lead to more stability. National economies would thus be less likely to plunge into unanticipated crises.

Fighting currency crises

The third objective of the Tobin tax, is to fight currency crises. Moreover, stable exchange rates are more conducive to trade and investment and would also make debt repayment of both developed and developing countries more predictable. As foreign trade and credit relations would be more predictable, it is likely that we would detect a rise in foreign direct investment (FDI), especially in developing countries (Wahl and Waldow, 2001, pp. 7–10).

Giving governments control over policy-making

The fourth objective is to give greater freedom to national governments in monetary and economic policy-making. In the current system, governments have lost a huge amount of autonomy, on the one hand because central banks no longer generate the same amount of capital as private investors do, on the other because speculation is occurring in relation to their currencies which forces them to act in accordance with predictions about them (Moreno, 1997, p. 1). Most researchers draw attention to the fact that, in reality, the autonomy that might be restored would remain limited regardless of whether they see it as a desirable outcome or not (Wahl and Waldow, 2001, p. 2; Frankel, 1996, pp. 59–60). Maybe this is not an area where the efforts of the Tobin tax proponents are likely to be most effective, which does not mean the tax is not necessary, it simply means it is not a remedy for all problematic aspects of international financial markets.

Dooley argues that 'before we arm governments with another distortion and charge them to "go forth and do good" we should carefully examine the historical record of what governments have actually gone forth and done...the record is not encouraging' (Dooley, 1996, p. 102). Whereas I am inclined to agree with Dooley, I would also argue that 'leaving things to the market' does not have such a great track record either. The problem is a political one: we should be trying to establish better systems of governance rather than turning our back on them and looking to market forces for salvation. What one perceives to be a better system of governance is, of course, linked to what one wishes to achieve. Here, I am calling for a shift in priorities, whereby a better system of governance would place human welfare at its core within a system that is democratic and accountable to those affected across national boundaries. The Tobin tax debate belongs to a category of research that seeks to shift the debate towards such concerns of cosmopolitan, egalitarian justice on a global scale, in which the human individual rather than the state is the referent object. In a Kantian spirit, universalizable maxims of justice are called for in a world in which all those who potentially have an effect upon each other have the duty to behave morally to one another (Linklater, 1999, p. 482). Redistribution on a global scale is part of this movement, which ties in with the final objective of the tax.[4]

Raising revenue

The final objective of the Tobin tax is to raise revenue in order to fund global health and environmental problems. There is sufficient evidence that poverty is widespread and is increasing (UNCTAD, 2001, p. 3). I would argue that much of it has to do with the inconsiderate behaviour within the global North, which has effects on the global South and upon disadvantaged groups within the global North. Furthermore, environmental issues that exceed national boundaries have never been as pressing as they are today. It is time we devised a mechanism of dealing with these issues on a supranational level. The Tobin tax could generate revenue between $50 billion and $300 billion per annum (Felix and Sau, 1996, cited in Patterson, 2002, p. 10). The revenue generated would depend on the tax rate (what percentage?), tax base (which type of transactions?) and the extent of tax evasion. Additionally, it should not be forgotten that the proclaimed goal of the tax is to diminish its own tax base. Its revenue would decline over time if it functioned properly, yet it would never be zero, as the goal of the Tobin tax is not to stop all currency transactions but to limit excess liquidity that fosters volatility (Wahl and Waldow, 2001, p. 5). Nevertheless, even at a minimal rate there would still be enough revenue generated, at the very least, to fund all UN spending and all official aid spending by OECD countries (Patterson, 2002, p. 10). This would be wiser than granting developing countries more loans that only create further problems of debt and dependence (Hayward, 1999, p. 6). One could argue that this reflects divergent political wills, whereby powerful institutions of the global

North do not want to release Third World countries from their dependency. However, the reality is more complex. Individuals shape norms and are in turn shaped by norms. Powerful discourses affect reality and people's perceptions of what type of society or change for the better is indeed possible, both on a theoretical and practical level.

Objections to the Tobin tax

As is to be expected, there are numerous objections against the Tobin tax. Many are technical and range from concerns about more volatility in the presence of a Tobin tax to warnings that a Tobin tax might not be enough to solve the problem. Further questions involve, for example, how high or low the tax rate should be and whether or not all participants should be taxed or whether governments and central banks should be 'trusted'. An additional set of questions asks what the tax base should be and to what extent evasion of it could be curbed; what if speculators move their transactions 'offshore' to non-participating countries, or trade in assets that are not covered by the tax, such as swaps, forwards, futures and treasury bills? Issues to be decided, further, include the problem of comprehensiveness: do all countries have to join, or does it suffice if countries with major financial centres join? There are fears that governments will not come to a consensus on the issue, meaning the tax would be too difficult to enforce. Problems could also occur around the effects of losses on companies. What would companies do to compensate for losses – would there be a knock-on effect on wages and employment? And practical issues, such as who should collect and distribute the tax and in what way, need to be settled. Should it be national governments, international institutions such as the IMF and the World Bank, should there be a new institution to avoid the pitfalls of existing governance structures reinforcing present unequal power structures within international political and economic relations? The beneficiaries of the tax fund also need to be established. Should developing countries get to keep all the revenue and developed countries give it away, should there be a halfway solution? And to what extent should specific circumstances be allowed to influence the level of the tax? Should there be a two-tier system whereby a minimal tax is levied at all times to generate the revenue desired but a surcharge levied in times of extreme volatility to deal with issues of instability, as proposed by Paul Bernd Spahn in 1996? Would it work? Finally, the question has been asked whether or not we should employ other forms of capital control such as direct capital controls on outflows or inflows, or the

'Chilean Model' (between 1991 and 1998 the Chilean government placed reserve requirements of a limited duration on capital imports, Patterson, 2002, p. 11).[5]

I would like to emphasize that questions of 'how' are most important even from an early stage as, given the unequal distribution of power and wealth in the international system, great care must be taken to hinder any implementation of the tax favouring those already in power. This is especially important when it comes to discussing revenue and who should collect and distribute it in what way. Those that need help must have a say now in how the tax is implemented or else they run the risk of being ignored at a later stage. The problem, therefore, is not one that only financial technocrats should be discussing.

Within the existing literature, discussions about how the tax can deal with such obstacles is taking place.[6] Nevertheless, the debate is presented as one in which it is argued whether the tax would work, which supposedly then provides a justification for whether the tax is desirable. Not everything we can do, also provides us with an action we should implement and vice versa. Continuing along such lines of argumentation can become circular if we do not disaggregate what ideological assumptions and visions of society underlie the different arguments within this debate. Through an analysis of the language used to justify certain positions, one can begin to unpack the underlying motivations of the participants in the debate in order to lay bare the divergent political projects. Using insights from Gramscian theory one can think about where power plays a role in fostering consent in situations in which an alternative is deemed impossible, rather than undesirable.[7] Deeming something impossible is a stronger argument than deeming something undesirable. In order to disentangle power, knowledge and ideology, I proceed to analyze why and how the proponents and opponents of the Tobin tax argue the way they do. By doing so, I hope to give a clearer picture of why opposition to the tax is more powerful at present and what the possibilities for change within the existing system are.

Constraints to the implementation of the Tobin tax

As Kenneth Kasa of the Federal Reserve Bank of San Francisco argued in 1999, 'whether a Tobin Tax is desirable depends on your beliefs about the efficiency of international financial markets' (Kasa, 1999, p. 1). The fact that Kasa used the word 'beliefs' is quite revealing as it shows that there is an underlying problem of ideology, namely, what does one 'believe' an international financial market should or should not be doing? In whose interest is this international financial market operating? One's view on how financial markets should operate is ultimately influenced by one's perspective on what or who they exist for. Theory and practice are in this sense inextricably linked as the Critical (International) Theorist Robert Cox states:

> Theory is always for someone and some purpose. All theories have a perspective. Perspectives are derived from a position in time and space, specifically social and political time and space...the more sophisticated a theory is, the more it reflects upon and transcends its own perspective...there is, accordingly, no such thing as theory in itself, divorced from a standpoint in time and space. When any theory so represents itself, it is more important to examine it as ideology, and to lay bare its concealed perspective.
>
> Cox, 1986, p. 207

With regards to the Tobin tax, theories that present the tax as unfeasible contain a perspective that does not desire a change in the present unjust economic system. The ideology of neo-liberalism is the powerful ideology that constructs itself as common-sense, perpetuated by those who benefit from it and who occupy influential positions within the existing system.

Obstinate resistance to the Tobin tax signals that massive economic interests are at stake for those benefiting from the current system, who happen to be those that control it. The introduction of a Tobin tax will take away profit opportunities of several billion US dollars from certain speculators (Wahl and Waldow, 2001, p. 5). In the remainder of this chapter I will analyze the arguments of the actors involved in the debate in terms of their interests and the underlying ideologies that inform their arguments in order to show that the real issue revolves around conflicting wishes and unequal power relationships that inform the theories employed and the policies adopted.

The actors involved in this debate are private investors, financial institutions such as banks and the IMF, international organizations such as the UN, NGOs, national governments, the EU, economists, academics, journalists and the general public. All have particular motivations for arguing in the way that they do. Private investors, financial institutions and economists that argue against a Tobin tax are the ones benefiting from the current situation. They argue that the Tobin tax is 'nonsense', 'unfeasible' and often appeal to complex technical arguments that they know any non-specialist will find difficult to understand. Furthermore, it is interesting to note the dismissive language used to make arguments more resonant: 'No competent economist in their right mind would support any form of capital control' (De Rosa, 2001; Bloomberg). Likewise:

> The French Socialist Party and some lunatic fringe Belgian Deputies are both clambering on board the Tobin train while there is no other news for journalists to write about...but don't worry, there is no chance of the [British] Government adopting this proposal...Let's hope that the Tobin tax will die with 2001 and that madcap politicians will come up with some other silly wheeze we can write about in 2002.
>
> Hetherington-Gore, 2001, p. 1

Although there is a great deal of sincere literature about the feasibility of the Tobin tax, I think it is revealing that such language is used by financial journalists, who are not thinking critically about the given context of the neo-liberal discourse. An example of how this discourse is constructed can be found in the language employed by Garber and Taylor in their article against the Tobin tax. They state that: 'A policy of throwing sand in the wheels of international finance would very likely amount to little more than a futile, Canutian attempt to command the tides of international capital flows' (Garber and Taylor, 1995, p. 180). This is a reference to the mythological figure King Canute, who thought he was so powerful he could command the tides of the sea and of course did not succeed (Markham-Rhodes, 2002; Viking). This implies that international capital flows are more powerful than the human beings that operate within them, meaning there is no point in trying to change the way they flow. Besides, the caricatured presentation of Adam Smith's theory of the 'Invisible Hand' of the market leads people to trust in unregulated markets. The example above also implies that they are not something created by human beings but are something that exists beyond them. This is a powerful metaphor but at the same time a questionable assertion that simply serves to reinforce the discourse that market forces are so powerful we cannot do anything to intervene. If we do, we are destined to be destroyed by the waves, in other words not succeed or bring greater problems upon ourselves. In mythology, those that try to meddle with nature usually bring great unhappiness upon themselves. Underlying the arguments outlined above is a specific interest in maintaining the status quo that is portrayed as 'inevitable' and 'beneficial'. What must be understood, however, is that the status quo is a reflection of the interests of a dominant elite, it is not the only or the most natural or the best way to construct the financial system. Arguments are constructed around the inevitability of open markets and a conception of liberalization and subsequent competition as 'good'. The problem is that because these groups dominate the financial arena, any opposition is thwarted as 'ignorant'. Following this line of thinking would imply that we are stuck with the present system. However, I would argue that such articulations merely serve to disguise the fact that this debate is about political will, not about feasibility: if we cannot do anything about it, then there can be no discussion; discussion being precisely what those who now benefit from the unregulated system are trying to eliminate. Increasingly, questions about the kind of society we wish to live in are being asked as processes of globalization open up the intellectual space and the practical necessity of doing so. The evolving field of global ethics is one which puts the element of choice first, which then leads to contemplations about how collective decisions can be translated into the sum of individual actions (Booth, Dunne and Cox, 2001). From this perspective, the goal becomes how we can make the Tobin tax, or any other ethical endeavour, work in practice, especially in light of our changing obligations and possibilities for action in a globalizing world, an issue which is discussed in more detail in Chapter 10 of this volume.

On the other side of the debate are those that are politically motivated, who are either not benefiting from the present system or who refuse to accept a society in which some are wealthy at the expense of the vast majority. Such people, some academics, some journalists, some members of NGOs and some individuals of the general public do not buy into the heralding of market forces and are far more cautious about its effects when left to its own devices. However, because most of them are not in positions of traditional political power, it is far more difficult for them to bring about change. Furthermore, it is difficult for them to attract the attention of the general public, many of whom are disillusioned by the difficulty of fighting for an alternative society or are influenced by doctrines that emphasize the inevitability of the present system coupled with libertarian notions that anyone who is poor should have done better for themselves in a world where opportunities are equal.[8]

National governments are increasingly under pressure to adhere to the interests of private capital, a movement that is only reinforced by the present financial system. The idea of a Tobin tax should actually be in the interest of governments as it could restore some of their monetary autonomy and raise revenue for projects that they should want to support. Yet the fact that most governments, except for France and Canada,[9] discuss the topic[10] and then do not implement the tax, shows that they are under much more pressure to satisfy business interests than those of their respective electorates. One might even argue that they benefit through collaboration with them. One of many examples is that of offshore banking. According to the Association for Accountancy and Business Affairs (AABA), the UK government could raise up to an extra £85 billion a year by tackling this leakage of revenues into tax havens (ATTAC London, 2002; Attac).

If a Tobin tax were implemented, governments might have more of an incentive to clamp down on offshore transactions; however the existence of offshore areas is used as a reason not to implement the tax. Furthermore, if governments were really concerned about offshore transactions, they could introduce a fee for transactions from such areas, which would make it more expensive for traders to retrieve their money (Wahl and Waldow, 2001, p. 7). Such behaviour does imply that business has a great hold over governments. As Hans Eichel, the German Minister of Finance explains, in reality, nobody in the industrialized states wants the Tobin tax (Eichel, cited in Schaefer, 2001, p. 1).

In 1999, the European Parliament decided against the Tobin tax, stating that a 'reimposition of restrictions on capital movement would signify a reversal of globalization' (Patterson and Galliano, 1999, p. 6). Within the official document there was no clarification of what the parliament means by 'globalization' and I can only conclude that they had a neo-liberal interpretation that emphasizes free trade and the deregulation of financial markets. Such an interpretation assumes that the market is best left alone and will ensure a fair distribution of goods and services (Rodrik, 1999, p. 1). There are two important points in this context. One is the fact that the term 'globalization' is used unquestioningly which signifies an insensitivity to the idea that 'globalization' is a term that can be employed to signify different kinds of processes and more importantly is not a process that is experienced in the same way by all of those affected (Steans and Pettiford, 2001, p. 145). Second, it is not questioned whether 'globalization' is actually a desired process. As van den Anker argues in Chapter 1 of the present volume, globalization is often posited as a process in which we cannot intervene successfully, rather than a political and economic project. The example used above shows that at this time, the European Parliament made a decision that benefited those who support the neo-liberal discourse that has such negative consequences, especially for the world's poor. The free flow of capital is presented as the solution to the woes of poor people and poorer countries within the global economy. Opposition to this is deemed 'protectionist' and 'antiquated' and no longer possible. This is not an unquestionable truth but a political discourse that does not have to be followed. What I wish to argue is that certain forms of regulation, like the introduction of the Tobin tax, can contribute to the development of a system that not only functions more smoothly in the absence of stark volatility and financial crises, but that refrains from causing harm to human beings.

According to Critical Theorists, change can be brought about when existing structures are called into question. Nevertheless, there is still the danger that a neo-liberal discourse will not accommodate criticisms and give concessions to petitioning voices to make people acquiesce to its harmful principles once more. Public education is crucial in this field where justifications for the present system rely upon keeping possibilities for change marginalized. Neo-liberalism is not an entirely independent structure that brings these problems with it, it is real people making real decisions that bring about the current system; this means real people can help to bring about real change in a future system. Slavery and the slave-like conditions poor people increasingly find themselves in today can be combated by taking a systemic approach to the problem and addressing causal links between the international financial system and the effects it has on ordinary people's lives. By doing so, systemic remedies can be devised, of which the Tobin tax is one. As van den Anker articulates at the beginning of this book, globalization does not only posit problems – within its discourse we can also find solutions.

Conclusion

I have sought to explain how a Tobin-style tax can change international economic management. I have identified five aims of the tax and have explained how it seeks to achieve them. In particular, this chapter looks at the debate itself in order to shed light upon what is really at stake. From a technical point of view both those that argue for it and those that argue against it have devised plausible mechanisms that suit their cause. This is where the real issue lies. Depending on whether one thinks that an unregulated market is efficient or not, depends on how one defines 'efficiency'. Those that benefit from the system as it is now have a vested interest in maintaining the status quo. Those that define efficiency in a broader way to include the repercussions that currency speculation has on the lives of human beings across the globe, wish to intervene to create a more just society. It is revealing to explore what types of arguments and what kind of language which actors use. Financial actors are concerned with technical debates of feasibility and often use language they know any non-economists will have difficulties understanding. Furthermore, they construct a discourse that emphasizes the inevitability of the existing system and therefore ridicule those that disagree. Political actors such as governments and international institutions mostly side with the economists, which reflects the vast amount of power business has in the existing system. This also means that arguments that favour an alternative and ultimately more just system have a difficult task in bringing about the change that they see necessary. This is why more must be done to educate the public so that a greater force can be established to bring about change. The debate about the Tobin tax throws up questions about what type of society we wish to live in and in particular draws attention to issues of democracy and accountability. To conclude, I would like to cite the American economist Joseph Stiglitz:

> Since the end of the Cold War, tremendous power has flowed to the people entrusted to bring the gospel of the market to the far corners of the globe...the culture of international economic politics is not democratic...this is what demonstrators shouting outside of the IMF...will try to say...not everything they say will be right. But if the people we entrust to manage the global economy...don't begin a dialogue and take their criticisms to heart, things will continue to go very, very wrong. I've seen it happen.
>
> Stiglitz, 2000

It can be argued that there are systemic problems within the present global economy that foster poverty and exploitation of vulnerable economies and the people dependent on them. Only by unpacking the assumptions of the theories that inform policy-making can we understand how to bring about change for the better by making a concern for human security our ontological point of reference based upon the theories of cosmopolitanism, egalitarianism and Critical Theory. From this perspective, the Tobin tax poses a viable solution to the problems it sets out to address as well as being able to contribute to a systemic alleviation of one of the causes of poverty – financial crises – and generate funds to alleviate poverty directly. The tax also opens up the conceptual space for debates about regulation and an ideological shift away from the present, harmful neo-liberal discourse. Poverty alleviation in terms of a restructuring of the present global economic system can go a long way to reducing and preventing contemporary slavery through fostering environments that are not conducive to the enslavement of one human being by another.

Notes

1. This is one of the oldest currency-trading companies whose services now include possibilities for individuals to engage in currency speculation online.
2. As outlined by Patterson, 2002, p. 3.
3. For actual calculations, see the table of figures in Patterson, 2002, p. 10.
4. See for example, Beitz, 1999, pp. 143–54.
5. See the following authors: Dooley, 1996; Kenen, 1995; Frankel, 1996; Garber and Taylor, 1995; Patterson and Galliano, 1999; Stotsky, 1996; Jones and Seguin, 1997; Hau, 2001; Hetherington-Gore, 2001 and Davidson, 1997 (not all of these authors are principally against a currency transaction tax; however, they are ones that predominantly discuss difficulties with it).
6. See the following websites and authors: www.attac.org.uk; www.waronwant.org; www.tobintax.org.uk; www.halifaxinitiative.org; Eichengreen *et al.* (1999); ul Haq, Kaul and Grunberg, 1996; Griffith-Jones, 1996; Felix and Sau, 1996; Kasa, 1999; Michalos, 1999; Moreno, 1997; Schmidt, 1999; Spahn, 1996; Wahl, 2001 and Wahl and Waldow, 2001 (again, these are authors that do recognize problems yet try to resolve them in favour of the tax).
7. For an explanation of Gramsci's theory of coercion and consent see Femia, 1981, pp. 35–45.
8. It must be pointed out that this is not necessarily their fault: certain information is often not released or is made difficult to access in an attempt to keep the public acquiesecent. Furthermore, people are educated into being deferent; politics is seen as something that must be 'left to those who know best'.
9. These two governments have recently passed decisions in favour of a Tobin tax (Patterson, 2002, p. 11); however, on a more cynical note, one could argue that they are placating the electorate as they both qualify that they will go ahead only if other governments do, knowing full well that this is not going to happen in the near future.
10. The European Commission published a report on the feasibility of the Tobin Tax in 1999 and updated its position in December 2001 (Patterson, 2001).

12
Modern Slavery and Fair Trade Products: Buy One and Set Someone Free

Ivan Manokha

Introduction

In its recent report on forced labour, the International Labour Organization (ILO) stated that:

> although universally condemned, forced labour is revealing ugly new faces alongside the old. Traditional types of forced labour such as chattel slavery and bonded labour are still with us in some areas, and past practices of this type haunt us to this day. In new economic contexts, disturbing forms such as forced labour in connection with the trafficking of human beings are now emerging almost everywhere.
>
> ILO, 2001, p. 1

Forced labour is not a relic of a bygone era, but a widespread practice which exists in the world today. According to the US Department of State's estimates, in 2001,

> at least 700,000, and possibly as many as four million men, women and children worldwide were bought, sold, transported and held against their will in slave-like conditions...Women, children and men are trafficked into the international sex trade for the purposes of prostitution, sex tourism and other commercial sexual services and into forced labor situations in sweatshops, construction sites and agricultural settings.
>
> US Department of State, 2002, p. 1

In 2001, *New Internationalist* estimated that there were about 27 million people who existed 'in a state to which the term slavery can be applied...This is higher than during the heyday of the colonial slave trade' (*New Internationalist*, 2001, p. 10).

Modern slavery and trafficking in persons are inseparable from extreme poverty and underdevelopment in Africa, Asia and Latin America and poverty and lack of opportunities in Eastern Europe, which create a socio-economic environment conducive to practices of forced labour and child labour. The US Department of State's report notes that:

> in countries with chronic unemployment, widespread poverty and a lack of economic opportunities, traffickers use promises of higher wages and good working conditions in foreign countries to lure people into their networks. Victims, who want a better life for themselves and their families, are easily convinced by the traffickers' promises.
>
> US Department of State, 2002, p. 1

For example, in Burkina Faso, 'most of the trafficking problems...result from a traditional regional pattern of poverty-driven mass migration of very young children in search of subsistence labor in mining, crafts, agriculture, and as domestics' and 'Burkina Faso is severely constrained in all its efforts against trafficking by its profound poverty' (US Department of State, 2002, p. 34). Debt-bondage is similarly related to extreme poverty. For example, a Human Rights Watch report states that:

> the poor remuneration of manual scavenging, agricultural labor, and other forms of low-caste employment often force families of lower castes or caste-like groups into bondage. A lack of enforcement of relevant legislation prohibiting debt bondage in most of the countries concerned allows for the practice to continue unabated.
>
> HRW, 2001

In India, for example, poor families send their children to work for creditors to pay off debts and loans and young children end up working for long hours in appalling conditions (*New Internationalist*, 2001, p. 11). According to the UN Working Group on Contemporary Forms of Slavery, about 20 million are caught in debt-bondage and India alone claims at least 10 million (*New Internationalist*, 2001, p. 11), while Human Rights Watch estimates that there are about 40 million bonded labourers in India (HRW, 2001). The ILO report also observes that there is a relationship between poverty and modern slavery:

'certain groups – such as women, ethnic or racial minorities, migrants, children, and above all the poor – are particularly vulnerable to these contemporary forms of forced labour (ILO, 2001, p. 2).

Now this, of course, is not to say that the relationship between poverty and slavery is that of direct necessity or inevitability, for there are many poor regions where slavery does not exist. However, it is undeniable that poverty facilitates slavery, as it facilitates sweatshops and extremely low-paid jobs, as well as child labour. These latter practices may sometimes resemble slavery, as conditions of labour are often slave-like. As a report by the Indian government observes, 'labour may be forced not only owing to physical force...but also owing to hunger and poverty which compels him [a worker] to accept employment for remuneration which is less than the statutory minimum wage' (cited in ILO, 2001, p. 9). However, slavery implies an important difference from sweatshops for it involves labour under threat or force of actual violence and the workers cannot leave (see Chapter 1 in this volume).

Modern slavery and extreme forms of exploitation such as sweatshops and child labour have, in recent years, generated campaigns and protests within the realm of global civil society, the 'supranational sphere of social and political participation' (Anheier, Glasius, and Kaldor, 2001, p. 4). A large number of NGOs, social movements and private think-tanks have tried to develop strategies for combating abuses of workers' and children's rights associated with forced labour and slave-like conditions of work. One such strategy has been Fair Trade which constitutes the subject of this chapter.

Fair Trade is an equitable and fair partnership between marketers in developed countries and producers in Asia, Africa and Latin America. A Fair Trade partnership works to provide low-income artisans and farmers with a living wage for their work (Fair Trade Federation [a]). It is a form of direct trade, which allows participating producers to sell their commodities not through the world market but directly to the distributors. As such, prices paid for their goods are higher and do not depend on the current world prices, although in some cases the economic difference to the producer may be insignificant as premiums are used for social investment in communities (see Chapter 9 in this volume). Fair Trade has been set up to contribute to development and poverty reduction by enabling producers to earn more money to sustain their businesses and by investing in communal development. According to the Fair Trade Foundation website, Fair Trade standards stipulate that traders must: (a) pay a price to producers that covers the costs of sustainable production and living; (b) pay a 'premium' that producers can invest in development; (c) make partial advance payments when requested by producers; and (d) sign contracts that allow for long-term planning and sustainable production practices. Fair Trade products include textiles, crafts and agricultural products. A Fair Trade label has been developed for use on coffee, tea, rice, fresh fruit, juices, cocoa, sugar, honey and sports balls.

In this respect, Fair Trade can be said to positively impact upon alleviation and/or prevention of forced labour for it renders the socio-economic environment less conducive to it, as we will see when we discuss some specific examples of Fair Trade initiatives. However, this chapter argues that despite a few encouraging experiences, Fair Trade does not deal with the underlying causes of poverty and underdevelopment perpetuated by the structure of world production and distribution, nor with the fact that the economies of numerous developing states depend virtually exclusively on exports of agricultural and primary products such as coffee, tea, cocoa or minerals. Such commodities are exported by many countries (encouraged by IMF and World Bank strategies) and as a result their abundant supply drives world prices down. Fair Trade does not question this arrangement and its historical roots; all it does is to ensure that certain farmers receive a better price for their produce. Nor does Fair Trade question the existence of global capitalism, of production for the market, of wage labour or of private property and accumulation of capital for its own sake. It presupposes these capitalist institutions, takes them for granted and contributes to their reproduction. Hence, the core argument that runs through this chapter can be summed up as follows: in the existing structure of global trade each one of us, in his/her routine daily shopping may make a difference to the lives of some individual producers and small communities by simply choosing products with a Fair Trade label; however, the root causes of poverty and practices of forced labour, associated with it, lie deeper and Fair Trade is not a sufficient strategy to deal with them.

Global poverty, global civil society and Fair Trade

The late-modern world has been characterized by two dialectical processes: perpetuation of human rights abuses on the one hand, and attempts to prevent or stop them, on the other. Many of the human rights abuses are, in one way or another, causally related with the growing power of transnational capital over the 'state/society complex' (van der Pijl, 1998), with liberalization of world trade and finance and impoverishment of different economies, particularly in the developing world, whose producers are unable to sustain competition (Tabb, 1997). For example, workers' rights abuses and child labour in sweatshops of multinational corporations (MNCs) in developing countries must be seen against the background of poverty in these states and the competition between them for foreign investment. The MNCs have been able to find cheap labour in poor Third World states where rates of unemployment and poverty are so high that even sweatshops with long working hours, appalling conditions and little pay seem a better option for many labourers than not working at all or than sticking with traditional livelihoods. At the same time, although such treatment of workers is universally prohibited and constitutes a violation of human rights, it is difficult for local governments to enforce regulations on corporations for the latter are highly mobile and may easily transfer the needed capital elsewhere. For example, in East Asian sweatshops of such multinational giants of the garment industry as Nike or Gap working conditions have been in violation of many international standards (O'Brien, 2001).

Modern slavery must also be examined against this background. In the world where enough food is produced to feed everybody, in many countries of Africa, Asia and Latin America millions of people still suffer from extreme poverty, hunger and disease. Today 800 million people suffer from hunger and are undernourished. Half of the world's population live on less than $2 a day. The gap between rich and poor is still growing. Today, 10 per cent of the world's population receives 70 per cent of its income, and the richest three men on earth have assets equal to the annual output of the 48 poorest nations. Since 1960 the polarization of income between the richest and poorest 20 per cent has tripled, to 90 to one (UNDP, 1998). Poverty makes people vulnerable and easier targets for slavery and trafficking as well as slave-like employment. 'Economic change and globalization have driven rural people in poor countries to the cities and into debt. These impoverished and vulnerable people are a bumper crop of potential slaves' (Bales, 2001, p. 14). For example, in Benin, according to the US Department of State report,

> children from poor rural and less-literate families are sent away to work as domestic and commercial helpers for wealthier relations or employers. Many of these children end up in indentured servitude, subjected to physical and sexual abuse. Beninese children are

trafficked to Ghana, Gabon, Nigeria, and Cote d'Ivoire, while children from neighboring Niger, Togo, and Burkina Faso, are trafficked to Benin. Some Beninese women are trafficked to European countries for prostitution.

US Department of State, 2002, p. 30

New Internationalist quotes a local UNICEF worker as saying: 'People come and offer the families money and say that their children will work on plantations and send money home. They give the family a little money, from $15 to $30 – and then they never see their children again' (Bales, 2001, p. 14). The same is true as regards child slavery in Ghana:

internally, Ghanaian children are sent from the poorest regions to work in the fishing industry and for domestic labor in urban areas. Many of these children, sold by their families to traffickers, suffer physical or sexual abuse and receive insufficient food, no wages, and no access to education.

US Department of State, 2002, p. 53

Liberalization of trade and capital movements around the world has played an important role in contributing to slavery. Introduction of free trade in cocoa in West Africa, for example, has had disastrous consequences for cocoa farmers. West African cocoa plantations, where reports of slave labour have been widespread, have long been subsidized by the state, which guaranteed a fixed price for farmers. With the liberalization of the cocoa market due to pressure from the World Trade Organization (WTO), cocoa producers now sell their products themselves at world market prices, which are unstable and generate lower returns (although, as Berlan in Chapter 9 in this volume shows, there are exceptions to this, such as Ghana). Slave labour allows these producers to reduce their production costs. In other words, trade liberalization and impoverishment of farmers cannot be said to directly lead to slavery, but they may be said to encourage forced labour to some extent. This conclusion is reached by Global Exchange, a non-profit research, education and action organization, whose experts argue that the causes of slavery are 'free trade, structural adjustment, and corporate control' (Global Exchange (a)). They further argue that:

severe poverty, child labor, and the reemergence of child slavery can be blamed, in part, by raw cocoa prices that are too low to provide farmers with enough income to meet their production costs, much less their basic needs. The effects of insufficient world market prices have been exacerbated by deregulation of agriculture in West Africa, which abolished commodity boards across the region, leaving small farmers at the mercy of the market. This economic crisis has forced farmers to cut their labor costs, and tragically that has meant relying on slave labor or pulling children out of school to work on family farms. These small farmers and their children remained trapped in a cycle of poverty, without hope for sufficient income or access to basic education or health care.

Global Exchange (a)

The power of capital over the 'state/society complex' has also manifested itself in the perpetuation of workers' rights abuses, the employment of child labour and also forced labour by Western MNCs in Third World countries. Sweatshops with slave-like conditions of work, beatings and sexual harassment and irregular, very low wages were operated – especially in the garment industry, by such giants as Nike, Gap and Adidas, particularly in East Asia (Clean Clothes Campaign; Corp Watch, 2002; BHRRC).

Multinational corporations have also been accused of using forced labour. For example, a lawsuit has been filed on behalf of 15 Burmese villagers, who allege that US oil company Unocal used forced labour in the construction of a gas pipeline (Alden, 2002). As the International Federation of Chemical, Energy, Mine and General Worker's Union (ICEM) reported in its newsletter:

together with French-based energy multinational Total and the Petroleum Authority of Thailand Exploration and Production Company, Unocal and MOGE are partners in a joint pipeline venture to bring gas to Thailand from the Yadana gas field off the Burmese coast. Since its inception, this project has stood accused of serious human rights abuses, notably the use of forced labour.

ICEM, 1996

Some famous brands are also accused of using forced labour on Saipan, one of the islands that make up the Commonwealth of the Northern Mariana Islands, a United States territory since 1976 (Barnes, 1997). Leslie Jermyn, a member of the Global Aware Co-operative, a co-operative of writers, academics, journalists and individuals, describes Saipan as 'an Export Production Zone that caters to such US American brand names as Polo, The Gap, Jones New York, Liz Claiborne, Calvin

Klein, Disney and JC Penny' (Jermyn, 2002). Among the most abused labourers, according to Jermyn, are women who come from China and the Philippines who accept debts of US$6,000–7,000, ending up in bonded labour with no right to leave, organize or change employers. Some have been forced to abort children when they became pregnant (Jermyn, 2002).

A number of US organizations filed a lawsuit against leading garment industries in 1999. In November 2001, a US district judge in the Northern Mariana Islands upheld the complaint in a lawsuit alleging sweatshop conditions on the Western Pacific island of Saipan. Directly addressing the plaintiffs' claims that the Saipan sweatshop industry is dependent on indentured foreign labour, the court stated:

> When the labour is tied to a debt owed to the employer and the employer physically coerces the worker to labour until the debt is paid or the consequences of failing to work to pay off the debt are so severe and outside the customary legal remedy that the worker is compelled to labour, a condition of peonage results, and this is the essence of plaintiffs' allegations.
>
> Labour Behind the Label, 2001

Slave-like conditions in sweatshops, abuses of workers' rights, child labour and different forms of slavery and forced labour have generated a movement against multinational corporations within the realm of global civil society comprising a multiplicity of NGOs, private think-tanks, students from different universities and colleges around the world and various celebrities. Fair Trade must be put within the framework of this movement, for although Fair Trade started in the 1960s, it is with the development of global civil society that it has acquired prominence worldwide. The movement against slavery and sweatshops may be described as consisting of two elements: the first includes strategies aimed at monitoring MNCs, forcing them to abandon malpractices, respect ILO regulations, and develop socially responsible codes of practice; the second element aims at dealing with the conditions that facilitate or encourage slavery and slave-like labour, namely, poverty and under-development. Fair Trade may be located at the intersection of these two strategies for, on the one hand, NGOs and Alternative Trade Organizations (ATOs) have developed or supported Fair Trade projects while, on the other, they have been trying to convince corporations to participate in Fair Trade, to make Fair Trade part of their socially responsible practice. Let us look at these strategies in more detail.

As regards the first strategy, a multiplicity of NGOs were established to monitor corporations' human rights records and mobilize public opinion. Examples include CorpWatch, NikeWatch, Multinational Monitor, Labour Behind the Label, Clean Clothes Campaign, Campaign for Labour Rights, and others. These organizations engaged in protests against corporations exposing malpractices and human rights abuses. They were actively supported by students. For example in 1997, student protests against Nike were conducted at a number of American universities. *The Economist* reports in this regard:

> in the past few years, Shell, BP, Rio Tinto Zinc, Disney, Reebok, Nike and Starbucks Coffee, among others, have been rocked by the public criticism of human-rights groups and labour unions. Levi Strauss, Macy's, Liz Claiborne, Eddie Bauer and PepsiCo have pulled out of Myanmar after being lambasted for doing business there. Oil giants Texaco and Amoco soon followed.
>
> *The Economist*, 1998

These protests have led to the development of codes specifying good business practice by corporations where commitment to corporate social responsibility is usually pledged.

> Codes of conduct, which set out the standards a multinational expects of its factories and contractors, have evolved from vague promises into detailed rules. The troubles of Nike, a firm making sports goods that fell foul of the activists in 1997, speeded up this transformation, as other multinationals scrambled to avoid similar boycotts. The best codes now tend to be monitored by outside auditors. Companies realize that merely making promises risks adding hypocrisy to the list of charges against them.
>
> *The Economist*, 1999

The ILO reports that today practically all corporations have a code of conduct (ILO, 1998).

Many corporations have gone further than just acknowledging the importance of labour standards and have engaged in various projects aimed at human rights advocacy, either on their own or in partnership with international organizations and NGOs. One example of such activities has been the Ethical Trade Initiative (ETI) developed by a number of corporations along with NGOs and trade union organizations. Ethical

Trade is a good preliminary to the analysis of Fair Trade, because it highlights the latter's more profound focus.

Members of ETI include such brands as ASDA, The Body Shop International, J. Sainsbury, Levi Strauss, Safeway, Somerfield and others, as well as such NGOs as Anti-Slavery International, Christian Aid, Fairtrade Foundation, Oxfam, Save the Children, Traidcraft Exchange, and so on. Participating corporations have declared commitment to business ethics and corporate responsibility, the promotion of workers' rights and human rights in general. In employment, ethical business includes working towards the ending of child labour, forced labour and sweatshops, looking at health and safety, labour conditions and labour rights (Ethical Trade Initiative).

These commitments do not aim at dealing with poverty and conditions forcing people to accept slave-like jobs and contributing to their vulnerability as regards slavery and forced labour. Such socio-economic conditions are objectives of Fair Trade initiatives, which constitute the second element of NGO strategy, namely, attempts to address the root causes of forced labour and sweatshops. For example, CorpWatch states the following as regards poverty among cocoa producers which often results in employment of slave labour: 'The Solution! Fair Trade Certification, which guarantees a minimum price of $0.80 per pound, would allow cocoa plantation owners to pay their workers a living wage AND cease the practice of child slavery' (CorpWatch, 2002). Anti-Slavery International says the same:

> Fair Trade is the only guarantee that products, such as chocolate, are slave free. All fair trade products have to meet strict conditions, including the guarantee that no forced or illegal child labour has been used. Fair trade goods also give producers a fair price for their produce, thus helping to challenge the unfair trading systems that keep people in poverty and often force them into slavery.
>
> Anti-Slavery International, 2003

The same position is taken by Global Exchange:

> Fortunately, there is a way to correct the economic imbalances of the cocoa system: Fair Trade...While the global price for cocoa hovers around 40 cents per pound, the Fair Trade system guarantees farmers 80 cents per pound, giving them the income to support their families with dignity.
>
> Global Exchange [b]

Fair Trade: achievements

The International Cocoa Organization (ICCO) estimates that there are approximately 14 million people directly involved in cocoa production. Ninety per cent of the world's cocoa is grown on small family farms of 12 acres or less. With the liberalization of cocoa trade the incomes of these farmers declined significantly and this encourages child and slave labour, which helps to reduce the cost of production (Global Exchange [c]). Fair Trade cocoa is produced by co-operatives representing about 42,000 farmers from eight countries: Ghana, Cameroon, Bolivia, Costa Rica, Nicaragua, Dominican Republic, Ecuador and Belize. To assess the achievements of Fair Trade organizations, this chapter will now look at three specific examples.

Fair Trade cocoa farmers in Bolivia: El Ceibo

El Ceibo co-operative was formed in 1977. It joined the Fair Trade system in 1997.[1] Sales through Fair Trade have been especially important to El Ceibo's development. Fair Trade ensures a minimum price of $80 cents per pound under long-term contracts, access to credit, and prohibits abusive child labour and forced labour. Fair Trade farmers are required to reserve a portion of their revenues for social projects, ensuring that community development and technical training for farmers will always be possible. Fair Trade also promotes environmentally sustainable practices such as shade cultivation, composting and minimization of chemical inputs, ensuring that farmers use cultivation techniques that are safe for the environment and public health. El Ceibo's Fair Trade sales amounted to 55 tons of cocoa beans and 35 tons of processed products in 1998, and 65 tons of cocoa beans and 20 tons of processed products in 1999. The co-operative began selling to the US Fair Trade market in 2002, which will ensure a fair price for more of the co-operative's harvest. El Ceibo's farmers receive especially good returns on their crop because organic cocoa yields an extra premium in both the Fair Trade system and the world market and the co-operative does some of its own processing. El Ceibo's Fair Trade premiums have supported agricultural improvement and community development in many ways. For example, the co-operative offers incentives for organic production, has a fund for community projects and activities, and a Safety Fund for medical emergencies.

Fair Trade cocoa farmers in Belize: TCGA

The story of Toledo Cacao Growers Association (TCGA), formed in 1986, is a perfect example of the extent to which Fair Trade makes a difference.

The co-operative has about 126 members and is located in the Toledo region of Belize, which is the poorest district in the country. In 1992–3 Belize cocoa farmers were forced to abandon cocoa production due to a dramatic fall in prices. Fortunately, the UK chocolate company Green & Black's offered a long-term contract for a stable supply of quality cocoa. They agreed to buy all the cocoa TCGA could produce at a price above the market price. The cocoa was used to create Maya Gold Chocolate, which was introduced in March 1994 bearing the Fairtrade Mark, denoting Fair Trade certification in the UK. For many individual families, Fair Trade premiums have meant the difference between being able to send children to school and having to keep them at home to work.

The above examples illustrate how Fair Trade directly improves the lives of farmers and their children and how it contributes to the prevention of slave labour and child labour. However, in 2002, out of 89 million pounds of cocoa produced by Fair Trade co-operatives only 3 million pounds were sold at Fair Trade prices (Global Exchange [c]). This shows that the share of the Fair Trade cocoa market is still very small, and that Fair Trade needs to be supported.

TARA projects, India

TARA (Trade Alternative Reform Action) Projects Association provides support services to the production and marketing of handicrafts on Fair Trade lines, and also looks after the community developmental needs of grassroot craftspeople to help them gain awareness, rights and human dignity in an area of approximately 200 kilometres in and around Delhi in north India. The goal of TARA is to

> fight exploitation and poverty of crafts-people and their communities who do not have any dignified identity and face inhuman exploit-ations and injustices in the traditional production and trade system. The project seeks to combat exploitation and poverty through fair trade, political and social lobbying, campaigns and rallies, education and proper development of crafts-communities.
>
> TARA

TARA Projects has been a leading advocate for the elimination of child labour in India.

TARA[2] earns enough money from its trading activities to fund some social development projects, like education centres. Such centres, for example, act as meeting points for women learning how to stitch and thread beads to make jewellery in the morning, with children being taught in the afternoon. Usually, students are originally from other areas and have migrated to Delhi to seek work. The skills they acquire through TARA-initiated schools enable them to make their own clothes. TARA also organizes meetings in villages where issues such as boycotting glass bangles made by children are raised. Finally, TARA directly supports craftspeople, and the survival of indigenous craft skills.

One of TARA's buyers is Traidcraft, the UK's largest Fair Trade organization. Traidcraft's experience is important in assessing Fair Trade results. According to Traidcraft, their suppliers around the world emphasize again and again that by getting a fair price/wage for their goods they are able to educate their children, rather than having to send them out to work (Traidcraft, 1999).

In 2002, the Fair Trade market in the UK was worth more than £60 million. For example, Sainsbury's alone now sells 1 million Fair Trade marked bananas a week. The Co-op supermarket chain has seen sales of Fair Trade products rise from £100,000 a year to £5.5 million a year since 1998. Cafedirect, a Fair Trade licensee, is now the sixth-largest coffee brand in the UK. The Fair Trade tea that they produce – Teadirect – is the fastest growing tea brand in the UK. In 2001–2 Traidcraft sales rose by 24 per cent to exceed £10 million for the first time, providing vital income for producers from over 30 countries (Traidcraft).

As regards Fair Trade statistics worldwide, the sales of Fair Trade-labelled products total $400 million each year. The value of unlabelled Fair Trade products is unknown. Of $3.6 trillion of all goods exchanged globally, Fair Trade accounts for only 0.01 per cent (Fair Trade Federation [b]).

The above examples show that Fair Trade does help the individuals and communities involved, and it plays an important role in addressing socio-economic conditions which facilitate slavery and slave-like labour. It aims at 'fighting poverty through trade', as Traidcraft's slogan states, and each one of us by choosing products with the Fair Trade label may contribute his/her bit to the prevention or alleviation of slavery, child labour and slave-like conditions of work.

But is Fair Trade a solution good enough to combat global poverty and growing inequality between the rich and the poor? In the next section we will examine Fair Trade critically and we will see that it is a 'problem-solving' measure which does not deal with structural causes of poverty and underdevelopment, leaving the world's unfair division of labour intact.

Fair Trade: system reproduced

Fair Trade helps to prevent or alleviate slavery and slave-like conditions of employment in local projects. Its objectives are more profound than those aimed at codes of practice for MNCs and their subcontractors, such as the ETI. Fair Trade is a partnership between the buyer and supplier, and joint initiatives in developing countries start from the needs of the supplier's community. This is in contrast to ETI-type initiatives that are dependent on the power exercised by supermarkets/Western buyers to bring about change in their supply chains. Such strategies may make the lives of people even worse, since working in extreme conditions for little money in the end may be a better option than having no income whatsoever. For example, when Reebok closed one of its factories where working hours were longer than 72 hours a week, *The Economist* labelled this 'corporate social irresponsibility':

> Doug Cahn, the company's head of human rights, talks about values, fairness and principles, with all the zeal of an anti-corporate lobbyist. He presents the news that Reebok has just decided to withdraw business from a subcontracted factory in Thailand as a proof of corporate caring. The reason: the 400 or so workers employed there to make shorts and shirts were working for more than 72 hours a week. It is responsible to press for better standards, but the supply of good jobs matters too. Workers at this Bangkok factory were paid above the minimum wage, with health-and-safety rights that few local manufacturers would offer... Since the most ethical way to do business is to attract investment and offer more people a way out of peasant labour, perhaps this practice should be relabelled corporate social irresponsibility.
>
> *The Economist*, 2002

Fair Trade attempts to help people out by offering them better alternatives and not just closing down the available ones. It attempts to create socio-economic conditions where families would be less vulnerable to offers from human traffickers to sell their children, and would instead be able to send them to schools.

Michael Barratt Brown, writing about Fair Trade, says the following:

> What then would be the nature of a 'fair trading' system in the world? What has to be challenged? And to answer that question one has to ask first how the world economy has come to this condition where

millions of peasants are subject to gross exploitation, so that we should enjoy our coffee, cocoa or tea, our tobacco and cane sugar, pineapple and other tropical fruits, our cotton, natural rubber and forest products...We shall have to look back at the period of colonial rule, and at the continuous interventions of imperial powers in the Third World, to discover how this rift occurred and how it can be healed.

1993, p. 11

The present structure of the world economy was established with force, conquest and plunder, slave trade and colonization, and later the preservation of the colonial structure of world trade after the colonies became independent. The creation of the present economic system started with the slave trade. Millions of Africans were captured and sold to work largely on sugar and tobacco plantations to cater for the rising demand for these two commodities in Europe. At the peak of the slave trade in 1750 about 65,000 slaves were taken every year. This trade in African slaves laid the foundations for British capital accumulation and industrialization, which would later allow Britain to build its colonial empire (Magdoff, 1969 and 1978; Blackburn, 1998). It constituted part of the 'triangular trade' with British manufactured goods being exported to West Africa and sold to African chiefs in exchange for slaves, who would then be transported to Caribbean colonies of Britain, Spain and France, to Brazil and southern states of North America and sold to work on plantations. The products grown at these plantations such as tobacco, sugar and cotton would then be exported to Europe:

> The results both for Africa and for America south of what became the United States were...disastrous. Africa lost the strongest and healthiest of her young men and women. The harsh rule of the chiefs was imposed with foreign guns upon the people who remained. Local handicrafts were destroyed by the competition of cheaper factory products.
>
> Barratt Brown, 1993, p. 15

This laid foundations for the division of the world into poor and rich, producers of manufactured goods and primary producers, developed and underdeveloped. Later on slavery and plunder were followed by colonization and the expansion of trade. As Britain attained industrial superiority, virtually the entire world was opened up to provide markets for her goods and raw materials for her industries.

Empire was only at first an instrument of merchant capital, merchant traders buying cheap and selling dear. It soon involved truly productive capital, local people being set to work to produce for the European and North American market, with all the processing and transporting being kept in European and North American hands.

Barratt Brown, 1993, p. 17

This structure of world production and distribution with colonies providing raw materials, agricultural products and minerals and serving as markets for European goods, remained virtually unchanged after the former colonies attained independence.

Fair Trade leaves the structure of such unequal exchange relations, established by force and conquest, intact. The fact that economies of many developing states depend on exports of a few agricultural products, sometimes a single crop, also exported by many other Third World countries, is left unquestioned. It is a starting point for the Fair Trade activists that cocoa exports constitute 40 per cent of earnings of the Ivory Coast and 30 per cent of those of Cameroon (Global Exchange [c]).

What is overlooked by Fair Trade activists is that products marketed through Fair Trade – such as bananas, cocoa, coffee, honey, orange juice, sugar and tea – are simply exported by too many states. This drives world prices down and Fair Trade can help at best only a few co-operatives, like the ones examined above. Significant expansion of Fair Trade is hardly possible, since this would considerably reduce profits of a number of marketing corporations and raise prices which risks reducing consumption and thereby damaging producers. But even if Fair Trade were universalizable, it would still leave the international division of labour, established with colonial expansion and operating at the advantage of developed countries, intact. This would reproduce enormous gaps in technological and industrial development between the rich and the poor nations.

As regards Fair Trade projects for crafts like TARA projects in India, it is indisputable that they do give to the poor an opportunity to acquire basic skills of craftsmanship and by paying them a fair price it contributes to their subsistence. However, how big is the market for such products and how many producers can it sustain? And even if they are relatively numerous, will their income from Fair Trade ever be comparable to the incomes of Western workers?

Fair Trade as such, is a 'problem-solving' measure, which does not aim at transcending the existing structures, but at making them function more smoothly. It does not challenge global inequality as a whole, but only its most extreme manifestations like forced labour, child labour and sweatshops. Nor does Fair Trade challenge global capitalism. Fair Trade presupposes the existence of certain relations which are fundamental to capitalism such as wage labour, production for the market, private property and capital accumulation. It takes for granted the fact that there are labourers and employers, that the former have no choice but to work for the latter. It does not question the inequality involved in this relationship. Instead, it implicitly includes these unequal relations as a set of unstated assumptions, taking their existence and historical origins for granted and it contributes to their normalization and objectification.

From this perspective, Fair Trade is an ideological concept, understood not in the sense of a political programme (such as liberalism or socialism) or false consciousness (as some Marxists authors do), but in the sense used by Marx particularly in *The German Ideology*. This meaning of ideology refers to forms of knowledge which distort and conceal certain relations of power, but which is not reducible to a deliberate project of an identifiable agency or class. It is a result of the fact that in capitalism certain relations look different from what they really are, and so do solutions to existing problems (Larrain, 1983, pp. 15–45; Maclean, 1988, pp. 308–9). For example, in capitalism individuals appear free and equal, but this is true of political and civil equality, while economically some people are richer and others are poor. In the production process some have no choice but to enter into a wage labour relation and sell their labour power to others. Economic inequality in capitalism appears as inequality of income and the solution seems to lie in a struggle for better wages. This, however, leaves relations of wage labour intact and reproduces the dominant position of the owners of means of production and subordination of those without them who must work for a wage. Fair Trade is an example of such ideological thinking in that it presupposes capitalist relations of production and reproduces them. Today, capitalism is global and there are no visible alternatives to it. The socialist/communist alternative not only failed and thereby contributed to the strength of victorious capitalism, but also contributed to its legitimacy as a social organization with free and equal individuals. This is because socialist/communist regimes were characterized by massive repressions, purges, torture, concentration camps and genocide. But this fact does not mean that capitalism is the best alternative form of social organization and that with the establishment of global capitalism history will end. The failure of the alternatives and their sometimes repugnant nature does not mean that we should stop thinking about a different way of organizing social life. Fair Trade does not do so and in this lies its conservative nature.

Conclusion

Within the existing structure of world production and distribution Fair Trade is unquestionably a positive practice. Fair Trade initiatives help prevent or alleviate instances of forced labour, child labour and slave-like conditions of work. Fair Trade is a strategy aimed at dealing with the causes and not just the consequences of poverty, unlike Ethical Trade and workers' rights campaigns against MNCs. As such, the position taken in this chapter is that Fair Trade must be supported and it is a duty of citizens of developed countries to choose Fair Trade products in the supermarkets, thereby improving the lives of individuals and communities in the Third World. However, Fair Trade does not challenge the existing division of labour whereby economies of numerous developing countries depend on exports of a few agricultural products and primary products, nor does it oppose global capitalism. It is a problem-solving ideological measure which takes the existence of capitalism for granted and contributes to its sustenance. Global capitalism is a result of European expansion which first used conquered territories as supplies of slaves and markets for goods, and then integrated them into the capitalist economy as producers of raw materials and consumers of manufactured goods. This structure of production and distribution has remained largely intact and Fair Trade contributes to its reproduction. What is needed to alleviate poverty, hunger, disease and related forced labour, child labour and slave-like working conditions, is the transcendence of global capitalism.

Notes

1. The following studies of two co-operatives in cocoa production, El Ceibo and TCGA, are based on Global Exchange studies (Global Exchange [d]).
2. Information on TARA projects has been obtained from correspondence between Traidcraft and Tara projects, kindly provided by Fiona Gooch of Traidcraft.

13
Slavery as Piracy: The Legal Case for Reparations for the Slave Trade[1]
Geraldine Van Bueren

The need for a bold, just and consistent approach

The purpose of any type of reparations for past wrongs, is the restoration of dignity: the dignity of survivors, the dignity of the memory of the dead and the dignity achieved by making restitution for past wrongs. The very act of reparation is to acknowledge respect. Reparations for consistent patterns of historic abuses, including slavery, should be discussed with this ethos and the building of a global community framework in mind. Respect is the spirit in which the question whether present generations should pay for the crimes of their ancestors and others to whom they are unrelated, should be answered.

The process of reparations, of uncovering the evidence and exploring causation, could also assist in the prevention of repetition of the harm done. For example, it is hard to imagine that the contemporary trafficking of human beings would have been ignored for so long by the international community or would have been able to flourish in a global community that had accepted full responsibility for the historical slave trade. In this chapter the argument for reparations is therefore made in the context of aiming for the complete elimination of contemporary forms of slavery, including trafficking in human beings. In order to make an argument for reparations, this chapter will focus on establishing the legal grounds for such a claim. A state commits an internationally wrongful act when it is in violation of an applicable rule of international law whether treaty or customary law. Most of the international laws cited in support of a slavery reparations claim are twentieth-century developments drafted and adopted after the cessation of the majority of slavery. It is difficult, therefore, to argue that they should be applied retrospectively when this was clearly not the intent lying behind the laws. Yet there are international laws which could succeed but which have not been used. In this chapter, a distinction is made between slavery and the slave trade. Second, the slave trade is reconceptualized as a form of piracy whereas piracy has been illegal for centuries. There is historical evidence to support this approach.

Any legal claim for reparations for the slave trade must be based on the enduring consequences of the legacy of slavery which continues to affect those living today. If it is argued that the period of time which has passed since the Atlantic slave trade is not critical, then why exclude other historical acts of slavery? As valid as the claim for reparations is, from Africa and descendants of those who once lived in Africa, it is not the continent which is the salient factor but the nature of the slave trade. Reparations should not necessarily be limited to the descendants of those enslaved in one continent or the descendants from that continent. Any claim for reparations for slavery, unless waived, ought to include the other continuing traces of slavery. What, for example, distinguishes African slavery from the slavery in South America? Reparations should be seen as a part of the honest acceptance of the past and of accepting moral and legal responsibility. Within this lens, compensation does not have to be considered in a narrow context. The discussions surrounding debt relief take on a completely different hue. In the past the linking of debt relief to poverty reduction has erroneously often been perceived as special pleading by African states. Yet, arguably, some of the debts owe their origin to remedying an impoverishment to which slavery may have contributed. The carefully targeted cancellation of this debt is, therefore, not an issue only of relief, but becomes a facet of compensation, and therefore of justice.

Reparations are a form of restitution: the return of unjust enrichment at the expense of others. They are not necessarily prompted by individual guilt; more by collective national shame. Guilt and shame have to be distinguished. Guilt is an immobilizing emotion allowing individuals the luxury of feeling bad while doing nothing; shame is not and need not be related to feelings of individual responsibility. Hence reparations focus on collective shame rather than an individual's sense of guilt. It is an acknowledgement of this shame which is so fundamental to survivors of historic abuses.

The claim for reparations is growing.[2] We should recognize that a bolder approach is needed. After all it was a new and bold approach that, in the first place, led to the development of the regional and international human rights system. Less than a century ago the violation of human rights behind the wall of a nation's borders remained principally that state's exclusive concern:

> States were obliged to abstain from interfering in the internal affairs of one another. International law was not concerned with the way in which a state treated its own nationals in its own territory. It is a cliché of modern international law that the classical theory no longer prevails in its unadulterated form.

Millett, 1999

We forget how new it was to place the individual at the centre of a system prior to the development of international human rights law and the extent of the resistance to this. When the Nuremberg Tribunal was held it was criticized by many, including international lawyers. However, 'whatever the state of the law in 1945, Article 6 of the Nuremberg Charter has since come to represent general international law' (Brownlie, 1990, p. 562). In other words, what was once considered an innovative mechanism issuing groundbreaking jurisprudence is now widely deemed acceptable. The Nuremberg Tribunal provides a lesson but it is not a parallel. The lesson is that reparations and accountability can be reconceptualized within a larger global justice framework and justice can still be attained. This is a call for an international charter to create a duty for governments, corporations and certain families or individuals to pay reparations for the slave trade.

Unreliable legal precedents

The most common legal examples cited in support of a claim for reparations for slavery do not suffice as legal precedents. The cases frequently cited are the judgement of the Nuremberg Tribunal and the subsequent reparations for the Holocaust and the United Nations Genocide Convention of 1948 and the damages paid to indigenous peoples, including Maori, for violations by non-indigenous settlers. Admittedly it is true that there are many similarities between slavery in Africa and Latin America and the German slavery and attempted extermination of the Jews. The dominant regimes characterized both groups as racially inferior. It is also true that both the Holocaust and the slave trade transported people in degrading and inhuman conditions across geographic borders: Jews were transported across Europe and the slave traders transported people out of Africa. However, on closer examination there are important legal differences between these claims and the claim for reparations for the slave trade.

The key issue is whether at the time of the commission of the slavery and the slave trade they were illegal acts either under domestic law or under international law. The Nuremberg judgement and the payment to indigenous peoples have been on the basis that there was a violation of law at the time of the commission of the offences. Article 6 of the Charter of the Nuremberg Tribunal[3] included within its definition of crimes against humanity 'enslavement, deportation'.[4] It is clear that slavery and the slave trade fall well within these definitions. This is unarguable. However, a careful reading of the judgement of Nuremberg shows that the tribunal held that many of the crimes committed against the Jews within Germany before the war, as 'revolting and horrible as many of these crimes were', were not established as being committed 'in execution of, or in connection with' any crime within the tribunal's jurisdiction.[5] The tribunal ruled that only after the war began were these acts held to have been committed in execution of war and were therefore crimes against humanity. Hence, even though before World War II had begun, 1 million Jews had been murdered (Gilbert, 1986), the Nuremberg Tribunal took a restrictive approach, some would argue unjustifiably and found only a crime against humanity if there was also proof of war crimes. This is an approach open to criticism but if we are relying upon legal precedents, then it is a restriction which has to be acknowledged.

In addition, in the reparations for slavery claim there is, unlike Nuremberg, no question of individuals being punished and this under-mines any argument for reparations for slavery and the slave trade based on Nuremberg. Nuremberg must also be placed in its historical context (Zalaquett, 1992). The reparations paid by Germany, Austria and Japan were among the terms for peace imposed by the victors and the con-ditions for reparations were set out in treaty form. Likewise the *United Nations Convention on the Prevention of and Punishment of the Crime of Genocide* 1948, which also includes within its definition of genocide 'killing members of the group', 'causing serious bodily or mental harm to members of the group' and 'forcibly transferring children of the group to another group',[6] does not apply retrospectively across the centuries.

The Austrian reparations agreement is also of little jurisprudential value for supporting claims for reparations for slavery and the slave trade as it established reparations only as personal to the survivor and not to descendants of survivors. The belated damages agreement by Austria was narrow in its ambit and was only for the survivors of concentration camps. Indeed if a survivor dies before the claim is settled, the claim dies with the survivor. Any claim with respect to African slavery would be a claim by the descendants and therefore beyond the Austrian crimes against humanity precedent.

The new Statute of the International Criminal Court also includes enslavement and deportation as crimes against humanity but again the court's jurisdiction will not be retrospective.[7]

Finally, there have been a number of acknowledgements of gross violations of human rights in previous centuries and reparation payments made to indigenous peoples. The Waikatu Raupatu Claims Settlement Act 1995, for example, under which the New Zealand government paid substantial compensation for seizure of Maori lands by British settlers, arose, arguably, because of the breach of an earlier 1840 treaty. The same is true of many other indigenous settlements. However, these could not be a legal precedent for reparations for slavery and the slave trade, since these were not illegal under existing international law at the time.

In conclusion, there are no obvious legal precedents for the reparations claim to be based on. Therefore, rather than relying upon Nuremberg or the Genocide Convention alternative approaches need to be found.

A new approach to legal precedents: piracy and the slave trade

It is wrongly assumed that at the time of the African slave trade there were no international laws of which the slave traders were in violation. The new approach developed in this chapter is to argue that there is sufficient precedent but it is found elsewhere and not in the Nuremberg trials or the Genocide Convention. Based upon this, there is sufficient precedent for a new charter to be negotiated to provide a framework for reparations for the slave trade. This approach bases itself on the underlying principle of international human rights law: that it is dynamic and purposive in the direction of greater protection of human rights.

For the sake of international legal precision it is necessary to distinguish between slavery and the slave trade. In the first Treaty of Paris, signed on 30 May 1814 between France and the United Kingdom, it was agreed to suppress the traffic in slaves although the nature of the co-operation was unspecified and the slave trade could continue for five years (Thomas, 1997, p. 583). The condemnation was reiterated at the Congress of Vienna in 1815. Between 1815 and 1880 over 50 bilateral treaties were concluded (Robertson and Merrills, 1992, p. 14). The General Act of the Berlin Conference 1885, signed by 15 powers, declared that 'trading in slaves is forbidden in conformity with the principles of international law'. This implies that the slave trade was illegal prior to the conclusion of the Berlin Conference Act as it is declaratory of existing general principles of international law. This begs the question of when the slave trade was illegal under general international legal principles. Was it sometime between 1814 and 1885 or was it earlier?

Critically, the slave trade was also regarded as piracy by the United States and Britain in 1823 (Thomas, 1997, p. 617). It is an approach which is consistent with an authoritative international legal definition of piracy *jure gentium*: 'according to international law, piracy consists in sailing the seas for private ends without authorization from the government of any state with the objection of committing depredations upon property or acts of violence against persons'.[8] This definition does not limit piracy to robbery on the high seas. Therefore, it would appear to cover a significant proportion of the slave trade. For example, piracy was clearly in breach of international law in the seventeenth century when Grotius (1583–1645) wrote *De Jure Belli ac Pacis* and considered the pirate to be beyond the protection of any state (Grotius, vol. 2, cap. 20, p. 40). Piracy was also made a crime under English law in 1536 with 'An Act for the punishment of pirates and robbers of the sea'.[9] This approach may bear much fruit as the reconceptualization of piracy means that at the time of the commission of the slave trade it was illegal.

An examination of comparative national jurisprudence on the slave trade is also helpful. In 1771, in England, in Somerset's Case, a slave (James Somerset) was held in irons on board a ship on the Thames bound for Jamaica. Counsel's clarion plea that 'the air of England is too pure for any slave to breathe', was upheld by the judge, Lord Mansfield, so implying that if an escaped or freed slave was not to be transported, then the English courts would not seek to uphold slave trading as a legitimate activity (Van Bueren, 1999, p. 52). Indeed the slave trade was regarded as 'worthy of condemnation and international response',[10] since it justified a violation of one of the fundamental principles of international law: freedom of the high seas. The United Kingdom first abolished the slave trade and then later slavery in the colonies in 1832. Earlier in the eighteenth century slavery itself was abolished in France by the French revolution, although Napoleon tried to resurrect it.

There are also precedents of national reparations where no violation of national law had been found at the time. In the United States the Civil Liberties Act 1988 sought to make restitution to Japanese Americans for losses due to relocation and internment of US citizens and permanent resident aliens of Japanese ancestry during World War II. The Act also includes in its purposes to 'Apologize on behalf of the people of the

United States'.[11] Yet, the Supreme Court in Korematsu versus United States ruled at the time, that such internment was constitutional.[12]

This form of comparative historical jurisprudence is necessary if reliance is to be placed on a legal precedent approach. However, there is a second approach which can succeed even against those who assert that the problem with claiming reparations for the African slave trade was that most of it was not in breach of international law or domestic law. This second approach overcomes the principal legal objection to a claim against reparations for slavery and the slave trade of retrospectivity.

The international legal system is still based largely upon state consent and states are legally able to agree among themselves, even in the absence of any judicial action, to the principle of reparations for slavery and to evolve a mechanism for restitution. There is nothing to prevent states deciding among themselves on how to consider the issue of reparations or to appoint a body to decide to whom, by whom, for what, as well as the issue of the form of reparations and quantum (the amount of compensation to be paid).

The worrying point for some states would be that in departing from such fundamental principles of international law, it leaves them more vulnerable to claims for other historical human rights violations including colonialism. However, this vulnerability is significantly diminished if the slave trade were acknowledged as a form of piracy. The alternative, a lack of acknowledgement for wrongdoings, which risks social amnesia, is much worse.

Having made a case for reparations based on the two complementary arguments of viewing the slave trade as piracy and motivating the international community of states to decide to move towards setting up a body to oversee reparations for the slave trade and slavery, we now have to look into some of the practical details which often cause objections to any form of reparations across such a long time span.

To whom, by whom and for what?

The first question is who is eligible for reparations for the slave trade. If we accept that reparations can be paid for violations which occurred in previous centuries but whose effects can still be felt today, then we have to question why reparations should be limited to Africa and the descendants of Africans. What distinguishes the African slave trade from the slave trade in South America, for example?[13] Vattel even justified such slavery, arguing that if it was to convert Indians to Catholicism then such treatment was in accordance with international law. It is at least arguable that for some of the populations in South America and the Caribbean the effects of the slave trade are still felt today. This is not to argue that all descendants from all forms of the slave trade through time are entitled to reparations, but the justifications for the boundaries have to be rigorously consistent for justice to be done.

The claim for reparations for the African slave trade is based on piracy, the destruction of civilizations, depopulation and the underdevelopment of African states. Millions were forcibly removed and 'a pattern of poverty and underdevelopment directly resulted' (Gifford, 1993).[14] It was a crime against humanity for economic reasons. Reparations would be an economic reinstitution for an economic crime. Much of the wealth of the United Kingdom, for example, was created from the slave trade.[15]

The claim for reparation has been strenuously resisted. In a debate in the English House of Lords, Lord Chesham resisted attempts to make Britain pay reparations by arguing that Benin and Niger Delta, where much of the slavery occurred, are now 'amongst the densely populated parts of Africa'.[16] He also cited General Obasanjo, as he was in 1991, on African impoverishment who argued that 'the major responsibility of our present impasse must be placed squarely on the shoulders of our leaders'.[17] However, this argument can also be turned around. Without excusing corruption and crimes by present and past African leaders, and the participation of Africans in the slave trade, the slave trade not only robbed those enslaved of their freedom but impoverished the societies from which they were taken. Reparations for the slave trade parallel actions against corrupt leaders for recovery of stolen funds. There are also those who regard reparations as unacceptable on principle; in Israel, for example, Menachim Begin held street demonstrations denouncing the Israeli government for accepting German 'blood money'. Prime Minister David Ben Gurion asked Israel to accept German reparations reluctantly and for weighty reasons such as to obey the

> final injunction of the inarticulate six million, whose very murder was a ringing cry for Israel to rise, to be strong and prosperous, to safeguard her peace and security, and so prevent such a disaster from ever again overwhelming the Jewish people.
>
> Schoenfield, 2000

Just as complex is the question of who ought to pay reparations. Historical evidence clearly shows the states that fostered and supported the slave trade. Such responsibility extends beyond Western states and includes the Arab slave trade along the east coast of Africa. Liability also extends beyond states to commercial entities and to particular families.

In the United States there have been apologies from companies that benefited financially from slavery. In March 2000 Aetna Insurance apologized – as have several newspapers which accepted advertisements from slave traders. In the United States at least ten cities including Chicago, Detroit and Washington have passed resolutions urging federal hearings into the impact of slavery (*The Times*, 2 January 2001). In January 2001 a Californian law required insurance companies to disclose policies they held covering losses incurred by slave owners when slaves died. In California the Slaveholder Insurance Policy Law as of March 2001 required all insurers whose businesses date to the nineteenth century to review their archives and reveal the names of insured slaves and their slaveholders. International reparations have also extended beyond the state. German companies agreed to pay £1.67 billion to those who survived Nazi slave labour atrocities.

There is also the question of slavery by Africans. In Ghana and in Benin chiefs have participated in ceremonies which offer apologies for the ancestors' complicity in slavery (Williams, 2001). The Ivory Coast film director, Gnoan M'bala, the director of *Adanggamanican*, an African film which looked at African involvement in the slave trade observes that, 'In our oral tradition slavery is left out purposefully because Africans are ashamed when we confront slavery. Let's wake up and look at ourselves through our own image' (Associated Press, 2001). If part of the purpose of reparations is for all of us to face the past and to educate ourselves, then reparations will be serving a similar role to that described by the Minister of Culture and Art in Burkina Faso, Da Bourdia, in reference to *Adanggamanican*, 'We need this kind of film to show our children this part of our history, that it happened among us in our own society.'

What form of compensation?

The international principle behind the purpose of reparations was originally laid down by the Permanent Court of International Justice (the predecessor of the International Court of Justice at the Hague) and is still valid today. 'Reparation must, as far as possible, wipe out all the consequences of the illegal act and re-establish the situation which would, in all probability, have existed if that act had not been committed'.[18] Reparations avoid a court judgement, although they do constitute a formal acknowledgement of a historical wrong and its continuing injury. It is symbolic of a commitment to redress, with the participation of the victims or their descendants for guidance, as to the nature and the quantum. A sum too small would be an insult and a sum too large would be unpayable.

Reparations for the slave trade provide an opportunity for a flexible, dynamic approach. There is likely to be very little reliance on individual claims. Indeed the nature of the reparations claim for the slave trade is the opposite of the individual claim. It is to restore dignity to groups and to acknowledge a mass wrongdoing and illegality.

The awards could be divided into three. First, those directed towards states as debt relief payments, paid directly to the state; second, those achieved through the lifting of specific trade barriers; and third, payments aimed at civil society groups focusing on social entitlements such as education and health. Reparations also address the barriers to enjoyment of human rights, promoting the survival and participation of groups who were once at risk of perishing. In this sense reparations are transformative.

The discussions surrounding both debt relief and the lifting of trade barriers would take on a completely different hue. Reparations for the slave trade also provide an opportunity to create a tool to address ongoing issues of inequality between developing and industrialized states. This does raise the question of whether the compensation culture is being used to replace a more equitable international order but it is not a question of either/or. In the past the linking of debt relief to poverty reduction and the lifting of trade barriers have often erroneously been perceived as goodwill in response to special pleading by African states. Arguably some of the debts owe their origin to remedying an impoverishment to which the slave trade may have contributed. Such an approach is supported by international human rights law. In a case against Surinam under the Inter-American Convention on Human Rights, the Aloeboetoe case, which is particularly apposite because of the difficulty in identifying the victim's descendants, the Court ordered the creation of trust funds and the reopening and staffing of a school.[19] Hence compensation does not have to be considered within a narrow context. The carefully targeted cancellation of debt and the lifting of punitive trade barriers are therefore not issues only of relief but become facets of compensation and therefore of justice.

The need for an international charter for reparations for the slave trade

Individual states could make reparations on an individual basis for the slave trade following the examples of the United States with regard to

Japanese Americans and Germany with regard to Holocaust victims but this would not be as equitable as an international settlement. If payments were on a national basis then the descendants of slaves in Brazil, for example, may receive nothing whereas descendants of slaves in America may receive compensation. This is not to argue against groups in individual countries taking action but rather to argue for an internationally co-ordinated approach. To have a consistent international approach there would need to be some form of international body or commission appointed to investigate the claim for reparations, to assess the quantum and to decide the form.

There has already been a claim for quantum. One body, the African World Reparations and Repatriation Truth Commission, has set the figure at $777 trillion from former colonial states for slavery at a meeting in Accra in August 1999. At first sight this may appear purely symbolic and a grossly inflated sum but Germany has paid some 4 million claims, and a total of $55 billion has been disbursed both to the state of Israel and to individual victims (Schoenfield, 2000). Germany's gross violation of human rights continued for less than 25 years, while slavery and the slave trade took place over a period of three centuries.

All of these issues are complex, but that is not a reason to shy away from them. Human rights have always been concerned with complex decisions. This is a good reason for an international commission to be established to investigate the nature of the claim for reparations, the claimants and the nature of the payment. For such a commission to have international authority it needs to be set up under an international mandate such as an international charter. It would enjoy greater authority if the commission were set up under the auspices of the United Nations. The United Nations Charter allows for this possibility. The representation on the commission needs not only to be global but also balanced as to gender.

If states, despite their responsibility for the slave trade and therefore piracy, refuse to agree to the establishment of a commission there still remains the possibility of a Slavery Reparations Commission established by civil society. This would be following the precedent of the Women's International War Crimes Tribunal 2000 on Japanese Military Sexual Slavery.[20] The authority would come not from a state but from the global community to whom beneficiaries of the slave trade have a duty under international law to render account. As with the Women's International War Crimes Tribunal, a Slave Trade Reparations Commission would step into the vacuum left by the states rather than replacing their role. It would also help bring the former slave-trading states to recognize their legal responsibility to provide reparations. The charter would not be the end of the process. The importance of the Slave Trade Reparations Commission is not only in its final result but also, as with the South African Truth and Reconciliation Commission, an educational and conscience-raising process both for the descendants of slaves and the descendants of the beneficiaries of the slave trade. Reparations for the slave trade is an opportunity for global society to reaffirm human values and to make a commitment against the repetition, in any form, of the trafficking of men, women and children.

Notes

1. This is an expanded version of a commissioned paper for the United Nations Durban Conference on Racism. I am grateful to the Consultative Council of Jewish Organizations for their support.
2. See, for example, Dolgopol and Paranjape, 1994, which includes arguments for reparations by Korean women, who were used as sexual slaves by Japan.
3. The United States, USSR, Britain and France concluded the London Agreement of 8 August 1945. The charter is annexed to the Agreement, 59 Stat. 1544, EAS no. 472.
4. Article 6(c) International Military Tribunal Charter defined crimes against humanity. Agreement for the Prosecution and Punishment of the Major War Criminals of the European Axis Powers and Charter of the International Military Tribunal, 8 August 1945 82 UNTS 279.
5. Opinions and Judgement at 84 'to constitute crimes against humanity, the acts relied on before the outbreak of war must have been in execution of, or in connection with, any crime within the jurisdiction of the Tribunal'. This would appear to narrow the charter, which is not so limited as Article 6 includes as crimes against humanity 'inhumane acts committed against any civilian population, before or during the war'. See also Schick, 1947.
6. Article 2(a), (b) and (e).
7. Rome Statute of the International Criminal Court reproduced in 39 ILM 999. Article 7 (c) and (d).
8. League of Nations Document C 196, M 70, 1927, V at 116.
9. Henry VIII. Cap. 15.
10. Randall, Universal Jurisdiction under International Law, 66 Tex.L.Rev. 785 at 794.
11. Purpose (2).
12. 323 US 214 (1944).
13. Indeed Thomas's book, *The Slave Trade* is subtitled *The History of the Atlantic Slave Trade 1440–1870*.
14. This is the first study of the legality of the reparations claim.
15. Viscount of Falkland in House of Lords debate on slavery and reparations. *Hansard*, 14 March 1996.
16. Lord Chesham resisting calls for British slavery reparations in House of Lords in *Hansard*, 14 March 1996.

17. African Leadership Forum Conference, Nigeria, cited in *Hansard*, 14 March 1996.
18. Factory at Chorzow Jurisdiction, Judgement No. 8 1927, PCIJ Series A No. 9, 21. Factory at Chorzow Merits, Judgement No. 13 1928, PCIJ Series A No. 17, 29.
19. Aloebeotoe *et al.*, Reparations, Judgement of Inter-American Court of Human Rights, 10 September 1993.
20. See the summary judgement on http//home.atte.ne.jp/star/tribunal. The judges were McDonald, Argibay, Chinkin and Mutunga.

Bibliography

Addison, A., Bhalotra, S., Coulter F. and Heady C. (1997) 'Child labour: a preliminary view', paper presented at the conference on Investment, Growth and Risk in Africa at the CSAE, University of Oxford.

Adelman, H. (1999) 'Modernity, globalization, refugees and displacement', in A. Ager (ed.) *Refugees. Perspectives on the Experience of Forced Migration* (London/New York: Pinter).

African Centre for Human Development (2002) *The Little Ghanaian Slaves Cry for Help, a Report of Child Trafficking in Ghana*.

Aguilar Martínez, R. (2000) *Investigación: Las Peores Formas de Trabajo Infantil* (Tegucigalpa: Save the Children).

Alden, E. (2002) 'The Americas: Unocal wants government to quash labour lawsuit', *Financial Times*, 9 August.

All Pakistan Federation of Labour (1989) *Bonded Brick-Kiln Workers – 1989 Supreme Court Judgement and After* (Rawalpindi: Cannt).

Alston, P. (ed.) (1994) *The Best Interest of the Child: Reconciling Culture and Human Rights* (Oxford: Clarendon Press).

Aman, K. (ed.) (1991) *Ethical Principles for Development: Needs, Capacities and Rights* (Upper Montclair, N.J.: Institute for Critical Thinking, Montclair State University).

Amersfoort, H. van (1996) 'Migration: the limits of governmental control', *New Community*, vol. 22, pp. 243–58.

Amersfoort, H. van and Doomernik, J. (eds) (1998) *International Migration. Processes and Interventions* (Amsterdam: Het Spinhuis).

Anderson, B. (1993) *Britain's Secret Slaves* (London: Anti-Slavery International and Kalayaan).

Anderson, B. (2000a) *Doing the Dirty Work? The Global Politics of Domestic Labour* (London: Zed Books).

Anderson, B. (2000b) 'Rabbits Head, Goose Head? Slaves and Scroungers', unpublished (available from Kalayaan).

Anderson, B. (2001) 'Just Another Job? The Commodification of Domestic Labour', *Gender and Development*, vol. 9, no. 1.

Anderson, B. and O'Connell Davidson, J. (2002) *Trafficking a demand led problem?*, paper presented at ASEM Conference held 7–9 October in Bangkok.

Anheier, H., Glasius, M. and Kaldor, M. (2001) 'Introducing Global Civil Society', in H. Anheier, M. Glasius, and M. Kaldor (eds), *Global Civil Society 2001* (Oxford: Oxford University Press).

Anker, C. van den (forthcoming 2004) *Global Social Justice: a Cosmopolitan Theory* (Basingstoke: Palgrave Macmillan).

Anti-Slavery International (1994) *Children and Forced Begging in West Africa*, report to the UN Working Group on Contemporary Forms of Slavery.

Anti-Slavery International (1997) India-Bonded Labour: the gap between illusion and reality. Submission made to the 60th Session of the United Nations, International Committee on Civil and Political Rights.

Anti-Slavery International (2000) *Rapport sur les Trafic des Enfants Entre le Bénin et le Gabon.*

Anti-Slavery International, 'Slave Trade or Fair Trade? The problem, the solution and how you can take action', available from <http://www.antislavery.org/homepage/campaign/slavetradevfairtrade.pdf>

Anti-Slavery International (2002a) *The Trafficking of Child Camel Jockeys to the United Arab Emirates*, report to the UN Working Group on Contemporary Forms of Slavery.

Anti-Slavery International (2002b) *Process Documentation of Kathmandu Meeting*, 19–20 August, unpublished.

Anti-Slavery International (2002c) *Karnataka Visit Notes: Bonded Labour in Karnataka*, unpublished.

Anti-Slavery International (2002d) *Report of The Workshop on Status and Abolition of Bonded Labour in Tamilnadu*, unpublished.

Anti-Slavery International (2003) Bonded Labour, at <http:www.antislavery.org/homepage/campaign/bondedinfo.htm>, visited 26 February 2003.

APFL: see All Pakistan Federation of Labour.

Archard, D. (1993) *Children: Rights and Childhood* (London: Routledge).

Ariès, P. (1962) *Centuries of Childhood* (London: Jonathan Cape).

ASI: see Anti-Slavery International.

Associated Press (2001) www.nandotimes.com.

Association for the Development of Education in Africa (2002) 'Ghana: the final stages of policy formation', *Newsletter*, vol. 14, no. 2, p. 19.

Attac www.attac.org.uk.

ATTAC (2002) 'No Convincing Arguments Against a Currency Transaction Tax', *ATTAC Newsletter Sand in the Wheels*, 20 February, www.attac.org

Bachman, S.L. (1995) 'Children at Work', Commentary, *San Jose Mercury News*, 16 July.

Bachman, S.L. (2000) 'The Political Economy of Child Labor and Its Impacts on International Business', *Business Economics*, vol. 35, no. 3, pp. 30–41.

Baer, S., Collins, C., Estrada, O. and Barra, R. (2000) *Y Todavía no Escampa: Niñez en Honduras después de Mitch*, 1st edn (Tegucigalpa, Honduras: Higueras, OFALAN/Save the Children UK).

Bales, K. (1999) *Disposable People. New Slavery in the Global Economy* (London and Los Angeles: University of California Press).

Bales, K. (2001) 'Going Cheap', *New Internationalist*, no. 337.

Bales, K. (2002) 'The Social Psychology of Modern Slavery', *Scientific American*, at http://www.sciam.com/2002/0402issue/0402bales.html.

Barnes, W. (1997) 'Escapees Tell of Pipeline's Slave Labour', *South China Morning Post*, 21 August.

Barratt Brown, M. (1993) *Fair Trade: Reform and Realities in the International Trading System* (London: Zed Books).

Bartell, E.J. (2001) 'Opportunities and Challenges for the Well-Being of Children in the Development of Latin America: An Overview', in E.J. Bartell and A. O'Donnell (eds) *The Child in Latin America: Health, Development, and Rights* (Notre Dame, Indiana: University of Notre Dame Press), pp. xiii–xxxi.

Basu, K. (1999) 'Child Labor: Cause, Consequence, and Cure, with Remarks on International Labor Standards', *Journal of Economic Literature*, no. 37, pp. 1083–119.

BBC *Correspondent* (2001) *The Slave Children*.

Becerra, L. (1999) *Cuando las Tarantulas atacan*, 5th edn (Tegucigalpa, Honduras: Baktun Editorial).

Beitz, C.R. (1979) *Political Theory and International Relations* (Princeton: Princeton University Press).

Beitz, C.R. (1983) 'Cosmopolitan Ideals and National Sentiment', *Journal of Philosophy*, vol. 80, no. 10.

Bhatty, K. (1997) 'Class Struggle', *India Today*, no. 22, pp. 69–73.

BHRRC (Business and Human Rights Resource Centre), http://www.business-humanrights.org.

Blackburn, R. (1998) *The Making of New World Slavery, 1492–1800* (London: Verso).

Bloomberg www.bloomberg.com

Booth, K., Dunne, T. and Cox, M. (eds) (2001) *How Might We Live? Global Ethics in a New Century* (Cambridge: Cambridge University Press).

Boyden, J. (1997) 'Childhood and the Policy Makers: A Comparative Perspective on the Globalization of Childhood', in A. James and A. Prout (eds) *Constructing and Reconstructing Childhood: Contemporary Issues in the Sociological Study of Childhood*, 2nd edn (London: Falmer Press), pp. 190–229.

Boyden, J. and Rialp, V. (1995) 'Children's right to protection from economic exploitation', in J.R. Himes (ed.), *Implementing the Convention on the Rights of the Child: Resource Mobilisation in Low-Income Countries*, UNICEF, International Child Development Centre, Florence (The Hague/London/Boston: Martinus Nijhoff Publishers), pp. 183–221.

Brammertz, S., Bernard, D., Gazan, F., Conings, L., Lecocq, P., Verbeke, D., Deridder, K., Bontink, W., Morreale, C. and Hongenaert, J. (2002) 'Policy and approach regarding trafficking in human beings in Belgium', paper presented at the European conference on preventing and combating trafficking in human beings: global challenge for the twenty-first century, Brussels, 18–20 September 2002, at belgium.iom.int/STOPConference/ Confdocs/ConfPapers.

Brownlie, I. (1990) *Principles of Public International Law*, 4th edn (Oxford: Clarendon).

Bull, H. (1977) *The Anarchical Society*, 1st edn (London: Macmillan).

Burman, E. (1996) 'Local, global or globalized: Child development and international child rights legislation', *Childhood: A global journal of child research*, vol. 3, no. 1, pp. 45–67.

Caballero, M.E. (2000) *La Paz no les ha llegado: Niños y niñas de la calle en Centroamérica* (San José, Costa Rica: Casa Alianza Internacional/CODEHUCA).

Carens, J. (1999) 'Reconsidering Open Borders', *International Migration Review*, vol. 33, pp. 1082–97.

Centrum voor gelijkheid van kansen en racismebestrijding (CGKR)(Centre for Equal Opportunities and Anti-Racism) (2000) *Strijd tegen de mensenhandel – Jaarverslag 1999. Tussen beleid en middelen: de diepe kloof?* (Brussels: CGKR).

Channel 4 Television (2000) *Slavery*.

Chin, K. (1997) 'Safe House or Hell House? Experiences of Newly Arrived Undocumented Chinese', in P.J. Smith (ed.) *Human Smuggling. Chinese migrant trafficking and the challenge to America's immigration tradition* (Washington, DC: CSIS).

Chin, K. (1999) *Smuggled Chinese: Clandestine Immigration to the United States* (Philadelphia: Temple University Press).

Clean Clothes Campaign 'Nike's Track Record 1988–2000', available from http://www.cleanclothes.org.

Cohen, J. (ed.) (1996) *For Love of Country: Debating the Limits of Patriotism* (Boston: Beacon Books).

Comisión Nacional para la Erradicación Gradual y Progresiva del Trabajo Infantil, IPEC/OIT, UNICEF, Save the Children UK (2000a) *Plan de Acción Nacional Para la Erradicación Gradual y Progresiva del Trabajo Infantil en Honduras* (Honduras, Centro América) draft version.

Comisión Nacional para la Erradicación Gradual y Progresiva del Trabajo Infantil, IPEC/OIT, UNICEF, Save the Children UK (2000b) *Diagnostico General de la Situación del Trabajo Infantil en Honduras* (Honduras, Centro América) draft version.

Commission on Global Governance (1995) *Our Global Neighbourhood* (Oxford: Oxford University Press).

Coomaraswamy, R. (1997) *Report of the UN Special Rapporteur on Violence Against Women, its cause and consequences, on trafficking in women, women's migration and violence against women*, submitted in accordance with Commission on Human Rights resolution 1997/44, paragraph 36.

Cornia, G.A., Jolly, R. and Stewart, F. (1987) *Adjustment with a Human Face: Protecting the Vulnerable and Promoting Growth*, vol. II (London: Routledge).

CorpWatch (2002) 'Vote for Fair Trade Chocolate', available from http://www.corpwatch.org/action/PAA.jsp?articleid = 2034.

Cox, R. (1986) 'Social Forces, States and World Orders: Beyond International Relations Theory', in R. Keohane (ed.) *Neorealism and its Critics* (New York: Columbia University Press).

Crawford, S. (2000) *The Worst Forms of Child Labour: A Guide to Understanding and Using the New Convention* (University of Edinburgh, DFID: www.dfid.gov.uk), accessed 1 July 2002.

Cuadrao, E. (1999) 'IPEC en América Latina: Avances y Perspectivas para la Acción', in E. Garcia Méndez and M.C. Salazar (eds) *Nuevas Perspectivas para erradicar el Trabajo Infantil en América Latina* (Santafé de Bogotá, Colombia: Editores Tercer Mundo and UNICEF).

CWIN (2002) *Far Away From Home: A Survey Study of Child Migrant Workers in the Kathmandu Valley* (Kathmandu: CWIN).

Daily Graphic (2001) 'More pupils go to school without food', 30 May.

Daily Graphic (2001) '60% of pupils in primary schools cannot read or write', 10 October.

Daily Graphic (2001) '652 schools cry out for teachers', 19 October.

Daily Graphic (2002) 'Boost for cocoa farmers', 14 March.

Davidson, P. (1997) 'Are Grains of Sand in the Wheels of International Finance Sufficient to do the Job When Boulders are Required', *Economic Journal*, vol. 107, pp. 671–86.

De Feyter, K. (1996) 'The Prohibition of Child Labour as a Social Clause', in E. Verhellen (ed.) *Monitoring Children's Rights* (The Hague: Kluwer Law International), pp. 431–44.

De Pauw, H., Broeckx, G., Defoer, S. and Van Nieuwenhove, G. (2002) *The Disappearance of Unaccompanied Minors and Minors Victim of Trafficking in Human Beings: dossier* (Brussels: Child Focus).

De Rosa (2001) 'Capital Controls Become the IMF's Latest Folly', www.bloomberg.com.

De Ruyver, B. and Fijnaut, C. (1994) 'De restauratie van het recht van onderzoek? Tevreden experten over de Parlementaire Onderzoekscommissie Mensenhandel (Restoration of the right to inquire? Satisfied experts of the Parliamentary Committee on Trafficking in Human Beings)' (Brussels: Panopticon).

De Ruyver, B., Van Eeckhoutte, W., Van Impe, K., De Somere, P. and Delcour, M. (1999) *Mensenhandel doorgelicht. De Filippijnen als case-study (An analysis of the phenomenon of human trade. A case study with the Philippines)* (Antwerp-Appeldoorn: Maklu).

De Ruyver, B., Van Heddeghem, K. and Siron, N. (2001) 'De strijd tegen mensenhandel: beleidsprioriteiten in België (Combating trafficking in human beings: the Belgian policy priorities)' *Tijdschrift voor Criminologie*, vol. 4, pp. 408–17.

De Ruyver, B. and Siron, N. (2002) 'Trafficking in migrants from a EU-perspective', in De Ruyver, B. Vermeulen, G. and Van der Beken, T. (eds) *Combating Transnational Organised Crime* (Antwerp-Appeldoorn: Maklu).

De Stoop, C. (1992) *Ze zijn zo lief, meneer. Over vrouwenhandelaars, meisjesballeten en de bende van de miljardair (They are So Sweet, Sir)* (Leuven: Kritak).

Doezema, J. (2002) 'Who gets to choose? Coercion, consent and the UN trafficking protocol', *Gender and Development*, vol. 10, no. 1.

Dolgopol, U. and Paranjape, S. (1994) *Comfort Women: An Unfinished Ordeal* (Geneva, International Commission of Jurists).

Dooley, M. (1996): 'Tobin Tax: Good Theory, Weak Evidence, Questionable Policy', ul Haq, M, Kaul, I. and Grunberg, I. (eds), *The Tobin Tax: Coping with Financial Volatility* (Oxford: Oxford University Press).

Doomernik, J. (1997a) *Going West. Soviet Jewish Immigrants in Berlin since 1990* (Avebury: Aldershot).

Doomernik, J. (1997b) 'Current Migration to Europe', *Journal of Economic and Social Geography*, vol. 88, pp. 284–90.

Doomernik, J. (1998a) *Labour Immigration and Integration in Low- and Middle Income Countries. Towards an evaluation of the effectiveness of immigration policies* (Geneva: International Labour Office).

Doomernik, J. (1998b) *The Effectiveness of Integration Policies Towards Immigrants and their Descendants in France, Germany and The Netherlands* (Geneva: International Labour Office).

Doomernik, J, Penninx, R. and van Amersfoort, H. (1997) *A Migration Policy for the Future. Possibilities and Limitations* (Brussels: Migration Policy Group).

Dower, N. (1998) *World Ethics – the New Agenda* (Edinburgh: Edinburgh University Press).

Dower, N. (2000) 'The Idea of Global Citizenship – A Sympathetic Assessment', *Global Society*, vol. 14, no. 4.

Dower, N. (2002) 'Against War as a Response to Terrorism', *Philosophy and Geography*, vol. 5, no. 1.

Dower, N. (2003) *An Introduction to Global Citizenship* (Edinburgh: Edinburgh University Press).

Drèze, J. and Gazdar, H. (1996) *Uttar Pradesh: The Burden of Inertia. Indian Development: Selected Regional Perspectives* (Oxford: Oxford University Press).

Eichengreen B., Tobin, J. and Wyplosz, C. (1995) 'Two Cases For Sand in the Wheels of International Finance', *The Economic Journal*, vol. 105, no. 428, pp. 162–72.

Eichengreen B. Mussa, M., Dell' Arriccia, G., Detragiache, E., Milesi-Ferretti, G. (1999) 'Liberalising Capital Movements: Some Analytical Issues', *Economic Issues*, no. 17 (IMF Publications), www.imf.org/external/pubs/ft/issues/issues17/index.htm

Einhorn, B. (1996) 'Gender and Citizenship in East Central Europe after the end of state socialist policies for women's "emancipation"', in B. Einhorn, M. Kaldor and Z. Kavan (eds) *Citizenship and Democratic Control in Contemporary Europe* (Cheltenham: Edward Elgar).

Elwert, G. (2000) 'Markets of violence', in G. Elwert, S. Feuchtwang and D. Neubert (eds) 'Dynamics of Violence: Processes of Escalation and De-escalation in Violent Group Conflict', Supplement no. 1, *Sociologus*, Berlin.

Ennew, J. (1994) *Street and Working Children: A Guide to Planning*, Development Manual 4 (London: Save the Children).

Ennew, J. and Milne, B. (1989) *The Next Generation: Lives of Third World Children* (London: Zed Books).

Ercelawn, A. and Numan, M. (2001) *Bonded Labour in Pakistan* (Karachi: PILER).

Ethical Trade Initiative: http://www.ethicaltrade.org

EU Council Directive (2002) *EU Council Directive on the Short-term Residence Permit Issued to Victims of Action to Facilitate Illegal Immigration or Trafficking in Human Beings who Cooperate with the Competent Authorities*, Brussels, 11 February 2002, COM 71 final.

European Commission (2000) *Combating Trafficking in Human Beings and Combating the Sexual Exploitation of Children and Child Pornography. Proposal for a council framework decision on combating trafficking in human beings*, 22 January 2001, COM 854 final /2.

Europol (1999) *General Situation Report 1996–7, Illegal Immigration*. The Hague, file no. 2562–52, p. 30.

EUROSTAT (1995) *Migration Statistics 1995* (Luxembourg: Office for Official Publications of the European Communities).

Fair Trade Federation (a), 'Membership Criteria', available from http://www.fairtradefederation.com/memcrit.html.

Fair Trade Federation (b), 'Fair Trade Facts', available from http://www.fairtradefederation.com/ab_facts.html.

Fair Trade Foundation, 'Fairtrade Standards', available from http://www.fairtrade.org.uk/standards.htm.

Felix, D. and Sau, R. (1996) 'On the Revenue Potential and Phasing in of the Tobin Tax', in M. ul Haq, I. Kaul and I. Grunberg (eds) *The Tobin Tax – Coping with Financial Volatility* (New York: Oxford University Press).

Femia, J.V. (1981) *Gramsci's Political Thought: hegemony, consciousness, and the revolutionary process* (Oxford: Clarendon).

Fetherston, A.B. (1998) 'Voices from Warzones: Implications for Training UN Peacekeepers', in E. Moxon-Browne (ed.) *A Future for Peacekeeping?* (London: Macmillan).

Firmo-Fontan, V. (2000) *Reassessing Women and War in Lebanon: historical-feminist and socio-psychological perspectives*, MA thesis, University of Limerick.

Firmo-Fontan V. (2003a) *Civil Peace in Lebanon: Endogenous patriarchy and social humiliation as dynamics in a developing re-creation process*, doctoral thesis, University of Limerick.

Firmo-Fontan V. (2003b) 'The media, conflict prevention and multi-track diplomacy: case study of Drvar', in M. Aguirre and F. Ferrandiz (eds) *International Media and Conflict Prevention* (Bilbao: HumanitarianNet).

Frankel, J. (1996) 'How Well do Markets Work: Might a Tobin Tax Help?', in M. ul Haq, I. Kaul and I. Grunberg (eds) (1996) *The Tobin Tax – Coping with Financial Volatility* (New York: Oxford University Press).

GAATW: see Global Alliance Against Trafficking in Women.

Gallagher, A. (2002) 'Trafficking, smuggling and human rights: tricks and treaties', *Forced Migration Review*, no. 12, pp. 25–8.

Galtung, J. (1975–1980) *Essays in Peace Research*, vols 1–5 (Copenhagen: Christian Ejlers).

Garber, P. and Taylor, M. (1995) 'Sand in the Wheels of Foreign Exchange Markets: A Sceptical Note', *The Economic Journal*, vol. 105, no. 428, pp. 173–80.

Ghana Living Standards Survey, at http://www.worldbank.org/html/prdph/lsms/country/gh/gh912doc.html

Ghosh, B. (1998) *Huddled Masses and Uncertain Shores. Insights into Irregular Migration* (The Hague: Martinus Nijhoff Publishers).

Gifford, (1993) 'The Legal Basis of the Claim for Reparations', paper presented to the First Pan-African Congress on Reparations, Abuja.

Gilbert, M. (1986) *The Holocaust: the Jewish Tragedy* (London: Collins).

Global Alliance Against Trafficking in Women (2001) *Human Rights and Trafficking in Persons: a Handbook* (Bangkok: GAATW).

Global Exchange (a), 'The Chocolate Industry: Slavery Lurking Behind the Sweetness', available from http://www.globalexchange.org/cocoa/background.html

Global Exchange (b), 'Fair Trade, Not Slavery, Child Labor and Poverty', available from http://www.globalexchange.org/cocoa/.

Global Exchange (c), 'Facts about Fair Trade and the Cocoa Industry', available from http://www.globalexchange.org/cocoa/facts.html.

Global Exchange (d), 'Fair Trade Cocoa Cooperative Profiles', available from http://www.globalexchange.org/cocoa/cocoacooperatives.html.

Global Foreign Exchange (website for foreign exchange transactions) www.globalforex.com.

Global Forex: see Global Foreign Exchange (above).

Godfroid, D.J. and Vinkx, Y. (1999) *Mensensmokkel* (Amsterdam: Meulenhoff).

Godrej, D. (2001) 'Of Human Bondage', *New Internationalist*, no. 337.

Government of India (1994) Country paper on India, presented at the Fourth World Conference on Women, Beijing, 1995.

Green, D. (1995) *Silent Revolution: The Rise of Market Economics in Latin America* (London: Cassell).

Green, D. (1998) *Hidden Lives: Voices of Children in Latin America and the Caribbean* (London: Cassell).

Griffith-Jones, S. (1996) 'Institutional Arrangements for a Tax on International Currency Transactions', in M. ul Haq, I. Kaul and I. Grunberg (eds) (1996) *The Tobin Tax – Coping with Financial Volatility* (New York: Oxford University Press).

Grootaert, C. and Patrinos, H. (1999) *The Policy Analysis of Child Labor: A Comparative Study* (New York: St Martin's Press).

Grosz, E. (1990) *Jacques Lacan: A feminist introduction* (London: Routledge).

Grotius, H. (1625) *De Jure Belli ac Pacis*, vol. 2, cap. 20 (The Hague: Martinus Nijhoff Publishers).

Groves, L. (2003) 'Implementation of ILO Child Labour Convention 182: Lessons from Honduras', *Development in Practice*, vol. 14, no. 1–2.

Gruzalski, B. (2001) *Gandhi* (Belmont, CA: Wadsworth).

Halifax Initiative, Ottawa, Canada, www.halifaxinitiative.org.

Haq, M. ul, Kaul, I. and Grunberg, I. (eds) (1996) *The Tobin Tax – Coping with Financial Volatility* (New York: Oxford University Press).

Harding, J. (2000) *The Uninvited. Refugees at the Rich Man's Gate* (London: Profile Books).

Hart, R.A (1997) *Children's Participation: The Theory and Practice of Involving Young Citizens in Community Development and Environmental Care* (London: Earthscan).

Haslam, D. (1999) *Caste Out: The Liberation Struggle of Dalits in India* (London CTBI publications).

Hau, H. (2001) *Estimating the Volatility Effect of a Tobin Tax*, www.banque-france.fr

Hayter, T. (2000) *Open Borders. The Case Against Immigration Controls* (London and Sterling, Virginia: Pluto Press).

Hayward, H. (1999) *Costing the Casino. The Real Impact of Currency Speculation in the 1990s*, www.waronwant.org/tobin/casinof.htm.

Heady, Ch. (2000) 'What is the Effect of Child Labour on Learning Achievement? Evidence from Ghana', Innocenti Working Paper no. 79 (Florence: UNICEF Innocenti Research Centre).

Held, D. (ed.) (2002) *Governing Globalization. Power, Authority and Global Governance* (Oxford: Polity).

Held, D. and McGrew, A. (2000) *The Global Transformation Reader* (Cambridge: Polity Press).

Hetherington-Gore, J. (2001) *A Last Gasp From the Tobin Tax as 2001 Ends*, www.tax-news.com/asp/story/story.asp?storyname=6825.

HRW: see Human Rights Watch.

Hudson, R. (2002) 'From Lara Croft to the Kosovo Girl', in M. Aguirre and F. Ferrandiz (eds) *The Emotion and the Truth: Studies in Mass Communication and Conflict* (Bilbao: University of Deusto).

Human Rights Watch (1999) *Small Hands of Slavery* (New York: HRW).

Human Rights Watch (2001) 'Caste Discrimination: A Global Concern', presented at the United Nations World Conference Against Racism, Racial Discrimination, Xenophobia and Related Intolerance, Durban, South Africa, September 2001, available from http://www.hrw.org/reports/2001/globalcaste/.

Human Rights Watch (2002a) *Backgrounder: Child Labor in Agriculture*, http://www.hrw.org/backgrounder/crp/back0610.htm.

Human Rights Watch (2002b) *Hopes Betrayed: Trafficking of Women and Girls to Post-Conflict Bosnia and Herzegovina for Forces Prostitution*, vol. 14, no. 9. (www.hrw.org/reports/2002/bosnia/).

Human Rights Watch (2002c) *Taking Cover: Women in Post-Taliban Afghanistan.*

ICEM (1996) 'The Burma Connection: Unocal Urged To Probe Alleged Drug Laundering Links', *ICEM Update*, no. 78/1996, 20 December, available from http://www.icem.org/update/upd1996/upd96-78.html.

IDB: see Inter-American Development Bank.

IHNFA (1998) *Análisis de Situación de Infancia, Mujer y Juventu* (Tegucigalpa, Honduras: IHNFA).

ILO (1975) Convention 143 Migrant Workers Convention, *Concerning Migrations in Abusive Conditions and the Promotion of Equality of Opportunity and Treatment of Migrant Workers.*

ILO (1996) *Child Labour: Targeting the Intolerable*, Report VI (1) of the International Labour Conference 86th Session (Geneva: International Labour Office).

ILO (1997) Workshop No. 2 – Globalization, Liberalization and Child Labour, Geneva, at http://www.ilo.org/public/english/comp/child/conf/amsterdam/workshop2.htm, accessed 28 June 2002.

ILO (1998) 'Overview of Global Developments and Office Activities Concerning Codes of Conduct, Social Labelling and Other Private Sector Initiatives Addressing Labour Issues, International Labour Organization', ILO doc. GB.273/WP/SDL/1.

ILO (1999) *A New Tool to Combat the Worst Forms of Child Labour*, ILO Convention 182 (Geneva: ILO).

ILO (2000) *Models of Control: a labour-status approach to Decent Work* (Geneva: ILO).

ILO (2001) *Stopping Forced Labour* (Geneva: ILO).

ILO (2002) *A Future Without Child Labour*, http://www.ilo.org/declaration, accessed 28 June 2002.

IMF: see International Monetary Fund.

Inter-American Development Bank (1998) 'Facing Up to Inequality in Latin America', *Economic and Social Progress in Latin America*, 1998–1999 Report, Washington, DC.

International Cocoa Organization (1999), website information, http://www.icco.org

International Institute for Labour Studies (1993) *Poverty: New Approaches to Analysis and Policy* (Geneva: IILS).

International Monetary Fund (2001) *Poverty Reduction Strategy Paper Honduras*, http://www.imf.org/external/np/prsp/2001/hnd/01/083101.pdf, accessed 1 July 2002.

International Monetary Fund and International Development Association (1999) *Honduras: Initiative for Heavily Indebted Poor Countries*, preliminary document prepared by the staffs of the International Monetary Fund and The International Development Association (in collaboration with the staff of the Inter-American Development Bank), Washington, November 23, 1999 (approved by Miguel E. Bonangelino and Jesús Seade (IMF), and Masood Ahmed and Donna Dowsett-Coirolo (IDA)).

IOM (2001) *Trafficking in Unaccompanied Minors for Sexual Exploitation in the European Union – Part I*, http://www.iom.int/documents/publication/en/trafficking%5Fminors%5Fparti.pdf.

Jermyn, L (2002) *Slavery Now*, http://www.globalaware.org/Artlicles_eng/slave_art_eng.htm.

Johnson, V., Hill, J. and Ivan-Smith, E. (1995) *Listening to Smaller Voices: children in an environment of change* (London: Actionaid).

Jones, C. and Seguin, P.J. (1997) 'Transaction Costs and Price Volatility: Evidence From Commission Deregulation', *The American Economic Review*, vol. 87, no. 4, pp. 728–37.

Jordan, A.D. (2002) 'Human Rights or Wrongs? The struggle for a rights-based response to trafficking in human beings', *Gender and Development*, vol. 10, no. 1; reprinted in *Gender, Trafficking and Slavery* (London: Oxfam).

Kaldor, M. (2000) *Neue und alte Kriege, Organisierte Gewalt im Zeitalter der Globalisierung* (Frankfurt am Main: Suhrkamp Verlag).

Kartush, A. (2001) *Reference Guide for Anti-Trafficking Legislative Review: with particular emphasis on South Eastern Europe* (Warsaw: Ludwig Boltzmann Institute of Human Rights, OSCE and ODIHR).

Kasa, K. (1999) 'Time For a Tobin Tax?', *Economic Letter*, no. 99/12 (San Francisco: Research Department, Federal Reserve Bank of San Francisco).

Kenen, P. (1995) 'Capital Controls, EMS and EMU', *The Economic Journal*, vol. 105, no. 428, pp. 181–91.

Knauer, S. (1999) 'Vom Tigerkäfig in den Wunderbus. Geldmaschine Knast: Die DDR verdiente Milliarden durch Zwangsarbeit und Häftlingsverkauf', *Der Spiegel*, no. 51.

Koser, K. (2000) 'Asylum Policies, Trafficking and Vulnerability', *IOM Quarterly Bulletin*, no. 20, pp. 91–108.

Labour Behind the Label (2001) 'News in Brief: Saipan', *Labour Behind the Label Bulletin*, no. 14, http://www.labourbehindthelabel.org/newsletters/14.htm.

Lansky, M. (1997) 'Child Labour: How the challenge is being met', *International Labour Review*, vol. 136, no. 2: pp. 233–57.

Larrain, J. (1983) *Marxism and Ideology* (London: Macmillan).

Linklater, A. (1998) *The Transformation of Political Community: Ethical Foundations of the Post-Westphalian Era* (Cambridge: Polity Press).

Linklater, A. (1999) 'The Evolving Spheres of International Justice', *International Affairs*, vol. 75, no. 3, pp. 473–82.

López-Calva, L.F. (2001) 'Child Labor: Myths, Theories and Facts', *Journal of International Affairs*, vol. 55, no. 1, pp. 59–73.

Ludwig Boltzmann Institute of Human Rights (2001) *Combat of Trafficking in Women for the Purpose of Forced Prostitution: Bosnia and Herzegovina Country Report*.

Maclean, J. (1988) 'Marxism and International Relations: A Strange Case of Mutual Neglect', *Millennium*, vol. 17, no. 2, pp. 295–319.

Magdoff, H. (1969) *The Age of Imperialism: The Economics of US Foreign Policy* (New York: Monthly Review Press).

Magdoff, H. (1978) *Imperialism: From the Colonial Age to the Present* (New York: Monthly Review Press).

Marcoux, A. (1997) 'The Feminization of Poverty: Facts, Hypotheses and the Art of Advocacy', *Sustainable Development Dimensions*. Food and Agricultural Organization of the United Nations www.fao.org/sd/wpdirect/wpan 0015.htm

Marcus, R. and Harper, C. (1996) *Small Hands: Children in the Working World* (London: Save the Children UK).

Margalit, A. (1999) *La Société décente* (Paris: Climats).

Markham-Rhodes, B. (2002) *King Canute*, www.viking.no/people/e-knud.htm

McGregory, D. (2002) 'Woman sacked for revealing UN links with sex trade', *The Times Online*, 7 August.

Menon, G. (1997) 'Bondage: Its Forms and Persistence in Tribal India' in *Enslaved Peoples in the 1990s* (Copenhagen: Anti-Slavery International and Work Group for Indigenous Affairs).

Meron, Th. (ed.) (1984) *Human Rights in International Law: Legal and Policy Issues*, vol. I (Oxford: Clarendon Press).

Meron, Th. (1989) *Human Rights and Humanitarian Norms as Customary Law* (Oxford: Clarendon Press).

Michalos, A.C. (1999) 'The Tobin Tax: A Good Idea Whose Time Has Not Passed', *Policy Options*, www. irpp.org/po/archive/oct99/michalos.pdf.

Millett, L. (1999) in R v Bow Street Metropolitan Stipendiary Magistrate ex parte Pinochet Ugarte (Amnesty International and Others Intervening) (No 3) 2 All E.R.97, 170.

Ministerio de Trabajo (1998) *Memoria Consulta Nacional sobre el Trabajo Infantil en Honduras* (Tegucigalpa, Honduras).

Mireilla Carbajar Education programme (1995) *La Salud del Adolescente y del Jóven* (Honduras: UNICEF Honduras).

Moens, B. (2002) 'Belgium', in E. Pearson, *Human Traffic, Human Rights: Redefining victim protection* (London: Anti-Slavery International), pp. 87–104.

Moreno, R. (1997) *Dealing With Currency Speculation in the Asian Pacific Basin* (San Francisco: Center for Pacific Basin Monetary and Economic Studies in conjunction with the Research Department, Federal Reserve Bank of San Francisco), www.frbsf.org.

Morrison, J. (1998) *The Cost of Survival. The trafficking of refugees to the UK* (London: The Refugee Council).

Myers, W.E. (1999) 'Considering Child Labour: Changing Terms, Issues and Actors at the International Level', *Childhood*, vol. 6, no. 1, pp. 13–27.

Navari, C. (2000) *Internationalism and the State in the Twentieth Century* (London: Routledge).

New Internationalist (2001) 'Of Human Bondage', no. 337.

Nivansah, B. (2000) *Environmental Studies for Primary Schools, Pupils' Book 2* (Accra: Ghana Education Service).

Nussbaum, M. (1996) 'Patriotism and Cosmopolitanism', in J. Cohen (ed.) *For Love of Country: Debating the Limits of Patriotism* (Boston: Beacon Books).

O'Brien, M. (2001) 'Labour', in E. Bircham and J. Charlton (eds) *Anti-Capitalism: A Guide to the Movement* (London: Bookmarks Publications).

O'Connell Davidson, J. (2002) *Beyond Contracts: Borders, Bodies and Bonds*, discussion paper for the ESRC seminar series at Warwick University.

OECD (1995) *OECD Environmental Data Compendium 1995* (Paris, France: Organization for Economic Co-operation and Development).

O'Neill, O. (1989) *Faces of Hunger* (London: Allen & Unwin).

OSCE (1999) *Trafficking in human beings: implications for the OSCE*, www.osce.org/odihr/documents/ background/trafficking.

Oxford Policy Management (2000) *Fair Trade: Overview, Impact, Challenges. Study to inform DFID's support of Fair Trade*, www. eftaFairTrade.org/pdf/ DFIB_ft_study.pdf. on Oxford Policy Management: www.opml.co.uk.

Patterson, B. (2001) 'Tax Coordination in the EU – The Latest Position', Working Paper Econ. 128, Directorate General, European Parliament, Luxembourg (http://www4.europarl.eu.int/estudies/internet/workingpapers/econ/pdf/128_en.pdf).

Patterson, B. (2002) *The Tobin Tax Proposal* (Luxembourg: European Parliament Research).

Patterson, B. and Galliano, M. (1999) *The Feasibility of an International Tobin Tax* (Luxembourg: European Parliament, Directorate General for Research, Economic Affairs Division), www.europarl.eu.int/workingpapers/econ/107_en.htm?textmode=on.

Payoke (2002) *Annual Report 2001* (Antwerp: Payoke).

Pearce, D. (1978) 'The Feminization of Poverty: Women, Work and Welfare', *Urban and Social Change Review*, no. 11.

Pearson, E. (2002a) 'Half-hearted protection: what does victim protection really mean for victims of trafficking in Europe?', *Gender and Development*, vol. 10, no. 1.

Pearson, E. (2002b) *Human Traffic, Human Rights: Redefining victim protection* (London: Anti-Slavery International).

Penninx, R. and Doomernik, J. (1998) 'Towards migration regulation in globalized societies', in H. van Amersfoort and J. Doomernik (eds) *International Migration: Processes and Interventions* (Amsterdam: Het Spinhuis).

Pijl, K. van der (1998) *Transnational Classes and International Relations* (London: Routledge).

PNUD (1999) *Informe Sobre Desarrollo Humano* (Honduras).

Pogge, Th. (1998) 'A global resources dividend', in D. Crocker and T. Linden, *The Ethics of Consumption* (Oxford: Rowman & Littlefield).

Pogge, Th. (2002) *World Poverty and Human Rights. Cosmopolitan responsibilities and reforms* (Cambridge: Polity).

Raman, V. (1998) *Globalisation and Child Labour*, Occasional Paper No. 31 (New Delhi, India: Centre for Women's Development Studies).

RESPECT Network (April 2001) *Accessibility of Services for Migrant Domestic Workers. Survivors of Domestic Violence: The Theory and the Reality*, unpublished (available from Kalayaan).

Robertson, A. and Misra, S. (1997) *Forced to Plough: Bonded Labour in Nepal's Agriculture Economy* (Kathmandu and London: Anti-Slavery International and INSEC).

Robertson, A.H. and Merrills, J.G. (1992) *Human Rights in the World*, 3rd edn (Manchester: Manchester University Press).

Rodrik, D. (1999) 'Making Openness Work', ODC Policy Essay no. 24, www.odc.org/publications/pe24bib.html.

Rodgers, G. and Standing, G. (eds) (1981) *Child Work, Poverty and Underdevelopment* (Geneva: International Labour Office).

Salazar, M. (2001) 'Child Work and Education in Latin America', in E.J. Bartell and A. O'Donnell (eds) *The Child in Latin America: Health, Development and Rights* (Notre Dame, IN: University of Notre Dame Press), pp. 171–97.

Salt, J. and Stein, J. (1997) 'Migration as a Business. The case of trafficking', *International Migration*, vol. 35, pp. 467–91.

Sassen, S. (1996a) *Transnational Economies and National Migration Policies* (Amsterdam: Institute for Migration and Ethnic Studies at the University of Amsterdam).

Sassen, S. (1996b) *Losing Control? Sovereignty in an Age of Globalization* (New York: Columbia University Press).

Save the Children Fund (2001) *Children's Rights: A Second Chance* (London: Save the Children UK).

SCF: see Save the Children Fund.

Schaefer, U. (2001) 'Lafontaine Light', *Spiegel Online*, www.spiegel.de.

Schick (1947) 'The Nuremberg Trial and the International Law of the Future', *American Journal of International Law*, no. 41.

Schmidt, R. (1999) *A Feasible Foreign Exchange Transaction Tax* (North–South Institute: Canada), pp. 1–20.

Schoenfield, G. (2000) 'Holocaust Reparations – A Growing Scandal', *Commentary*, September.

Scholte, J.A. (2000) *Globalization: A Critical Introduction* (Basingstoke: Palgrave).

Sen, A. (1999) *Development as Freedom* (Oxford: Oxford University Press).

Shaw, M. (ed.) (1999) *Politics and Globalization. Knowledge, Ethics and Agency* (London: Routledge).

Singer, P. (1972) 'Famine, affluence and morality', *Philosophy & Public Affairs*, vol. 1 and, extended (1979), 'Rich and poor', in P. Singer (ed.) *Practical Ethics* (Cambridge: Cambridge University Press).

Singer, P. (1991) *Companion to Ethics* (Oxford: Blackwell).

Siron, N. and Van Baeveghem, P. (1999) *Trafficking in Migrants through Poland. Multidisciplinary research into the phenomenon of transit migration in the candidate Member States of the EU, with a view to the combat of traffic in persons* (Antwerp-Appeldoorn: Maklu).

Smith, P.J. (ed.) (1997) *Human Smuggling. Chinese migrant trafficking and the challenge to America's immigration tradition* (Washington, DC: CSIS).

Somerset, C. (2001) *What the Professionals Know: the trafficking of children into, and through, the UK for sexual purposes* (London: ECPAT UK).

Spahn, P.B. (1996) 'The Tobin Tax and Exchange Rate Stability', *Finance and Development*, vol. 2, no. 33, pp. 24–7.

Steans, J. and Pettiford, L. (2001) *International Relations, Themes and Perspectives* (Harlow: Pearson Education [Longman]).

Stiglitz, J. (2000) 'The Insider – What I learned at the World Economic Crisis', *The New Republic*, vol. 17, no. 4, www.thenewrepublic.com/041700/stiglitz041700.html.

Stiglitz, J. (2002) *Globalization and its Discontents* (London: Allen Lane).

Stiglmayer, A. (ed.) (1994) *Mass Rape: The War Against Women In Bosnia-Herzegovina* (Lincoln and London: University of Nebraska Press).

Stotsky, J. (1996) 'Why a Two-Tier Tobin Tax Won't Work – Reply to Paul Bernd Spahn', *Finance and Development*, vol. 2, no. 33, pp. 28–30.

Tabb, W. (1997) 'Globalisation Is *An* Issue, The Power of Capital Is *The* Issue', *Monthly Review*, vol. 49, no. 2.

TARA Projects http://www.peoplink.org/tara.

The Economist (1998) 'The Power of Publicity', 5 December.

The Economist (1999) 'Sweatshop Wars', 25 February.

The Economist (2002) 'Ethically Unemployed', 14 December.

The Economist Intelligence Unit (2001) *EIU Country Report 2001: Honduras* (London: EIU).

The Independent on Sunday (2002) 'Sweet success for anti-slavery lobby', 19 May, http://news.independent.co.uk/business/news/story.jsp?story=296494.

Thijs, E. and De T'Serclaes, N. (2000) 'De mensenhandel en prostitutie in België. Verslag namens de subcommissie "Mensenhandel en prostitutie" (Trafficking in human beings in Belgium. Report on behalf of the sub-commission "trafficking and prostitution")', *Parl. St. Senaat*, 1999–2000, 2–152, 1–166.

Thomas, H. (1997) *The Slave Trade: The History of the Atlantic Slave Trade 1440–1870* (London: Picador).

Traidcraft (1999) 'Fact Sheet', September.

Traidcraft, 'Fair trade makes a difference – to lots of people!', available from http://www.traidcraft.co.uk/fs_diff.html.

UK Government (2000) 'Eliminating World Poverty: Making Globalisation Work for the Poor', *Second White Paper on International Development*, www.globalisation.gov.uk.

UNCTAD Secretariat (2001) *Global Economic Trends and Prospects*, www.unctad.org/en/docs/pogdsm21.en.pdf.

UNDP (1998) *UNDP, Human Development Report 1998* (New York: Oxford University Press).

UNHCR, United Nations High Commissioner for Refugees (2002) *Statistical Yearbook 2001. Refugees, Asylum-seekers and Other Persons of Concern – Trends in Displacement, Protection and Solutions* (Geneva: UNHCR).

UNHCHR. Fact Sheet No.14, http://www.unhchr.ch/html/menu6/2/fs14.htm, visited 27 February, 2002.

UNHCHR (2002) *Status of Ratifications of the Principal International Human Rights Treaties*, http://www.unhchr.ch/pdf/report.pdf.

UNICEF (1997) *The State of the World's Children 1997: Focus on Child Labour* (New York: Oxford University Press).

United Nations (2001) *Protocol to Prevent, Suppress and Punish Trafficking in Persons, Especially Women and Children, Supplementing the United Nations Convention against Transnational Organized Crime*, G.A. res. 55/25, annex II, 55 U.N. GAOR Supp. (no. 49) at 60, U.N. Doc. A/45/48 (Vol.I); online at http://www.uncjin.org/Documents/Conventions/dcatoc/final_documents_2/convention_%20traff_eng.pdf.

United Nations Convention against Transnational Organized Crime, http://www.uncjin.org/Documents/Conventions/dcatoc/final_documents_2/convention_%20traff_eng.pdf.

United Nations Economic and Social Council (2002) *Social and Human Rights Questions: Human Rights*, session, 1–26 July.

UNPD, United Nations Population Division (2000) *Replacement Migration: Is it a Solution to Declining and Ageing Populations?* (New York: United Nations).

United Non-Profit, http://www.united.non-profit.nl/pages/presandlist.htm.

US Department of State (2002) 'Victims of Trafficking and Violence Protection Act 2000', *Trafficking in Persons Report* (Washington, DC: USDoS).

Van Bueren, (1999) 'Alleviating Poverty through the Constitutional Court', *South African Journal of Human Rights*, no. 52.

Vandenberg, M.E. (2002) *Testimony on Trafficking of Women and Girls to Bosnia and Herzegovina for Forced Prostitution*, presented to the House Committee on International Relations Subcommittee on International Operations and Human Rights, 24 April 2002; online at http://www.hrw.org/backgrounder/wrd/trafficking-testim-april.pdf.

Van Impe, K. (2000) 'People for Sale: The Need for a Multidisciplinary Approach towards Human Trafficking', *IOM Quarterly Bulletin*, no. 20, pp. 113–30.

Vermeulen, G. (2002) 'International Trafficking in Women and Children', *Revue Internationale de Droit Pénal*, no. 3 and no. 4, pp. 837–90.

Viking www.viking.no.

Vile, G. (1989) *Zorg en hoop: analyse van enige grondbegrippen van Maslow* (Haren: Sassenhein).

Wahl, P. (2001) 'ATTAC antwortet auf Spiegel Gespraech: "Streiten Sie mit uns, Herr Tobin" (ATTAC answers to the Spiegel Interview with James Tobin: "Argue with Us, Mr Tobin")', *Spiegel Online*, www.spiegel.de.

Wahl, P. and Waldow, P. (2001) *Currency Transaction Tax – A Concept With a Future* (Bonn, Germany: World Economy Ecology and Development Association [WEED]).

War On Want (2002) *Tobin Tax Update – A Digest of News and Action for the UK Campaign for a Tax on Currency Speculation*, www.waronwant.org.

Watson, M. (2002) 'Sand in the Wheels, or Oiling the Wheels of International Finance? New Labour's Appeal to a New Bretton Woods', *British Journal of Politics and International Relations*, vol. 4, no. 2, pp. 193–221.

Weiner, M. (ed.) (1993) *International Migration and Security* (Boulder: Westview Press).

Weiner, M. and Teitelbaum, M.S. (2001) *Political Demography, Demographic Engineering* (New York/Oxford: Berghahn Books).

Westin, C. (1999) 'Regional analysis of refugee movements: origins and response', in A. Ager (ed.) *Refugees. Perspectives on the Experience of Forced Migration* (London/New York: Pinter).

White, B. (1999) 'Defining the Intolerable: Child work, global standards and cultural relativism', *Childhood: A Global Journal of Child Research*, Special Issue: Understanding Child Labour, vol. 6, no. 1, pp. 133–44.

Williams, B. (2001) 'The Case for Slavery Reparations', at http://news.mpr.org/features 20011/13_Williamsb_reparations/.

Williams, J. (2002) 'Good International Citizenship', in N. Dower and J. Williams (eds) *Global Citizenship: A Critical Reader* (Edinburgh: Edinburgh University Press).

Williams, Ph. (ed.) (1999) *Illegal Immigration and Commercial Sex. The New Slave Trade* (London/Portland: Frank Cass).

World Bank, (1995) 'Workers in an Integrating World', in *World Development Report 1995* (New York: Oxford University Press).

World Bank (1999) Country Brief on Honduras for May 1999, http://lnweb18.worldbank.org/external/lac/lac.nsf/c2e12c369e771d17852567 d6006b402b/281fa5f69683b753852567d900735efd?OpenDocument.

World Bank (2000) 'Making Markets Work Better for Poor People', in *World Development Report 2000/2001*, www.worldbank.org/poverty/wdrpoverty/report/ch4.pdf.

World Bank (2001) 'Global Economic Prospects for 2002', www.worldbank.org/prospects/GEP2002.

World Bank (2002), http://www.worldbank.org/hipc/about/hipcbr/hipcbr.htm, accessed 17 August 2002.

Zalaquett, J. (1992) 'Balancing Ethical Imperatives and Political Constraints: The Dilemma of New Democracies Confronting Past Human Rights Violations', *Hastings Law Journal*, no. 43.

Zecchini, L. (2003) 'Cinq cent policiers de l'Union Européenne ont pris le relais de l'ONU en Bosnie', *Le Monde*, 25 January.

Index